THE ROMANS IN SCOTLAND

THE ROMANS
in
SCOTLAND

GORDON S. MAXWELL

JAMES THIN
THE MERCAT PRESS

1989

EDINBURGH

Published by
JAMES THIN
The Mercat Press
53–59 South Bridge, Edinburgh

First published 1989

© GORDON S. MAXWELL

Design, typography, layouts by
T. L. Jenkins, Edinburgh.

ISBN 0 901824 76 3

Printed and bound in Great Britain by
Billing & Sons Ltd., Worcester.

Contents

Photographs

The air photographs are characterised by extremely fine detail and wide tonal range, and in attempting to translate these features successfully from the continuous tone of superb photographic prints through screened negatives necessary for commercial printing, there was a risk of losing some of their quality in the process.

Conventional halftone methods were likely to fail this test to some degree, because they are limited to a camera setting for both highlight and shadow which restricts the other tones. The name Hislop & Day of Edinburgh has long been synonymous with high quality in this field, and with the advent of electronics their new DIATONE process gave us some promise of success.

These 16 plates here listed have been reproduced using their unique 'diatones', and give a remarkably high quality of reproduction – very much better than ordinary halftones would have achieved.

. . . These plates are inserted between pages 36−37 and 84−85

Dedication

to Kathleen, Amanda
and Rebecca

with thanks for their indulgence

Preface

IT IS OFTEN MAINTAINED that the Roman occupation of Scotland attracts more than its due share of publicity. There is some justice in this claim, although the matter is not beyond debate. What cannot be denied is that the Romans occupy a disproportionately prominent position on the stage of national history. Their presence in this northern kingdom did not extend beyond three episodes, which together spanned no more than fifty years. Yet such is the power of the 'Roman factor', that these brief intervals of foreign domination are accorded keener public curiosity and deeper academic research than many centuries of domestic development in prehistory – or even more recent times. The reason probably lies in the readiness with which we find, in the events of that long-dead occupation, a parallel to our common experience. Whatever may be our perception of national identity, we trace an intellectual line of descent from Graeco-Roman civilisation. Our acquaintance with the classics and Roman history, even at the most basic level, helps us to recognise the characters in this military drama as people like ourselves, belonging to a society not totally dissimilar from our own.

It was a society with taxes, government officials, and a professional army; a society that was no stranger to foreign policy, colonial possessions, and inflationary spirals. On the other hand, if we readily recognise the human lineaments of the oppressors, we in Scotland can also sympathise with the oppressed. The tale of an overpoweringly resourced southern neighbour making dramatic interventions north of Cheviot strikes a familiar note. The long trail trodden by Agricola and Severus was traced and retraced in later centuries by Northumbrian, Edwardian, and Hanoverian armies. The events of the Roman occupation are therefore not remote from our understanding; they are the first recognisable manifestation of a series of influences which have continued down through the ages and persist today in a more subtle guise, no less formidable for being cultural and economic rather than military in character. It is for these reasons that authors return again and again to the topic of Roman conquest.

In the case of the present work there is another reason – the repayment of a debt. For more than thirty-five years the history and monuments of Roman Scotland have provided the author with an unfailing source of interest and pleasure. It has been a privilege to be engaged upon a quest that led through so many happy discoveries to the widening of our knowledge of the period. To communicate the excitement of the chase and to share that pleasure with others through lectures and site-visits has always seemed the very pitch of felicity. The invitation from the Mercat Press to write a book on this subject has thus allowed the author to give back a little of what he has received. In the event, my choice has been to make a selection of those areas of Roman studies which I, from personal experience, have found particularly rewarding, because closest to recent discoveries. This, as I am well aware, has led to scant recognition of the contribution made by several fields of specialist study – epigraphy and numismatics, for example, or the role played by students of pottery and other artefacts. I should also like to have said more about the work of the field-surveyors, especially about O. G. S. Crawford, the most illustrious of the Ordnance Survey's Archaeology officers. In addition to this selectivity there have been other, more paradoxical, disadvantages: the accelerated tempo of fieldwork, excavation, and aerial survey has made it difficult to keep abreast of the times, despite – perhaps because of – close personal involvement. I am all the more conscious of that defect since the writing of these chapters has been a leisure-time activity, of necessity spread over years rather than months.

Acknowledgements

For his consistent help and encouragement during this lengthy gestation I am deeply grateful to James Thin, as I am to Tom Jenkins, in whose hands has lain the design of the format and layout of the book itself. For the design of the dust-jacket and the preparation of all but a few of the line-drawings that enhance its pages I owe sincerest thanks to my colleague John Borland; the remainder (Figures 1.1, 1.2, 4.7, 6.2, 6.3, 8.3, 8.5, 9.6–9.8), are from the hand of the author. For permission to use photographic material from the National Monuments Record of Scotland (Plates 3–13 and 16; Figures 1.5 and 1.6) the author and publishers are grateful to the Royal Commission on the Ancient and Historical Monuments of Scotland; we are also indebted to the Scottish Record Office for permission to reproduce Figures 1.1 and 1.2, which are based on material in its archive.

And finally, for financial assistance in the production of the illustrative material we wish to express our appreciation and warm thanks to the Russell Trust and to the Carnegie Trust for the Universities of Scotland.

ABBREVIATIONS

C.I.L.	*Corpus Inscriptionum Latinarum*
D.E.S.	*Discovery and Excavation Scotland*, Council for British Archaeology, Scotland
G.A.S.	Glasgow Archaeological Society
Pan. Lat. Vet.	*Panegyrici Latini Veteres*, ed. R.A.B. Mynors. 1934. Oxford
R.C.A.M.S.	Royal Commission on the Ancient and Historical Monuments of Scotland
R.I.B.	*Roman Inscriptions of Britain* vol. 1. (R.G. Collingwood and R.P. Wright) 1965. Oxford
S.H.A.	*Scriptores Historiae Augustae*
Stat. Acct.	*The Statistical Account of Scotland* (1791–9). Edinburgh.

1

Scottish Antiquaries and the Romans in Scotland

T O MANY PEOPLE the studious antiquary, with his mildly monomaniac pursuits, may seem a figure of fun; hardly less so his modern successor, the archaeologist. To some he may conjure up not unattractive associations with the quest for the Romantic element in life; to others his dedication to the search for fragments of our ancient past provides yet another example of academic self-indulgence, an extravagant expenditure of public money which brings no material reward and in the present economic situation seems scarcely to be justified. That such caricatures enjoy wide acceptance should cause no surprise, for there can be few, even among those professing an interest in their country's past, who are fully aware of either the range of disciplines embraced by modern archaeology or the nature of the contribution made to humane studies by past generations of antiquaries. Yet, on the stage of Scottish life and letters the latter present a familiar character, whether commanding our amused affection as the learnedly credulous Jonathan Oldbuck of Scott's *Antiquary,* or provoking our less tolerant despair in the persons of John of Fordoun (died *c.* 1384) and Hector Boece (died *c.* 1536) – historians for whom tradition and truth were inextricably intertwined.

Such liberties as were once taken with the historical record might be pardoned, according to the standards of the times, and even commended if they succeeded, as they did, in feeding a healthy curiosity about the nation's past. For the early writers, in particular, knew that there was also a practical purpose, that of documenting the evolution of the Scottish people as a political entity. Threatened as it was by a richer and more powerful neighbour to the south, the Scottish nation required literary proof of its separate identity in order to justify to the world abroad the rejection of foreign domination, and foster at home the spirit of independence which was necessary for survival.

The preamble to the Declaration of Arbroath, written in 1320, furnishes an early instance of this type of historical fiction:

> 'from the chronicles and books of the ancients we find that among other famous nations our own, the Scots, has been favoured with wide renown. They travelled from Greater Scythia by way of the Tyrrhenian Sea and the Pillars of Hercules, and for a long time lived in Spain among the most savage tribes, yet nowhere could they be conquered by any nation, however barbarous. Twelve hundred years after the people of Israel crossed the Red Sea, they left Spain to settle in their present western home, where they still live today. First of all they drove out the Britons, and then they totally destroyed the Picts, and, although attacked countless times by Norwegians, Danes, and the English, they held that home by victory after victory and untold labours.'

Some 360 years later the same sentiments were expressed by Stair in the introduction to the first edition of his *Institutions of the Law of Scotland*.

> 'We (the Scots) do not pretend to be among the great and rich kingdoms of the earth; yet we know not who can claim preference in antiquity and integrity, being of one blood and lineage, without mixture of any other people, and have so continued above two thousand years; during all of which no foreign power was ever able to settle the dominion of a strange Lord over us . . .'

If Stair was concerned, above all things, to define and describe the foundations upon which a truly independent system of jurisprudence might rest, he was further aware, in a period over which the impending Act of Union cast a long shadow, that national identity was also at stake. His thoughts were cast back over past struggles for independence, both political and religious, to a much earlier period of history, when open conflict between Scots and English was foretokened by the frontier wars waged between the Romans and North Britons:

'It is yet a greater glory that you (Charles II) . . . and your subjects in Scotland have been least under the yoke of Rome in your sacred or civil interest. Their arms could never subdue you; but they turned on the defensive; and to exclude your valour, two of their most famous Emperors, Severus and Hadrian, were at an incredible cost to build two walls from sea to sea, the foundations of which are yet known, and a great part of Hadrian's wall from Carlisle to Newcastle is still standing'.

The reference to the two mural frontiers – Hadrian's and the Antonine Wall, as we now know them – indicates not only that Stair expected his readers to identify with the pre-Scottic British tribesmen of the second and third centuries AD as typifying the resistance to southern domination, but also that he presumed in them a familiarity with the antiquities to which he referred. Such expectations were not unreasonable. For more than a century and a half educated Scotsmen had been able to read, either at first hand or as reported in the less fictional pages of Hector Boece's *Scotorum Historiae*, the uniquely detailed account of the first Roman conquest of North Britain written by the Roman historian Tacitus. No longer was it necessary to rely upon the scanty information to be gleaned from such early post-Roman sources as Gildas, Nennius, and Bede, or upon the embroidered fantasies of mediaeval chronicles in which the former were incorporated. But it was not just to the renascent interest in classical *literature* that this heightened awareness of the past was due; increasingly in the sixteenth century it came to be appreciated that the *material* relics of remote antiquity constituted an equally important form of evidence, which might serve to complement the documentary sources. In other words, it was a period which saw the infancy of Romano-British archaeology.

The first person to apply the archaeological method in Scottish historiography was George Buchanan, tutor to both Mary, Queen of Scots, and the young James VI. In his *Rerum Scoticarum Historia*, published posthumously in 1582, Buchanan treated the period of the Roman occupation with an assurance which reflected a thorough mastery of the classical texts; yet he did not disdain to consider the testimony of the Roman inscribed stones which were then beginning to attract not only local but also more widespread international attention as, for example at Inveresk (Maxwell, 1984c). The reference to three inscriptions from the Antonine Wall in the continental scholar Scaliger's *Thesaurus*, printed at Leyden in 1606, is more than just an early indication that scholarship knows no frontiers; it may in fact derive ultimately from the author's personal acquaintance with Buchanan.

From the appreciation and acquisition of Roman artefacts, enquiring minds were now proceeding to the location and examination of ancient structures. The English antiquary William Camden (1551–1623) was the first to undertake and successfully publish such researches on a country-wide basis. His *Britannia*, whose first edition (written in stylish Latin) was issued in 1586, set the pattern and the standard for antiquarian works for almost two centuries. In Scotland the pioneer work in actual survey of the monuments was conducted by Timothy Pont (1560–1614), elder son of Robert, the Scottish Reformer. Pont was an accomplished mathematician and cartographer, the first projector of a Scottish atlas, an enterprise which eventually saw light of day as part of Blaeu's Atlas (Amsterdam, 1654); to a keen interest in Roman antiquities he brought the trained eye of the surveyor, a combination which allowed him to identify, for example, many of the forts and related structures of the Antonine Wall (Fig. **1.1**). Some of these have subsequently been lost to view, only to be rediscovered in more recent times, but many have been overlaid with modern works, so that their authenticity is unlikely ever to be verified. It is doubly unfort-unate, therefore, that none of Pont's papers or original 'designments' – presumably field-sketches of the sites – now survives. Later antiquaries, rarely generous in their appreciation of predecessors, thought highly of this material: Sir Robert Sibbald, discussing the same sites a century later, admitted (1707, 27) that Pont had 'viewed them more accurately than these did who came after him', although one of the reasons for this was that the pace of land improvement had begun to accelerate and ancient monuments were beginning to vanish before the plough; air photography has only recently revealed the scale of the destructive process which was then afoot (see below, pp. 45, 48–9).

Pont's most notable successors were David Buchanan (c. 1595–1652) and Christopher Irvine (c. 1635–85), both of whom took pains to visit and record their impressions of Roman remains in Scotland; tragically, apart from a summary of observations made by the latter, nothing now survives of their once voluminous field-survey reports, but the valuable clues furnished, for example, by Sibbald's references (1707, 28-31) indicate how much we have lost. Some estimate of the value and character of their work may be gained from a leaf of the notebook belonging to Alexander Edward, the Scottish architect (1651–1708), which shows a sketch of an inscribed slab from Castlehill on the Antonine Wall (Fig. **1.2**). The brief explanatory note accompanying the sketch may contain a reference to a long unsuspected fortlet adjacent to the better-known fort (Keppie, 1980).

As one might expect, the decades of exploratory research undertaken by these and other workers in the field were followed by a period in which various authors sought to synthesise the results of their labours. Among these, three antiquaries were pre-eminent : Sibbald, Gordon, and Horsley. Sir Robert Sibbald (1641 – 1727), whose slim but invaluable volume *Historical Inquiries* appeared in 1707, was a polymath of note – the first holder of the chair of medicine at Edinburgh, physician to Charles II, founder of the Royal College of Physicians and the Botanic Garden in Edinburgh, geographer and antiquary. A contributor to Gibson's edition of Camden in 1695, Sibbald possessed the trained physician's appreciation of the importance of accurate observation, as he makes clear in the preface to his *Inquiries*:

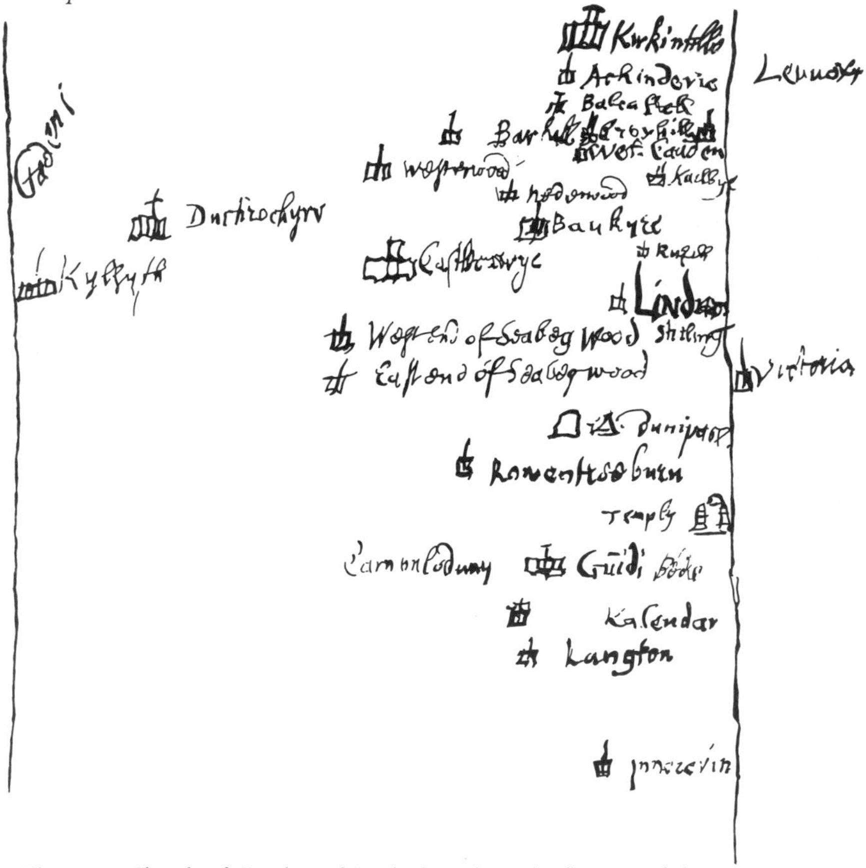

Fig. 1.1   Sketch of Gordon of Straloch's schematic diagram of the Antonine Wall, based on the work of Timothy Pont *c*.1600.

'And I must intreat pardon for the liberty and boldness I have assumed, having broken the ice first in this way of writing of our antiquities. I have been very sparing in giving conjectures about the names of places; where I have not an ancient author to guide me, I have kept by the vestiges of the Walls, and of the forts, and I found my opinion for the most part upon the vestiges of the camps and buildings, and the inscriptions found in the place, or near to it.'

Thereafter any writer touching upon the Roman antiquities of North Britain ignored the archaeological method at his peril. It is instructive to note how many of those involved in Antiquarian Studies at this time were exponents of one or other of the applied sciences and crafts — medicine, cartography, geography, and architecture — as well as scholars in other, more 'academic' disciplines.

Alexander Gordon (*c.* 1692–1750), however, may scarcely be assigned to either category. A man of great curiosity and considerable drive, not to say ambitions, he appears to have acquired a taste for antiquarian studies in the course of a Grand Tour. A university education at Aberdeen had given him sufficient acquaintance with classical learning to make it possible to mount a three-year long survey of the Roman monuments of northern Britain, and in 1726 to publish the results in a publicly subscribed work, *Itinerarium Septentrionale*. The illustrations of both artefacts and sites were the work of the author, who appears to have been a draughtsman of some ability (Plate **1**), although evidently not always concerned to reproduce precise detail or exactitude, and the uneven quality of the drawings accords well with that of the text; in this it may also reflect the character of Gordon himself, whose qualities and foibles have been variously described by his

Fig. 1.2

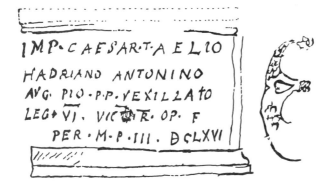

Sketch of notebook draught on an Antonine Wall Distance Slab from Castlehill made by Alexander Edward c.1699. (illustration by permission of the Earl of Dalhousie and with the approval of the Keeper of the Records of Scotland. SRO ref. GD 45/26/140)

patrons and colleagues (Wilson & Laing, 1873 ; Macdonald, 1933, 32 – 40). Yet, if Gordon can be accused of numerous deficiencies, both moral and professional – the alleged plagiarising of Horsley's unpublished researches on the Hadrianic frontier is a case in point – his enthusiasm for and dedication to field survey are surely compensating virtues, regardless of their results. In particular, Gordon's account of the Antonine Wall represents a significant advance on the work of earlier scholars, being based on personal observation made during a comprehensive programme of survey and measurement which was the first to be undertaken on the northern barrier.

It is perhaps in the preface to the *Itinerarium* that Gordon gives the clearest picture of the changes which had taken place in Scottish historiography since the days of Boece and Fordoun or their imitators, whose fabulous concoctions, as he noted, had rightly drawn the censure of Stukely. Antiquity may now be seen not as a weapon of political propaganda, but rather as an intellectual exercise practised as much for its aesthetic as its educational rewards. The Roman monuments of Scotland thus no longer serve as an example of extreme domination but as an integral part of the country's historical and archaeological heritage, in which the present inhabitants might take due proprietorial pride:

> 'But if we consider this grandeur amongst us with regard to the military scene in Britain, they [the Romans] have left here such remains of magnificence, that Italy herself can scarcely boast of greater: for who can, even to this day, take a view of those stupendious [sic] Walls made cross the island from sea to sea by sundry Emperors and their lieutenants, but must confess . . . that the whole world cannot show a greater sight of amazing grandeur, than what the Romans have left behind them in Cumberland, Northumberland, and Scotland?'

That a similar enthusiastic pride may be recognised as the driving force of Jonathan Oldbuck in the pages of Scott's *Antiquary* is not wholly surprising, for, as Macdonald noted (1934, 76n.), some of the fictional antiquary's more ingenious archaeological theories appear to be directly based on elements in the *Itinerarium*. Moreover, it must be admitted that such enthusiasm would not have been uncongenial to Scott himself, although, as we learn from his correspondence, he fully realised that objective examination of the material remains was an essential basis to any study of the past, however romantic an interpretation might subsequently be put upon it; and in any case it would be foolish to consider that the Romantic ideal had no part to play in the motivation of archaeological research, even in modern times. To trace its development would, however, require more space than is available here.

The Northumberland archaeologist John Horsley (1685–1732) provides the perfect antithesis to Gordon, whose relationship with him has already been mentioned. A Nonconformist minister and schoolmaster, with a wide range of interests, which included mechanics and hydrostatics, meteorology, and Roman antiquities, he graduated from Edinburgh University and, according to one authority (Macdonald, 1933, 4–6), may even have been born at Pinkie House on the outskirts of the city. His great work, *Britannia Romana*, was the result of much patient labour and judicious scholarship of a range and standard not previously displayed by students of the subject. The almost astringent objectivity of his approach to both the material remains and literary evidence was to become the single quality which distinguished the best of his successors. Although his situation and the relative frequency of surviving remains determined that most of his work should be conducted on the southern side of Cheviot, Horsley nevertheless also took Scottish sites into consideration, his account of the Antonine Wall being particularly valuable.

In many ways the publication of *Britannia Romana*, sadly preceded by its author's death, represented both high-water mark and watershed in Romano-British archaeology. A little over a dozen years later, the North of Britain was convulsed with war as, in the course of the second Jacobite Rising, opposing armies again marched and countermarched over country that had once seen the legions of Agricola and Severus. Although peace returned in 1746 the presence of the military in the North, with its attendant programme of fort-building and road construction, could not fail to remind people either that history repeated itself, or that, as Gordon had emphasised in his preface, the Roman monuments of Scotland were 'made by military hands'. Hence it is not altogether surprising that for the next century most of the running in Roman archaeology, so to speak, was made by members of the military profession. The greatest of these was General William Roy (1726–1790), a native of Coulter in Lanarkshire, who is justly considered to be the father of the Ordnance Survey. His book *Military Antiquities of the Romans in North Britain*, published posthumously in 1793, was compiled as a result of interest aroused early in his career, when engaged in the military survey of mainland Scotland, as a member of the staff of the deputy-quartermaster-general in North Britain; the opening paragraph of his prefatory introduction admirably sets forth the context of his own involvement in archaeological fieldwork:

'Among those studies which some proportion at least of the speculative part of mankind are imperceptibly led into, for private amusement only, Antiquity is the one which hath always commanded a considerable share of the attention of such as have engaged in it: each, according to his particular taste, inquiring into that favourite branch that pleases him most; and in this choice he seems generally to be directed by the relation which it bears to his ordinary employments in life. Hence it is that military men, especially those who have been much accustomed to observe and consider countries in the way of their profession, in reasoning on the various revolutions they have undergone, or on those which, in certain cases, they might possibly suffer hereafter, are naturally led to compare present things with the past.'

Roy, who went on to serve in Germany during the Seven Years War and whose later achievements in surveying were to gain him in 1785 the Copley medal of the Royal Society, was thus able to bring to Roman frontier studies what had till then been conspicuously lacking – a soldier's practical experience in the managing of military affairs and the reading of terrain. To this he added a lively curiosity about the campaigns of Roman commanders in North Britain, particularly Agricola, and an excellent working knowledge of the ancient military texts. The outcome of this felicitous combination of skills and interests may be seen in the *Military Antiquities*, the most important element in which is the series of magnificently presented plates of more than fifty Roman military sites in Scotland and northern England (Plate **2**, *a*), as well as a map of the entire length of the Antonine Wall. The quality of surveying undertaken to produce these diagrams far surpasses anything formerly attempted, and many of the site-plans may still be used at the present time as a basis for structural interpretation – a test which several surveys of more recent date might fail to pass! Being especially fascinated by the campaigns which Julius Agricola (governor of Britain A.D. 77-8–83-4) conducted against the northern tribes, Roy naturally paid close attention to the remains of the great marching-camps – a category of field-monument hitherto inadequately considered.

From this seminal treatment by Roy, inspired by the reports and discoveries made by a fellow-officer, Captain Robert Melville (Stuart,

1868), we may ultimately derive the present-day recognition that the temporary works of the Roman army in the field constitute as vital a body of evidence about the history of Roman Scotland as the more enduring permanent forts and frontiers. In modern times the former have proved to be particularly susceptible to detection in the course of aerial survey (see below, pp. 48–9), but before this facility was available their identification on the ground was a signal achievement. Indeed, the period of nearly 150 years which followed Roy's pioneering work in the middle of the eighteenth century would have been almost devoid of significant Roman discoveries in the field had it not been for the experienced eyes of officers who succeeded him in the survey task of the Royal Engineers. Chance finds, of course, continued to be made from time to time, notably during the construction of the monuments of the Industrial Revolution, e.g. the discovery of altars in a pit at Auchendavy on the Antonine Wall in 1771 while work was in progress on an adjacent stretch of the Forth and Clyde Canal. Nevertheless, there was no outstanding contribution to archaeological research to compare with the intensive activity and progress of the period 1700–1750, which is not altogether what one might have expected, considering that this was also a time when the Enlightenment was producing its maximum effect on architecture, law, literature, philosophy, and science. Historians there certainly were, but of the trio that springs immediately to mind – Maitland, Chalmers, and Stuart – only the last could be said to have made a really valuable contribution to the study of Roman Scotland, and that, as he makes plain in the honourable but unnecessarily apologetic preface to his *Caledonia Romana*, was motivated by a desire to supply the want of an up-to-date record of Roman discoveries in his native land. The result was what has been identified as the last in the long tradition of 'antiquarian' treatises; the future now lay with the 'archaeologist', and archaeological research amplified not only by observation but also by excavation.

Appropriately, therefore, amongst those to whom thanks were duly expressed in the editorial preface of the posthumous second edition of Stuart's *Caledonia* was Dr Daniel Wilson, who conducted the first planned excavation of a Roman site to be reported in any Scottish archaeological journal (Wilson, 1851). This was the examination of the fortlet known as Castle Greg in West Lothian (Plate **2,** *b*), which still impresses the visitor by its splendid state of preservation, with a turf rampart 8m thick rising more than 2m above the level of the enclosing defences. Doubtless it was this which drew Wilson to examine it, but to judge from the sparseness of the report, trenching in the interior, including excavation of the well to a depth of 3.3m, produced a meagre haul of artefacts, none of which was described in detail. As the finds themselves were subsequently lost, it is still uncertain when the fortlet was constructed or occupied; no plan was published, probably because all the internal buildings were of timber and their fugitive traces were consequently not recognised by the excavator. The results hardly represented a promising start to the new era, but perhaps too much should not have been expected of an archaeologist whose contribution to the subject had little to do with the Roman period; indeed, Wilson was the first scholar to use the term 'prehistoric', and his interests were rather in the artefactual than the structural side of archaeology. His attitude is indicated by a passage from the *Prehistoric Annals of Scotland* where an account of Iron Age cultures is prefaced by a brief sketch of the Roman period (Wilson, 1863, ii, 26):

> 'The history of the Scoto-Roman invasion is different ... It affects only a small portion of the country, and constitutes a mere episode, which might be omitted without very greatly marring the integrity and completeness of the national annals.'

Times had indeed changed, when the 'grandeur of Rome' could be so dismissively treated!

The next excavation to be reported, however, was more successful. Conducted in 1892 by Walter Laidlaw, then custodian of Jedburgh Abbey, it was designed to test the hypothesis that a Roman station had guarded the point where Dere Street, the Roman road that led from Corbridge to the Forth, crossed the Kale Water 4km E. of Jedburgh. In this case, the excavator was fortunate that some of the internal buildings were stone-built and not too severely damaged by cultivation. The published report (Laidlaw, 1893) was illustrated by a plan (Fig. **1.3**), which deserves to be better known, being the very first of its kind in Scotland; it gives no information about the fort's defences − the enclosing ramparts were of turf and too denuded to be easily identified, even if they had been specifically sought; yet the buildings of the interior appear to have been carefully uncovered and planned. The buttressed building is clearly a granary of standard plan, although of no great size, and the structure with what seems to be an internal courtyard to the west may be a form of headquarters building, or the commanding officer's residence. Unfortunately Laidlaw had chosen to examine a fort which was too small to house a complete military unit, and the internal layout was therefore non-standard and of limited use in illustrating the usual appearance of a Roman frontier-post. The report is nevertheless a workmanlike statement of what was discovered, and the catalogue of finds is adequately detailed, with proper emphasis placed on the importance of the commemorative slab erected by the Twentieth Legion, which was found during excavation. The discovery of the slab marks another significant turning-post in the development of Roman studies in Scotland, for it represents the first occasion on which the association of an artefact of archaeological value with a known site had been demonstrated as a result of planned exploration, and not just by chance. Not that chance discoveries had failed to produce material of the utmost value; during the 19th century as many as seven out of nineteen known or suspected Distance Slabs from the Antonine Wall were found more or less by accident (see below pp. 154–6), and down to the present day serendipity has continued to operate with as much force and success as carefully planned research.

The two excavations described above were, in fact, little more than disinterments, in scope and aims not unlike the uncovering of the works on the Hadrianic frontier, such as John Clayton's progressive clearing and refurbishing of the central sector between the North Tyne and the Irthing from 1840 till the 1880's. However, developments on Hadrian's Wall

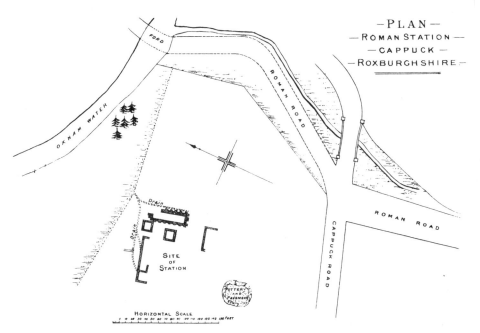

Fig. 1.3   Laidlaw's plan of Cappuck 1892.

thereafter, particularly as a result of the series of planned excavations undertaken on the instigation of the Cumberland and Westmorland Antiquarian Society, powerfully influenced archaeological thinking in Scotland, where considerable interest was already being aroused by work on the Roman frontier in Upper and Lower Germany. The thorough exploration of Hardknott fort in Cumberland by Calverley and Dymond in the years following 1889, and the institution of the Reichs-Limeskommission in Germany in 1892, gave added impetus to a feeling that study of the Roman monuments of Scotland should be put on a more regular footing.

The first concerted action came, as so often in the succeeding history of Roman studies in Scotland, from the Glasgow Archaeological Society, which between 1890 and 1893 conducted a programme of excavations and exploration on the line of the Antonine Wall. The project was guided by a committee comprising an inspector of schools, a landowner, a factor, an architect, and a procurator-fiscal, who compiled a report (G.A.S. 1899) which far surpassed any antiquarian work hitherto undertaken in Scotland, combining lucid presentation of the archaeological data with judicious assessment of the literary and epigraphic evidence; the measured section-drawings were produced with a careful attention to detail that ensured their continuing usefulness to later generations of field-workers. The report did not concern itself, however, with the wall-forts, but only the various elements of the running barrier itself. The time had now come for a similarly intensive examination of the various posts which had held the Roman army of occupation throughout the country.

Thus in 1895 the Society of Antiquaries of Scotland decided to embark upon a series of excavations, acting on a suggestion made by the Dumfries and Galloway Antiquarian Society, who pointed to the desirability of a practical examination of the Roman fort at Birrens, near Ecclefechan, and the Roman siege-works at Birrenswark, some 10km to the north. Work commenced at Birrens at the beginning of June in the same year, the direction of the excavation being in the hands of a Committee of eight, initially with a force of four workmen, later increased to eight. Although overall management remained in the hands of the committee, day-to-day supervision of the task was entrusted to a clerk of works, Mr Thomas Ely.

Individual members of the committee, especially those living close at hand, or with a particular interest in the work like James Barbour, might spend considerable lengths of time on site, but it was the clerk of works in this and succeeding excavations promoted by the Society of Antiquaries who bore the brunt of the task. To those accustomed to the hierarchical organisation of a modern excavation, with professional directors, the method seems more than a little haphazard, but there can be no doubt that, within their limits, the combined efforts of skilled labourers and painstaking clerks of works produced remarkable results, and it is perhaps to them rather than to the supervisory committees that we should be grateful for the early progress in site exploration. There is every reason to believe, however, that Lord Abercromby's direction of work at Inchtuthil in 1901 was a notable exception to this rule (Abercromby et al., 1902). The photographs taken during excavation (Plate 3) indicate the attainment of standards evidently unsought under other directors. One can only speculate how great a loss was occasioned to Roman studies by Abercromby's subsequent quarrel with the Society.

Thanks to the perceptive eyes of Ely and Barbour, as well as the draughting skills of the latter, who was an architect in Dumfries, the excavation of Birrens produced as complete a plan of a Roman auxiliary fort as had ever been revealed on the Roman frontier in Britain (Fig. 1.4). Modern excavation (see below, pp. 22–3) has refined some of the identifications then made, but it has not materially altered the general picture presented by Barbour's pioneering plan (Christison et al., 1895). In time it was joined in the annals of archaeology by the report on excavations of such forts as Housesteads on Hadrian's Wall (1898), Gellygaer in Wales (1903), and Melandra Castle in Derbyshire (1906), but in Scotland it long stood as an exemplar against which all other sites might be judged, as well as providing a memorial to the vision of those early members of the Dumfries and Galloway Society.

Although the next fifteen years saw a veritable spate of excavations on Roman sites in Scotland, few were able to match, in completeness of record, the results won at Birrens. For this there were various reasons, but the most important was the state of preservation of the remains. The sites selected – Ardoch (1896–7), Birrenswark (1898), Camelon (1899–1900) Lyne and Inchtuthil (1901), Castlecary (1902), Rough Castle (1903), Bar Hill (1902–5), and Newstead (1905–10) – represented the most imposing Roman defensive works in the country, which had already figured largely in antiquarian studies. What could not be known, however, was that, unlike many of the sites uncovered in Northern England, where the occupation of Roman sites had continued till the later fourth century AD and most of the internal structures had been robustly built (and re-built) in stone, a great number of the Scottish forts contained a high proportion of timber buildings, only the central range being constructed in stone. Moreover, the life-span of the Scottish forts, and therefore the depth of

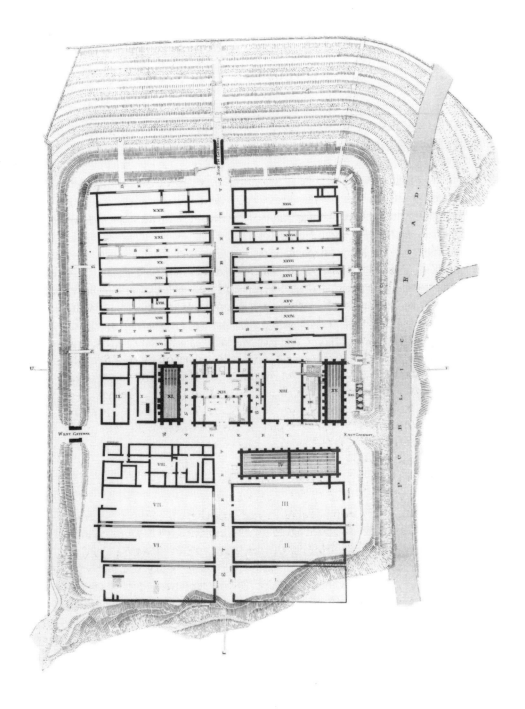

Fig. 1.4 Plan of Birrens as excavated in 1895.

stratification within them, was much less than in the case of their English counterparts, with the result that the former had been afforded correspondingly less protection against the erosive processes of cultivation and other forms of land-development.

It is not surprising, therefore, that many of the plans of this period display areas which are either blank or occupied by fragmentary traces — areas which we now know would have contained the remains of barracks built entirely of wood, or with a wooden superstructure resting upon stone sills; in either case the buildings were such as to leave only the most fugitive of traces. All the more credit, accordingly, that in some cases the former existence of timber structures should have been identified and their outline recovered. The honour of being the first excavator in Scotland to make this discovery belongs to Thomas Ely, when acting as clerk of works at Ardoch (Christison et al., 1898, 445-6; see below, pp. 115–18), but Alexander Mackie was doubtless behind the recognition of the post-trenches of barracks at Lyne and Inchtuthil, his invaluable services as clerk of works being retained at seven out of the ten pioneering explorations listed above. At Bar Hill, the survival of the wooden posts themselves enabled the excavators to recognise the position of at least one of the garrison's barrack-blocks; in this case too the recognition probably resulted from the skill of the overseer, John McIntosh, forester on the Gartshore estate, to whom 'the duty of immediate supervision' was entrusted by the 'archaeologists'. The dependence of the various excavating committees or directors of excavation upon their respective clerks of works is amply demonstrated by a telling passage in the preface to James Curle's report on the fort at Newstead (Curle, 1911, vii):

> 'The excavations were begun on 13th February, 1905 and continued without interruption until 19th May, 1909. After an interval of some months, work was resumed on the 22nd December of that year, and finally brought to a close in the middle of September, 1910. During these periods of work my residence within a mile of the site enabled me to make frequent, and often daily, visits to follow the progress of the digging ... Throughout the whole period of our working, Mr Alexander Mackie acted as Clerk of Works. Mr Mackie had gained experience under the Society in their excavations at Birrenswark, Inchtuthil and Lyne ... and was thus able to render valuable service in working out the problems of the site. He stuck to his post undeterred by weather, and by his shrewd observation

contributed in no small measure to the success of the
undertaking. The photographs of the foundations were all taken
by Mr Mackie.'

In this series of excavations there were other, largely unsung heroes;
the draughtsmen and surveyors. The contribution of James Barbour has
already been mentioned at Birrens; Thomas Ross, co-author of a major
architectural survey, *The Castellated and Domestic Architecture of Scotland*,
advised or assisted in the planning and surveying at Camelon, Inchtuthil,
Lyne and Newstead. The published plans of all these sites are straightforward and, in the main, trustworthy accounts of what was discovered by
the excavators, not always at a scale large enough to permit critical examination of the individual buildings, but of a satisfactory clarity; where they
fell short as illustrative records of the excavation was in the lack of strati-
graphic documentation. Such section-drawings of defences or internal
structures as chanced to be published were at too small a scale and too
rudimentary to be of any use to later generations of scholars. In their
defence, it must be admitted that although the importance of stratigraphy
had long since been demonstrated by Pitt-Rivers, it was not yet appreciated
by the archaeological world at large; it could hardly be expected, therefore,
that two practising architects should give it any degree of prominence.
Nevertheless, the work of T.H. Cunningham, a civil engineer and
Treasurer of the Society of Antiquaries, and the trained surveyor Mungo
Buchanan, demonstrated what could be achieved by site-directors who
were really interested in the techniques and mysteries of scientific excavation. Cunningham's plan and sections of Ardoch are still worthy of the
highest praise: the former produced at 1:500, or thereby, represent a
masterly interpretation of a complex and extensive series of earthworks, on
which it would not be easy to improve; the latter were reproduced at about
1:150, and although somewhat lacking in detail, still offer a basis for
discussing the structural development of the site (see below, pp. 165–9).
Buchanan, from his style, would seem to have been a freer spirit, for his
plans and sections have an almost atmospheric quality (Fig. **1.5**); an
attractive blend of pen and colour wash, they constitute subjective comment rather than objective reporting, and although the results may be less
reliable, considered as measured drawings, there can be no doubt that they
are the product of sensitive observation – a talent which appears to have
been all too rare in the early excavators. The published illustrations of the
Camelon report must be considered his finest work; the detailed sections
and elevation of the best preserved buildings, reproduced at 1:60, and the

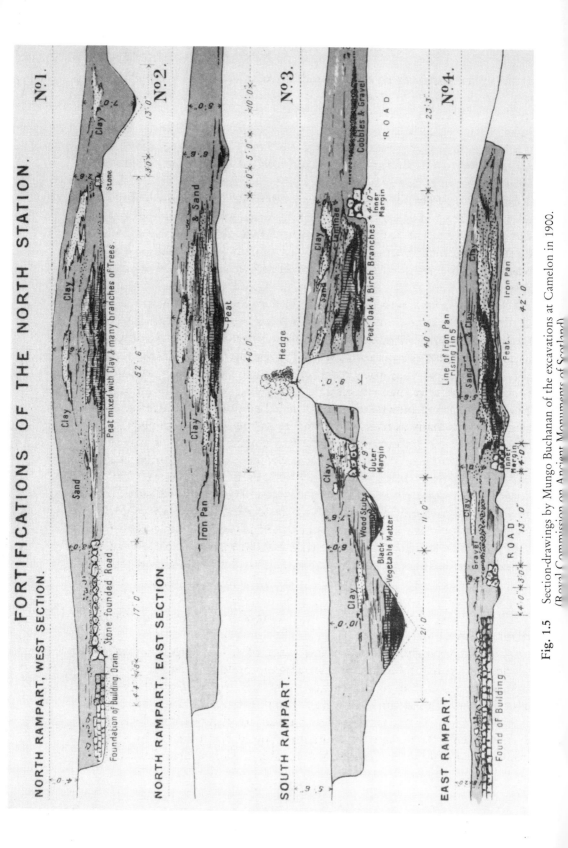

Fig. 1.5   Section-drawings by Mungo Buchanan of the excavations at Camelon in 1900.
(Royal Commission on Ancient Monuments of Scotland)

section-drawings of the defences, published at *c.* 1:170, particularly the latter, reveal the enquiring mind that is the essential attribute of the modern excavator. The original drawings, now housed in the National Monuments Record of Scotland, were first drawn in pencil and then worked up with pen and ink and watercolours, the full range of which is not shown by the two-tone blocks of the actual publication. Finally, the drawings were annotated to illustrate the diverse nature of the stratification, layers of clay, sand, gravel, and laminated turf being duly distinguished, and the presence of peat, brushwood, vegetable matter, charcoal, and lines of iron pan carefully indicated. The result was a standard of graphic recording which had not been previously attained and which was not to be surpassed or even approached in Scotland for more than thirty years.

The excessive length of this interval may be explained partly by the character of those directing the succeeding series of site-excavations, partly by the change of pace and direction which occurred in the study of Roman Scotland after the First World War. In a sense, this was inevitable after almost two decades of breathtakingly rapid advance. A process which began as little more than site-clearance had developed into a tool of some discrimination. At Newstead, James Curle had not only succeeded in distinguishing as many as five separate structural periods – establishing it as perhaps the most important multi-period Roman site in Scotland – but had even been able to identify the respective dates of the different occupations. His examination of the great wealth of small finds recovered during excavation itself represented a work of considerable scholarship and an almost immeasurable advance on what had been attempted up till then; it also underlined the importance of comparative study, both of structures and artefacts, pointing out to the student of Roman archaeology, as was already obvious to the prehistorian, that Scotland was an integral part of a much broader scene. It is a mark of James Curle's achievement that his report on the excavation at Newstead (1911) continues to be both consulted for enlightenment and – rare distinction among archaeological reports – read for pleasure.

Not surprisingly, the depth and range of scholarship manifested in Curle's report had the effect of discouraging random 'site-clearance'. The way ahead was now seen to be through scholarly appreciation of the wider context in which Roman sites were set and by selective use of excavation as a scientific research-tool. This new philosophy, if such it may be termed, derived even greater support from its espousal and practice by Curle's friend and mentor, Sir George Macdonald. If ever a man bestrode his professional world like a colossus, that man was Macdonald in the field of Roman British studies. He was the son of Dr James Macdonald, headmaster and scholar, who had himself made a notable contribution to the subject as author of several articles on Roman roads in Scotland (1894, 1895) and, more notably in 1897, of *Tituli Hunteriani,* an authoritative account of the extensive collection of Roman stones in the Hunterian Museum of the University of Glasgow. George Macdonald had thus been brought up in an atmosphere in which scholarship and Roman archaeology had been happily blended, and his own considerable intellectual gifts, heightened and refined in a scholastic career of exceptional brilliance, ensured that those first affections for antiquity were developed and tested within the framework of an exacting academic discipline. In the words of Curle's obituary (1940), he possessed an equipment such as has rarely fallen to the lot of Scottish antiquaries; Macdonald made excellent use of it.

The first major contribution to archaeology was in his numismatic studies. As lecturer in Greek at the University of Glasgow he had been appointed honorary curator of the Hunter Coin Cabinet in 1893, and his powers of discrimination and organisation were soon amply displayed in the work of systematising and publication by which he made available the treasures of that collection to the scholarly world. In 1902 he assisted in the excavation of the fort at Bar Hill on the Antonine Wall, eventually collaborating with Alexander Park in the compiling of the report (1906). Although now a busy administrator in the Scottish Education Department, Macdonald continued to pursue his studies into the northern frontier-line and, following up an opportunity presented by his delivery of the Dalrymple Lectures in 1910, produced in the succeeding year the first edition of his now classic work *The Roman Wall in Scotland.* In this he drew together all that could possibly be learned about the Antonine Wall – from early antiquaries, from inscriptions, from the surviving traces on the ground, and from what little had been revealed by excavation. Like Curle's *Newstead,* the *Roman Wall* set standards by which all subsequent treatment of the subject might be judged; indeed, as a work of reference, it was not to be surpassed until the issue of the second edition in 1934. That the history of Roman studies in Scotland between the two World Wars is largely the history of research into the Antonine Wall reflects the enormous influence of Sir George – he was made a Knight Commander of the Bath in 1927 – throughout the country. Not that his own interests were confined to that monument alone, as a glance at the range of his published articles will demonstrate; but the final chapter of the first edition of the *Roman Wall* had contained a plea for proper examination of the barrier to be mounted before the destructive agencies of modern development could remove further traces of an important national monument.

Macdonald himself set an example with a comprehensive programme of observation in the field, tested where necessary by excavation, his early experience at Bar Hill and the results of S.N. Miller's work at Balmuildy fort in 1912 – 14 having shown what an increase in knowledge might be expected from a carefully directed exploration. With the support of the Glasgow Archaeological Society, which had long (understandably) looked upon the investigation of the Antonine Wall as its peculiar responsibility, further large-scale excavations were also undertaken. In 1923 – 4 S.N. Miller examined the western terminal fort at Old Kilpatrick; and in 1929 – 31 John Clarke directed work at Cadder, where the Antonine Wall is crossed by the Forth and Clyde Canal. Two years earlier, Macdonald and A.O. Curle had collaborated to investigate the fort at Mumrills in an excavation promoted by the Society of Antiquaries, while in 1931 Macdonald alone had embarked upon an exploration of the fort at Croy Hill which was to be continued intermittently until 1936.

Reading the reports of these excavations, from Balmuildy published in 1922, to the latest examination of Croy Hill, one is struck by the degree of uniformity which they exhibit. For the most part, they share with their predecessors a lack of interest in the evidence presented by stratification, and the standard of illustrations depicting site- and building-plans is generally disappointing; although when the working relationship between Macdonald and C.S.T. Calder (of the Royal Commission on the Ancient and Historical Monuments of Scotland) became established, presumably after Macdonald's appointment as a Commissioner in 1924, things began to improve. Calder's draughtsmanship, which embellishes the second edition of *Roman Wall* with its simple elegance, seems first to have been called into play for the Mumrills report (1929), but even its attractive qualities cannot hide the fact that the actual techniques of excavation had not progressed much beyond what was being achieved by Ely and Mackie at the end of the preceding century. The full photographic record, to which generous resort was made for publication, amply demonstrates the limitations which the old-fashioned methods necessarily imposed. Indeed, it is ironical that the increased use of photography, itself an instance of one of the improvements on earlier exploration, should now serve to highlight the inadequacy of the approach. At Mumrills, for example (Plate 4), the prints reveal with impartial candour (Macdonald & Curle, 1929, *passim*) such vistas of apparent devastation that it is surprising so comprehensible a plan could have been extracted from its midst.

It was, in fact, only as a result of Macdonald's highly trained powers of observation and deduction that a credible story could be wrung from such unpromising materials. But increasingly this apparent lack of concern for technique became an unnecessary obstacle to place in the path of site-exploration; as is made clear by Sir George's description of the arrangements for his latest work at Croy Hill, where Samuel Smith was to act as his deputy-supervisor:

> 'Residing within manageable distance, he (Smith) never lost contact with the work for a day, an ideal which it would have been hopeless for me to aim at ... His gift of observation, coupled with his appreciation of the possible importance of seemingly trivial appearances, was a guarantee that nothing of moment was being missed, and he never failed to summon me if any new feature emerged.'

No matter that such reports incorporated the results of the most judicious consideration of artefactual evidence, while the survey of historical context and comparative material shed a comprehensively illuminating ray, and rigorously impartial scrutiny of the structural evidence reduced the hypothetical element to an irreproachable minimum; if the structures themselves were not to be revealed in all their complexity, the greatest intellect in the world might travail in vain to interpret them. In short, if further progress was to be made in the study of Roman Scotland, the high intellectual standards established by Macdonald had to be combined with a more sympathetic approach to the technical skills of excavation.

Fortunately such a combination had already been realised on Hadrian's Wall, where the decade 1930−9 saw yet another torrent of work, which laid the foundations of our present understanding of the origin and development of the southern barrier. Foremost among the leaders and promoters of this comprehensive programme were F.G. Simpson, Parker Brewis, Eric Birley, and Ian Richmond; the last two, representing the younger generation of archaeologists, carried that interest in the Roman frontier northwards into Scotland and thus effectively filled the gap which had opened in the study of the Roman period beyond Solway and Cheviot.

It is not surprising, in view of their origin, that one of the first sites which attracted Birley and Richmond was Birrens, lying immediately north of the western terminal of the Hadrianic frontier. In 1936−7 their re-examination of the fort by selective trenching furnished evidence of the successive re-casting of the defences and re-construction of the internal structures; more accurate assessment was now made of the various periods of occupation, and a case made out for the recognition of the fort as an outpost of Hadrian's Wall when other stations in Scotland had been abandoned. Birley and Richmond were to work together on other Scottish sites later in their careers, but for the former Hadrian's Wall was to remain his main sphere of activity, while Richmond was destined to make a contribution to Roman archaeology in Scotland which is in every way comparable with that of Sir George Macdonald (Fig. **1.6**).

Since the publication of his first article in the *Proceedings* of the Society of Antiquaries in 1922, on the subject of the Ptolemaic Map of Scotland, Richmond had developed an interest in the earliest penetration of North

Fig. 1.6   Sir Ian Richmond in the field in 1949; an 'action photograph' taken as he was carried across the Borthwick Water on the line of Dere Street, the porter being Angus Graham, then Secretary of the Royal Commission. In the official archive this view is reputedly filed: 'Graham, A., see under Richmond'! (Royal Commission on Ancient Monuments of Scotland)

Britain by the Roman army. Consequently, when the chance presented itself in 1936 to examine what seemed likely to be an early castellum on the outer frontier at Fendoch, in the very mouth of the Sma' Glen in Perthshire, he commenced operations with a will. Richmond's intention was to uncover as complete a plan of the interior as possible, but with economy of effort (and minimal disturbance of the remains). Having defined the position of the defences, he drove a series of exploratory trenches obliquely through the various divisions of the interior, supplementing the evidence thus obtained and confirming the outline which they partially revealed by sinking test pits at crucial points. Given the strictly limited object of his enquiry, the method was extremely successful, particularly on sites like Fendoch, where only one period of occupation was to be encountered (Fig. 5.3). On more complex sites it was admittedly less informative, but the comparatively symmetrical and orderly layout of Roman military works helped to ensure that gross errors were avoided. The technique was also admirably suited to elucidating the plan of timber structures and, as Richmond showed, all the internal buildings at Fendoch had been made of timber; the slots and pits in which the sole-plates and uprights had once stood were clearly recognisable as disturbed areas in the virgin gravel subsoil which formed the floor of each exploratory trench. The pioneering work of Thomas Ely at Ardoch, after forty years of comparative neglect, had at last been brought to fruition, and archaeology was finally equipped with the skills necessary to explore the great series of earth-and-timber forts of the Scottish *limes*.

Although the outbreak of the Second World War put a temporary halt to the onward flow of archaeological research, by the time peace had been restored, younger colleagues with similar outlook and training had appeared to swell the tide of reconnaissance and excavation. Richmond went on, now a professor at the University of Oxford, to locate or examine various Roman works, notably in 1947 the great fort at Newstead and the presumed siege-works at Woden Law, Roxburghshire. In much of his research he either collaborated with or drew upon the skills of J.K.S. St Joseph of Cambridge, whose espousal of aerial survey as an archaeological research tool was to alter almost beyond recognition the face of Roman Britain (see below, pp. 48–9). It was as a result of air photography of the legionary fortress of Inchtuthil taken by St Joseph that the great programme of excavation at that site was begun in 1952 and continued until Richmond's tragically early death in 1965; in this project the techniques of exploratory trenching could be said to have reached their apotheosis, with the result that the complete plan of a Roman fortified enclosure, 53 acres

(21.5ha) in extent, the key position of the northernmost frontier of Britain in the first century, was made available for study (see below, pp. 100–5). In the same period, Anne Robertson, Keeper of the Hunter Coin Cabinet and the Cultural Collections in the Hunterian Museum, Glasgow, presided over the pursuit of Roman studies in western Scotland, with particular responsibility for the Antonine Wall, while Kenneth Steer, as an officer, and later Secretary of the Royal Commission on the Ancient and Historical Monuments of Scotland, maintained watch and ward over more easterly regions, especially the eastern and central Borders, where the Commission was active in the 1950s and 1960s. While Professor Robertson may be said to have traced her descent from the tradition represented by Macdonald, Dr Steer, as a Durham-trained graduate, reflected the influence of the 'Hadrianic' school, the two essential strands of modern Roman archaeology thus being united in their combined contribution to the subject, the background of which was the mounting roll of discoveries effected by the brilliantly successful aerial survey of Professor St Joseph. All three have now retired, but in the light of their researches and in the hands of those who succeeded them, the work of exploring and understanding Roman Scotland has continued to develop, as it did in the days of their predecessors.

2

Emperors, Generals, and Conquest

*T*O THE BEST OF OUR KNOWLEDGE, the interval which elapsed between the invasion of Britain under the Emperor Claudius in AD 43 and the first Roman military penetration of Scotland was approximately thirty-five years. The history of Rome's piecemeal annexation of the British mainland in this period records a chequered career of relentless, apparently imperturbable advance, of sudden checks, and the slow grinding campaigns of attrition by which resisting tribes in sequestered upland fastnesses were gradually brought to heel. It took roughly four years to overrun the lowland areas of England, the line of the Rivers Trent and Severn being reached by c. AD 50 and all Britons to the south and east disarmed. The work of Romanisation, of converting a conquered people into loyal citizens of a supranational empire might now begin, while an apparently invincible army began the long haul against the nations of the Highland zone. To the north, stretching from sea to sea on either side of the Pennines, lay the confederate tribes of the Brigantes, whose farthest marches extended northwestwards from the Tyne to the lower reaches of Annandale. As yet, this great potential source of danger to the infant province of Britannia was neutralised by diplomatic means, the Brigantian queen Cartimandua having perceived that a Roman alliance was preferable to Roman occupation.

Accordingly, the attention of the provincial governors could be turned to the tribes of the west, initially the Decangi or Deceangli of Flintshire and the Silures of South Wales and Monmouthshire. By AD 60, however, the governor of the day, Suetonius Paullinus, was still campaigning in North

Wales, when the great rising of Boudicca, queen of the Iceni of Norfolk, drew him back from an assault on the Druidic centre in Anglesey. The revolt of the Iceni, who were joined by their neighbours the Trinovantes of Essex, had almost plunged the province into total ruin before Paullinus brought the rebel forces to battle on a field of his own choosing and re-established the superiority of Roman arms. But it had been an extremely close-run thing, and for the next eight years, until the fall of Nero in AD 68, priority was given to repairing the damage and restoring stability. In the meantime, the centre of the empire itself was subject to destabilising in-fluences, and AD 69 saw four emperors succeed one another on the imperial throne, the final victor being Vespasian, originator of the Flavian dynasty and one of the officers to whom Claudius had entrusted the work of the invasion in AD 43. Although the task of conducting military operations in the province did not cease while Italy was convulsed with the struggle for power, there was no consistently guiding hand to ensure that the wisest policies were being followed. With Vespasian in supreme com-mand however, a new spirit of confidence and purpose manifested itself in Britain. First of all Petillius Cerealis (71–74) and then Julius Frontinus (74–77) were appointed to the governorship: the former marched his troops into the North Country, overrunning the lands of the Brigantes; the latter, after a quarter of a century of desultory warfare waged by his predecessors, completed the subjugation of the tribes of South Wales.

The governor who succeeded Frontinus, arriving late in the cam-paigning season, nevertheless reacted to a recent atrocity committed by the Ordovices of North Wales, and leading his columns into the heart of their mountainous domain, virtually wiped out the entire tribe. By this prompt and decisive action, which included the final conquest of Anglesey, the new governor won immediate golden opinions, as people wondered what his next exploits might be. His name was Gnaeus Julius Agricola, and in seven whirlwind years he was destined to penetrate the very heart of Caledonia (Fig. **2.1**).

When Agricola assumed the governorship in AD 77 or 78 (the actual year is uncertain) he found himself in control of an army comprising four legions and probably at least ninety auxiliary regiments of foot and horse. At any given time an appreciable proportion of these troops would have been engaged in garrison duties of one sort or another, the mobilisation of a field force occurring only during the campaigning season, between March and October. The legions, composed of freeborn Roman citizens, were each about 5500 strong and they represented the flower of the Roman army; they were subdivided into ten cohorts, the first of which was 1000

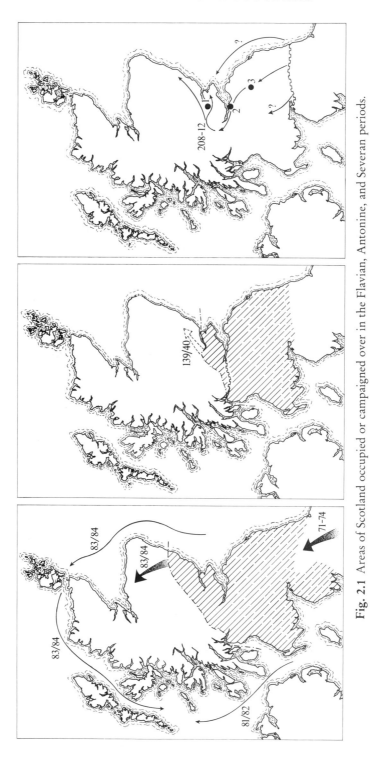

Fig. 2.1 Areas of Scotland occupied or campaigned over in the Flavian, Antonine, and Severan periods.

men strong, (or milliary), the others containing only 500 (quingenary). Each quingenary cohort was formed of six centuries of eighty men apiece, commanded by a centurion; the first cohort comprised five double centuries. The auxiliary regiments (which were for the most part recruited from non-citizens), took the form of quingenary and milliary cohorts of infantry, also composed of centuries, and cavalry squadrons (*alae*) of similar strengths, subdivided into sixteen troops (*turmae*) of thirty-two men respectively, each *turma* being commanded by a decurion. Some of the auxiliary cohorts were composite units, a proportion of their strength (about a quarter) being mounted; these were known as *cohortes equitatae*. Although all Roman soldiers were superbly trained and equipped, the legions provided the extra specialist services that in the modern army would be provided by a separate corps. Thus, the legionaries numbered amongst their ranks personnel skilled in artillery, engineering tasks, signalling, transport, and medical services, to name but a few; there was even a small cavalry element. The four legions stationed in Britain during Agricola's governorship were *II Augusta*, based at Caerleon, *II Adiutrix* at Chester, *IX Hispana* at York, and *XX Valeria Victrix* at Wroxeter, but in the summer months vexillations, or major subdivisions, of each legion, comprising several cohorts, would have been put into the field to form the backbone of the campaign force.

Where that force was deployed in the years from 77 to 83 (for convenience, only the earlier dating will be used) we learn from the pages of one of Rome's foremost historians, Tacitus, to whom Agricola had the good fortune to entrust his daughter in marriage. Tacitus's account of his father-in-law's career, *de vita Agricolae*, represents the most detailed description of any series of Roman frontier campaigns ever written, but it was also a literary creation, and in the absence of directly confirmatory archaeological evidence for any particular statement – which is quite frequently the case – extreme caution must be exercised in its interpretation, as will be seen later (e.g. pp. 54–6). Nevertheless, it is an indispensable guide to the general course of events in these seven momentous years.

In the second year of campaigning, Tacitus tells us that Agricola gave further display of his active leadership, carrying out a reconnaissance in an area of forests and estuaries, giving the enemy no rest from ceaseless harrying, yet often winning the day by diplomacy, and finally enmeshing the defeated peoples in a network of roads and garrisons. The description of the terrain thus covered (Tacitus, *Agricola*, 20) is too vague to offer any possibility of precise identification, but we may be reasonably certain the field of operations lay in northern England among the Brigantes. The means of access into Scotland, first glimpsed afar off by Petillius Cerealis, were now secured ready for invasion. The third season (79) brought the Romans into contact with hitherto unknown tribes, and the enemy were harassed perhaps as far north as the estuary of the Tay; the panic caused by this lightning advance was such that there was little resistance, and the army had leisure to engage in fort-building – an operation which would normally have been left to the following season when the tide of war had surged far beyond the newly conquered areas (*Agricola*, 22). In 80, presumably taking advantage of this unexpected passivity, Agricola set about consolidating his gains, making sure of his grasp on the land he had overrun by establishing a chain of stations across the Forth-Clyde isthmus (*Agricola*, 23).

The next year, the fifth of his governorship, was the occasion for more open warfare against tribes not previously encountered, but success once more crowned his troops' endeavours, and he began to prepare bases in the coastal areas facing Ireland, in case it might prove possible to invade and conquer that island also. His hope was that in so doing he might remove a possible source of trouble on his western flank (*Agricola*, 24); but this was not to be, for in the succeeding season, 82, fears of hostile action by natives living north of the Forth, in that part of Britain which Agricola knew as Caledonia, committed him to combined operations, with fleet and field-army working in conjunction – an innovation in military tactics according to Tacitus – which had a considerable psychological effect on the natives opposing him. By this time the emperor Vespasian had been succeeded by his younger son, Domitian, after the brief reign of the elder son, Titus. Military success in Britain could not have been unwelcome to an emperor newly established upon the imperial throne, and it was thus, presumably, with Domitian's entire approval that Agricola again moved north. Taking a considerable risk, he divided his landforces into three battle-groups, hoping that he would thus more easily locate the enemy's line of march and avoid being outflanked; his concern at this stage must have been very real, for the Caledonian tribes had already given an earnest of their intentions by an open assault on a number of frontier forts. At one stage it almost seemed that Agricola's gamble might not after all come off, for the enemy, learning that the battle-group formed around the Ninth Legion was the weakest of the three, launched a night assault upon it. By good luck, however, as they moved in for the attack, their tracks were picked up by scouts, and Agricola was informed in time to lead a flying column to the rescue; what had been threatening to become disaster now blossomed into victory, and the Caledonian forces melted swiftly away into the surrounding swamps and thickets (*Agricola*, 25–27).

The last of Agricola's campaigns, which at the outset served to occupy his mind when the grief of losing an infant son weighed heavily upon him, was directed at bringing the entire Caledonian forces to bay in a set-piece battle. With the fleet harrying the coastal districts, a battle-group unencumbered by the usual baggage-train, and therefore equipped for speedy action, set forth to meet the Caledonians. The latter, showing a rare unanimity, had gathered together a force numbering more than 30,000 men at a hilltop site known to Agricola as *Mons Graupius*, which the Roman army finally reached comparatively late in the campaigning season. After exhortation from their respective commanders – the Caledonians had chosen a warrior named Calgacus, 'the Swordsman', as their leader – battle was joined.

To begin with, the Romans laid down a barrage of javelins and other long-range missiles, but these did not seriously inconvenience the native troops, who were drawn up, rank on serried rank, along the heights of *Mons Graupius*, overlooking the Roman line of battle. Eventually, the word was given to come to close quarters, and the auxiliary regiments began to push the enemy slowly back up the hill, aided by squadrons of cavalry, who caused instant alarm amongst the native ranks. However, as the resistance grew fiercer and the ground steeper, the advance came gradually to a halt, and fresh elements of the Caledonian army began to descend the hill in an attempt to outflank the now-victorious auxiliaries. For such a counter move Agricola had been waiting, and the cavalry regiments he had kept in reserve were instantly despatched on each wing to meet the developing threat. With this move the defeat of the native forces became a rout, and, before night fell, up to 10,000 of the enemy had fallen at the cost of only 360 Roman lives. It was a signal victory, but the approach of winter made it impossible to penetrate as far as the success of arms had warranted. Marching down to the coast, Agricola made contact with his fleet, which he now sent on into northern waters to confirm that Britain was indeed an island, while the land forces slowly retraced their steps to winter quarters (*Agricola*, 29–38).

Of the succeeding years of occupation Tacitus tells us nothing save for an epigrammatic description of the fate of the province in the later years of the emperor Domitian : *perdomita Britannia et statim omissa* – 'Britain was completely mastered and then immediately thrown away'. Indeed, for the history of events in Britain from AD 83 until the end of the second century we must rely on similar comments, embedded in the accounts of imperial achievements that were, both literally and metaphorically, closer to the heart of the Empire; the contrast with the literary evidence available for the Flavian period could not be greater. Thus, the withdrawal from Scotland under Trajan (AD 98 – 117) and the subsequent construction of the Stanegate system of forts guarding the Tyne-Solway isthmus go unrecorded in Rome's surviving annals. Even the building by his successor Hadrian of the great stone and turf wall between Wallsend and Bowness on Solway merits only the brief comment that Hadrian visited Britain, 'instituted many reforms, and was the first to build a wall 80 miles long to separate the barbarians from the Romans' (*SHA*, Hadrian, 11). Without the fruits of archaeological research we should know nothing of the changes of plan which took place before Hadrian's Wall in its final form was constructed on the southern isthmus.

A similar brevity characterises the references to the operations which brought the Romans back into Scotland on the accession of the Emperor Antoninus Pius in AD 138 (Fig. **2.1**). Although it is now thought unlikely that hostile pressure in Britain was the only reason that compelled him once more to take the offensive, the Augustan History states bluntly that Pius 'engaged in many wars through his legates (provincial governors); for he conquered the Britons through Lollius Urbicus, the legate (in control of Britain), and, driving back the barbarians, constructed another wall of turf' (*SHA*, Pius, 5,4). The wall which was then erected spanned the narrower, northern isthmus between Bridgeness, near Bo'ness on the Forth, and the right bank of the Clyde at Old Kilpatrick, on the north-western outskirts of Glasgow. The preceding British victory that won Antonine his second Imperial acclamation is recorded on coins of AD 142 or 143; these depict Britannia in a subdued or dejected pose which contrasts sharply with the proudly confident demeanour represented on modern British coins. Similar coin-types issued in AD 154 – 6 have been taken to indicate that there was a rising on the northern frontier at that time, which brought the first Antonine occupation of Scotland to an abrupt end. Archaeological evidence, nevertheless, shows that the country between the Tyne-Solway isthmus and the Tay was soon re-occupied, but not for long, and it is now reckoned that the end of this second Antonine period coincided with the war that threatened to break out early in the reign of the succeeding emperor, Marcus Aurelius, when Sextus Calpurnius Agricola was despatched (*c*. 163) to take control of the situation.

It is uncertain whether another reference to the imminence of war in Britain under Marcus Aurelius represents a separate outbreak or a confusion with that already mentioned, but in the early 180s, under his successor Commodus, we learn from the historian Cassius Dio (lxxii, 8) that the tribes in Britain 'crossed the wall that separated them from the encampments of the Romans, caused great havoc, and slew a Roman general with the troops under his command'. Ulpius Marcellus, the governor whom Commodus sent to take charge of the situation, meted out harsh punishment to the invading tribes and, if we may believe the testimony of coins dated to 184, won a convincing victory which justified the emperor in adding the epithet 'Britannicus' to his titles. Although it is clear that such a victory could not have been won without some form of campaigning, probably to the north of Hadrian's Wall, there is as yet no firm evidence to show that a re-occupation of the lost lands beyond the Tweed was ever contemplated. Indeed, there is reason to believe that the outpost forts which had guarded the way north from Cheviot to the Tweed – the last of all the Antonine foundations – were now abandoned for good.

However, history records one last interlude of Roman rule in Scotland before the equivalent of prehistoric obscurity once more descended. This brief episode (Fig. **2.1**) originated in one of the most troubled periods of imperial and provincial history, the final decade of the second century. By AD 192 opposition to the wayward and tyrannical follies of Commodus had grown to a head, and on the last day of the year the emperor was assassinated. His successor, Publius Helvius Pertinax, a former governor of Britain, was removed from power within three months, to be replaced by Didius Julianus, who won this position of supreme power, not by force of arms or personal qualities, but by making the highest bid for the support of the Praetorian Guard. His appointment was greeted with a mixture of

| 1 | 2 | 3 | 4 |

Fig. **2.2**   Coin-portraits of the emperors Vespasian (1), under whom the conquest of Scotland began *c*. AD 79, Domitian (2), who may have rejected total conquest, Antoninus Pius (3), who authorised the northern Wall, and Septimius Severus (4), who died campaigning against the northern tribes in AD 211.

anger and derision by the governors of those provinces whose military strength had already endowed their masters with almost imperial authority. Foremost amongst these were Pescennius Niger, commanding the army of Syria, Lucius Septimius Severus, governor of Pannonia (a province on the middle Danube), and Decimus Clodius Albinus in Britain. The first to make a move was Pescennius Niger, who speedily annexed the ten legions of the eastern provinces, but the shrewdest tactics were displayed by Septimius Severus. Knowing that control of the city of Rome counted almost as much as military might and legal right, he marched swiftly and successfully into Italy, at the same time taking the wind out of Clodius Albinus's sails by offering him the rank of Caesar (or junior imperial colleague). There followed several years of campaigning against Pescennius Niger in the East, and a series of operations against the Parthians, Rome's most dangerous enemy on the eastern frontier. Before these had been brought to a successful conclusion, Albinus, realising that in all probability his turn was next, chose to go on the offensive rather than be caught like a rat in an insular trap. Claiming the imperial throne in his own name, he assembled an expeditionary force from the garrison of Britannia and crossed over into Gaul, where on the 19th of February 196 he narrowly failed to defeat the army of Severus, and committed suicide.

It was long thought that to support his claim Albinus had stripped the northern frontier of the majority of its garrison, leaving the province defenceless before the onslaughts of the northern barbarians, but archaeological evidence once identified as representing the traces of a tempest of destruction at the time, is now seen to be of a more equivocal character. It is in any case most improbable that even the lure of supreme power would have blinded Albinus to the folly of removing the bulwarks of the province. Thus, when Virius Lupus, the new governor appointed by Severus, arrived in Britain he may have found the frontier under pressure and the northern tribes restive, but it is less than likely that he was faced with widespread scenes of devastation. Nevertheless, it is clear that whatever trouble there was came from the North. Soon after his arrival Lupus was forced to purchase peace from a tribe known as the Maeatae, who had evidently already clashed with Roman forces, for they now returned some prisoners (Dio, lxxv, 5). The Maeatae were about to be assisted in this belligerence by the Caledonii, their northern neighbours, despite promises that had been made in some earlier treaty not to combine against the Roman province. We are told that these two tribes were confederacies who had swallowed up all the lesser peoples of Northern Britain, who had not yet been won over to the side of Rome or brought within its realms. On

the south, the Maeatae probably marched with the Dumnonii, who
occupied much of Central Region and Strathclyde, and the Votadini of
Lothian and Berwick; it has, however, also been suggested that the Maeatae
should really be identified as the tribes of Southern Scotland, Caledonian
territory commencing north of the Forth. Whatever their location, these
two peoples continued to tax the abilities of successive governors for over
a decade. Finally in 207, despite initial successes, one of them, Alfenus
Senecio, reported to the emperor that the rebellious tribes of the north
were getting out of hand, and only an imperial expedition, or substantial
reinforcements, could retrieve the situation. For various reasons — the
desire for military glory, the need to instil a little discipline into his sons
Caracalla and Geta, a real concern for the safety of the province and the
morale of the troops — Septimius Severus began to amass a suitably
equipped field-army and by 208, or at latest in 209, he was ready to campaign in strength beyond the line of Hadrian's Wall.

The achievements of Severus and his sons in North Britain were recorded by two historians, Herodian and Cassius Dio, but these accounts
are only partially preserved, and what is left contains much that is mere
literary 'padding'; like most classical authors writing about events that
took place at some distance from Rome, Dio and Herodian display an
irritating nonchalance about dates and geographical details. Nevertheless, it
seems reasonably certain that, when the imperial army established itself at
its northern bases, the hostile tribesmen at first decided that it might be best
to parley. Their overtures were turned down, however, and the vast
Roman war-machine lumbered northwards over the frontier into enemy
territory, seeking the kind of victory which Agricola had won at *Mons
Graupius* more than a century before. Not surprisingly, the Maeatae and
Caledonians declined to engage in a set-piece battle, preferring to use
guerilla techniques, which, in conjunction with the natural obstacles
encountered on the march, made the Romans pay dearly for every day's
advance; 50,000 men were said to have been lost during the campaign — a
hopelessly exaggerated total, but at least indicative of the perceived severity
of the losses. At length, when Severus had led his forces to what is described
as the very extremity of the island, the Caledonians — who seem to have
been the primary target — came to terms, and were compelled to give up
a large part of their territory. Thus, with victory of a sort as his reward, the
emperor presumably retired to spend the winter, probably that of
209–210, at York. Since coins issued in the years 208–209 allude only to
the preparation and troubles of the campaign, with the crossings of rivers,
estuaries, and 'Ocean' itself (the English Channel — in Roman eyes a

symbolic as well as a physical barrier between Britain and the continent) it may perhaps be assumed that Severus did not consider his work was finished; it was not until 210–11 that coins with explicit reference to a British victory began to appear (cf. Robertson, 1980).

However, if he was in any doubt about the nature of the peace which his northern expedition had secured, the uncertainty was dispelled within a year by the revolt of the Maeatae, and a second campaign, more ruthlessly punitive than the first, was set on foot. But the emperor was now a dying man, and it seems probably that such operations as took place in 210 were under the direct control of Caracalla. On the death of Severus on 4 February 211 at York, Caracalla is reported to have immediately abandoned his father's conquests, including several fortified positions (Dio, lxxvi, 15), but the archaeological record suggests that this represents at least a telescoping of events, if not outright libel. Whatever the truth of the matter, the Severan plan for Scotland, evidently incorporating a Roman presence north of Cheviot, either in the form of isolated strong points or a more general occupation, was soon given up in favour of the Hadrianic solution, a frontier lying in the Tyne-Solway isthmus. Indeed, historical accounts of the reconstruction of the southern wall by Severus (e.g. *S.H.A.*, Severus, 18,2) carried such weight with the later chroniclers and annalists that it was not until the middle of the nineteenth century that Hadrian was generally acknowledged to be its true father.

Yet it was not only in the history books that the Severan (in essence, the Caracallan) reorganisation made so abiding an impression, for the frontier policy adopted after the last retreat from Scotland was to endure with minor modifications until the last days of Roman rule in the North. Moreover, it would appear that the final victory won by Severus and Caracalla had ensured, whether by force of arms or shrewdness in negotiation, almost a century of peace.

When war came again, the frontier was menaced by new enemies, or at least old enemies under a new name – the Picts. Although it is possible that the Picti (or Pecti, as they are sometimes called) had existed as an important tribal group in the time of Severus (Rivet & Smith, 1979, 438–40), it seems more likely that considerable political changes had occurred in the intervening years, and a new alignment of the tribes north of the Forth now presented a threat not just to the northern military zone, but to the whole province. In part, the gravity of the threat was the result of political instability within the province itself. This had manifested itself in Britain's brief adherence to the Gallic Empire under the usurper Postumus from 260–73. It was signally evident again in the attempt by

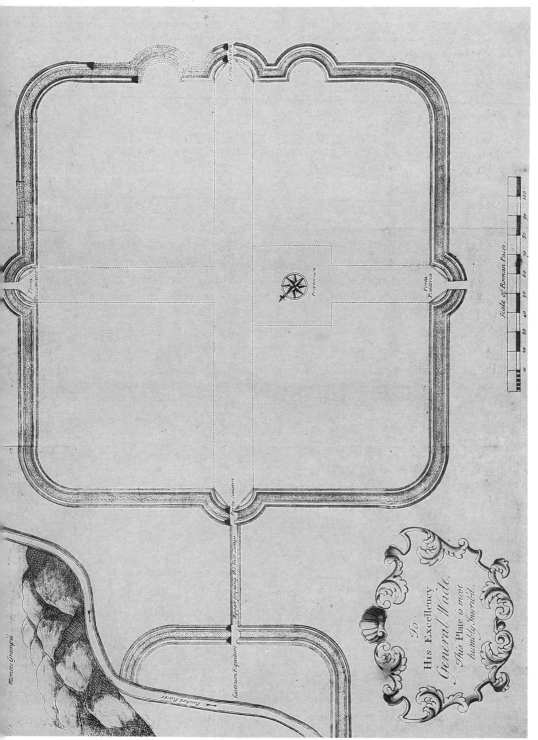

Montes Grampius

Rutha River

Castrum Equitum

Report shewing the two Camps

Porta Sinistra

Porta Praetoria

Praetorium

Porta Victoria

Porta Decumana

To
His Excellency
General Wade,
This Plate is most
humbly Inscribed.

Scale of Roman Paces.

10 20 30 40 50 60 70 80 90 100

Plate 1   Plan of Dalginross by Alexander Gordon, published 1726.

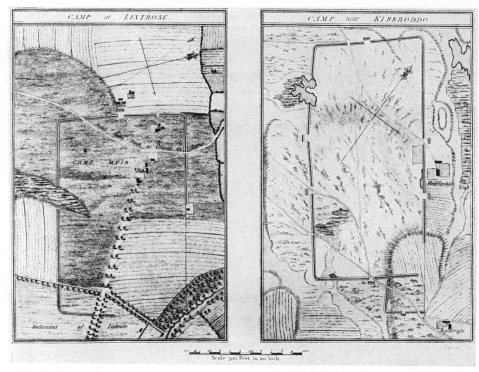

Plate 2a Plans of Lintrose and Kirkbuddo camps by William Roy, surveyed *c.*1750.

Plate 2b Air photograph of Castle Greg fortlet under snow, excavated by Sir Daniel Wilson in 1851.

Plate 3   Abercromby's excavation of the legionary bathhouse at Inchtuthil in 1901. (Royal Commission on the Ancient Monuments of Scotland)

Plate 4
Sir George Macdonald excavating at Mumrills *c.*1927, when day-to-day supervision of extensive trenching was still largely in the hands of foremen and clerks of works. (Royal Commission on the Ancient Monuments of Scotland)

Plate 5a   Air photograph of cropmarks showing outline of two-period marching-camp at Castledykes near Lanark.

Plate 5b   Air photograph of Roman road at Huntingtower, near Perth, revealed by cropmarks of quarry-pits on either side.

These two photographs by permission of Royal Commission on the Ancient Monuments of Scotland.

Plate 6

Air photograph of the Roman road Dere Street near the crossing of the Teviot in Roxburghshire. The course of the road is indicated mainly by the straight line of field-boundaries leading northwards to the distant Eildon Hills. (Royal Commission on the Ancient Monuments of Scotland)

Plate 7

Air photograph of Bochastle fort, near Callander; crop-marks, crossed by a disused railway-line, reveal the defence-system of the fort, with the darker lines of the ditches curving in at each gate. (Royal Commission on the Ancient Monuments of Scotland)

Plate 8

Air photograph of the Cleaven Dyke, probable prehistoric ritual monument, once thought to be a Roman defensive work. The parallel cropmarks show the pair of flanking ditches to be irregularly cut.

Carausius, one-time commander of the British Fleet, to establish himself as emperor of Britain and Northern Gaul in 286; after seven years Carausius was assassinated by Allectus, his minister of finance, and Allectus in turn fell to the imperial army of retribution, commanded by Constantius Chlorus in 296. Anonymous panegyrics of 296–7 and 306 indicate or imply that the Picts seized the opportunity offered by these internal dissensions to assault the northern frontier (*Pan. Lat. Vet.*, vi (vii), 7, 2; viii (v), 2, 3) only to be defeated by an expeditionary force under Constantius, who was by then senior Augustus. Some sixty years later, according to the contemporary historian Ammianus Marcellinus (xx, 1, 1), the frontier regions were again being ravaged by the Picts in alliance with the Scots of Ireland, apparently in contravention of some form of agreement; but it was not until 367, when, in an event known as the 'Barbaric Conspiracy', Britain was nearly overwhelmed by the concerted assaults of all the barbarian nations — Picts, Scots, Saxons, and Attacotti — that a victory was won to bear comparison with the achievements of Agricola or Severus. This time, however, it was not just the embattled garrisons of the north that needed help. Raiding bands were roaming the countryside not far from London, and it took two years at least before the province was brought back into a semblance of order. By then, if we may believe the eulogistic phraseology of the court poet Claudian, the ablest military mind of the day, Theodosius, had taught the northern tribes that the arm of Rome was still long enough to reach beyond the frontier Wall with punitive effect.

It was, however, probably the very last time that such operations could be mounted in force, for already the shadows were gathering, not just on the periphery of the Empire, but at its very heart, and affairs in Britain , whose guiding an emperor had once considered the greatest glory of his reign (*S.H.A.*, Severus, 18, 2), were now only nominally the concern of Rome. Henceforth, Britain's destiny lay with the Britons themselves, on either side of the frontier, and more especially with those barbarian invaders, who were to shape the later history of the country, giving its constituent parts the names and nationalities by which we recognise them today. The emperors and generals were to conquer no more.

3

Armies on the march

THE HISTORICAL EVENTS discussed in the preceding chapter involved, for the most part, the movement of men and materials on a scale that Northern Britain had never before witnessed, and indeed, was not to see again for almost a thousand years. The armies that marched and countermarched in those eventful centuries, though often tens of thousands strong, nevertheless required to look well to their security, surrounded as they were by tribesmen committed to defending both their country and their freedom. Even when the campaigning was over and a Roman victory won, the land had still to be held by force of arms; the permanent garrisons planted for that purpose at regular intervals and in strategic positions still required to communicate with each other, sending out patrols and stationing pickets in outposts, to keep watch and ward along the intervening tracts. The military structures that allowed these several operations to be undertaken in relative safety constitute the two classes of Roman field monument in which Scotland is particularly rich – temporary camps and roads. In fact, it would not be wrong to claim that, in the case of the former, this country may boast a wider variety of examples, and in greater numbers, than any other part of the Roman Empire. There are various reasons for this, not least the fact that any knowledge of temporary works depends very greatly on the availability of aerial reconnaissance – a means of archaeological prospection in which Britain has led the field, with particular benefit to the study of the Roman period (St Joseph, 1976).

'Temporary camp' is the technical term for the defended bivouac in which bodies of Roman troops rested while on the march or while engaged in other field-operations, such as training exercises, fort-building, or the like. When on campaign in hostile territory, a Roman commander would have ensured that everything was done 'according to the book': a due order was necessary on the march, with scouts sent ahead and, if necessary, cavalry screens operating on the flanks, the pace of the column geared to the slowest units; these would normally have been the baggage-train carrying the *impedimenta*, heavy items, such as the leather tents used by the troops, and possibly other wheeled vehicles required for transporting the artillery — the spring-guns and mangonels (the latter given the name of *onager* (wild ass), presumably because they had, as we would say, a kick like a mule. The average column may thus have extended over several miles, its irresistible snakelike progress through the winding river valleys of the Southern Uplands or up the broad reaches of Strathmore as potent a token of the superiority of the Roman military machine as the evident excellence of its equipment or its discipline in the fight. At the end of each day's march — indeed long before the end — a suitable site would have been chosen for the bivouac of the succeeding night, scouts and surveyors having been sent ahead to ascertain how the land lay.

Choice of ground was vitally important if the army was not to be put at a disadvantage in a military sense, or deprived of what comforts might reasonably be expected even on campaign; according to the manuals, the site had to enjoy sufficient natural strength to give its occupants a tactical edge should they come under attack, although, whenever possible, a commander would avoid camping in an area where assault was likely. The camp site also had to be close to a source of running water, enough to satisfy the needs of several thousand men and animals. On the other hand, for comfort and convenience of communication within the camp, the area enclosed by the defences could not include too much poorly drained ground, or frequent water-courses, or, by contrast, ground that was excessively steep or uneven, which would have made it difficult for the troops to pitch their tents in rows. It would seem at first sight that it was no easy task to find such a spot at about the right distance from the last night's camp-site, and there are in fact a number of examples of camps which one might cite as exemplifying infringements of one or other of these rules. Nevertheless, the careful observer will note that in many more cases the ground appears to have been shrewdly read, with the camp situated just at the right point to make the best possible use of natural advantages, with the line of defences, for example, drawn cunningly along the break of slope, or the whole defence-work sited in such a way as to enclose a local ridge or summit and thus incapable of being overlooked.

The choice of ground made, the next task would have been to mark out the perimeter of the camp, so that on the arrival of the main body, the construction teams could immediately begin their work. The surveying called for specialists, the *mensores* or *gromatici* on the permanent strength of each legion, whose function was to calculate the total area required for the body of troops engaged, lay out a defence perimeter of sufficient extent, accommodating its shape as necessary to fit the available terrain, and then to allot individual spaces within the interior to each of the units composing the whole army. When that had been done it should have been possible for each soldier to know, at the end of the march, precisely what part of the camp he was responsible for constructing, and where, eventually, he would pitch his tent for the night.

We know something of the size and appearance of these temporary works from two main sources: archaeology and the writers of military manuals, or historians. The latter include the historian Polybius of the second century BC, who incorporated descriptions of Roman camps in his account of campaigns against the Carthaginians; Hyginus Gromaticus, of uncertain date but probably of the second century AD, who dealt specifically and in detail with the internal ordering of the temporary camps; and Vegetius, writing in the latter part of the fourth century AD, who also devoted considerable space to the description of the defences of temporary works. From these we learn that a Roman camp could be of practically any geometrical shape, but that square or rectangular forms were preferred; the majority of sites would have been girdled by defences consisting of a ditch and rampart, but these might have varied in scale depending on the nature of the ground, the strength of the position, or the materials available. In sandy or stony areas, a bank alone could suffice, or in situations where no hostile activity was expected the legionaries might have been content with a minimal defence consisting of a mere bank of sods crowned by stakes. The smallest *fossa legitima*, or regular ditch, appears to have measured five Roman feet wide by three deep, and the military handbooks offered a sliding scale of width ascending in stages of odd feet to a maximum of 17 feet (Vegetius, i, 23−5, iii, 8).

While there is no need to believe that such directions were followed implicitly on every occasion, it seems likely that high standards of ditch-digging and rampart-building were nevertheless observed, even in the construction of temporary works. The complimentary remarks that are recorded as having been addressed by the Emperor Hadrian to troops engaged in field-exercises at Lambaesis in North Africa (*C.I.L.*,viii,18072) include specific praise for their careful cutting of ditches, care evidently having been taken to smooth the ditch-scarps to the correct profile. The responsibility for this would have lain with the centurions, who supervised the work of the separate work-parties into which the field-force was subdivided; the rivalry which we may presume existed between the gangs of different units would naturally have served to expedite the wearisome task. When faced by a resolute enemy, the speed with which the entrenching proceeded could be almost unbelievable, especially to the foe, as at least one has openly testified (Josephus, *Bell. Jud.*, iii, 84).

The interior of the camp, as we know it from military authors (especially Hyginus), was laid out in accordance with principles which were in part military and practical, in part augural and religious (Fig. **3.1**); the nerve centre was the commandant's quarters, or *praetorium*, which lay at the crossing of a T-plan street system. The main street, or *via principalis* representing the bar of the T, ran across the entire width of the camp between two principal gates, while the *via praetoria*, forming the upright, extended from the *praetorium* to the front gate. A third road, the *via quintana* was drawn parallel to the *via principalis* immediately in the rear of the *praetorium*, but this did not always issue through the defences on either side, access to the rear of the camp being by means of the gate known as the *porta decumana*. A space sixty feet wide, the *intervallum*, was left free of obstruction or buildings all round the perimeter of the camp immediately behind the rampart, thus providing an unencumbered approach to the defences should there have been a need to man them in an emergency. Within the *intervallum* the interior was divided into three main areas: the *praetentura*, on either side of the *via praetoria*; the *retentura*, to the rear of the *via quintana*; and the *latera praetorii*, flanking the *praetorium* itself.

All these sub-divisions of the camp would have been crossed by a network of minor streets, separating century from century, cohort from cohort, and legion from legion; where a mixed field-force was concerned, provision would also have been made for auxiliary troops. Hyginus suggests (*de munitionibus*, 2) that non-legionary units were not trustworthy enough to be placed next to the defences, and should therefore be allotted a position within the heart of the camp. We do not know if such precautions were taken in every case, but in the Flavian period, when armies were constantly on the march, the Romans throughout the Empire were unlikely to have forgotten the near-disaster of AD 69, when Batavian *auxilia* in Lower Germany had risen in revolt under Claudius Civilis; in Britain, where local tribesmen were now being formed into auxiliary regiments, there would also have been memories of the bloody rising of

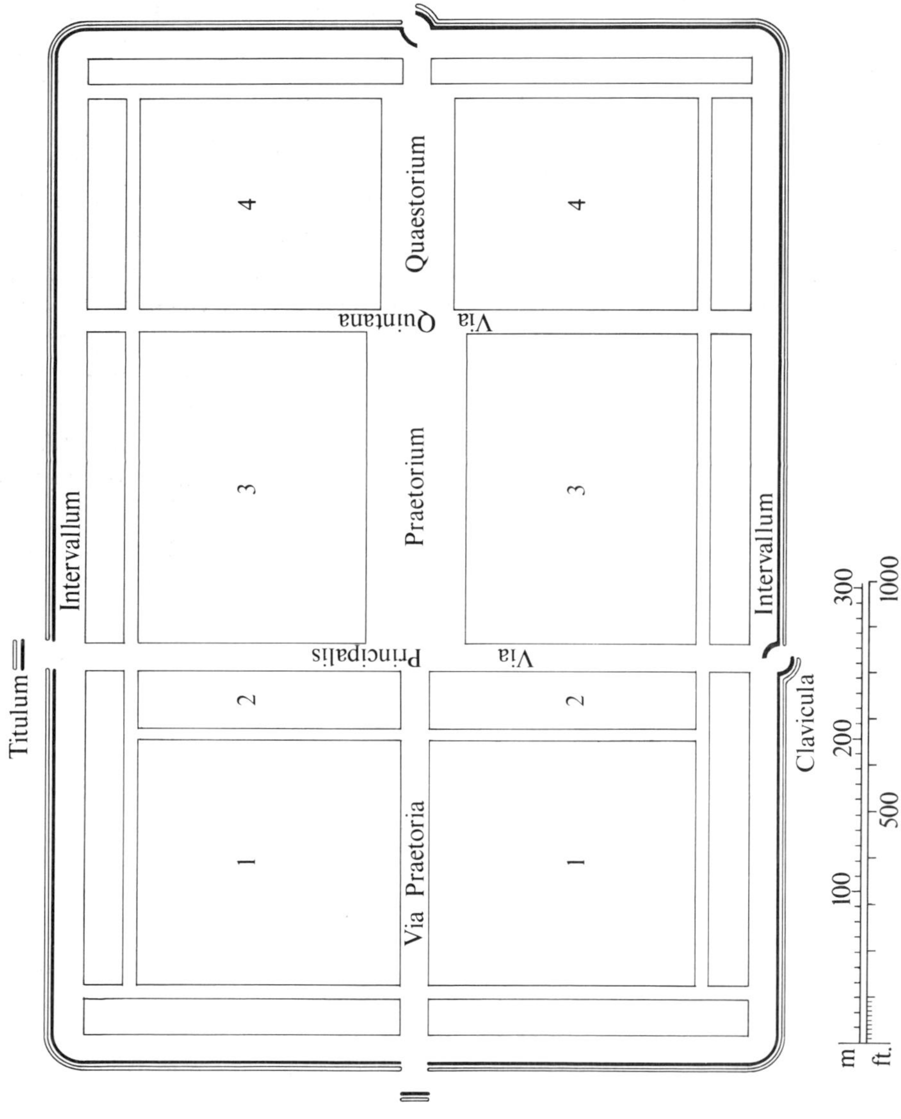

Fig. 3.1

Schematic diagram of a Roman camp:

1. *praetentura*

2. senior officers' quarters

3. *latera praetorii*

4. *retentura*; legionary cohorts' accommodation disposed around periphery

60–1 in which Queen Boudicca of the Iceni had so nearly succeeded in throwing off the Roman yoke once and for all. Awareness of these things may well have heightened the tension as the invading army of Agricola pushed ever deeper into Caledonia and further from the security of the established province.

It would be wrong, however, to give the impression that much is known for certain about the actual dispositions inside a typical marching-camp; we may picture the tent lines arranged neatly in block and file by century and cohort, but where the individual units lay, or of what pro-portions of auxiliary and legionary troops an army might be composed; or – most important of all – how large an area each unit occupied, these are questions to which we may never know the answer. As regards the capacity of temporary camps, much ink has been spilt in modern times to demonstrate the degree of fidelity with which the ancient authors should be followed, but it is impossible, for example to compare the data provided by Polybius to describe the state of affairs relating to the second century BC with those of Hyginus which refer to the practice of perhaps three centuries later. Moreover, even when one assumes the correctness of the figures given by Hyginus for individual *pedaturae* (the areas allotted to specific units' tent-lines), quite divergent figures for the total area to be assigned to a single marching legion may be argued (cf. Grillone, 1977, xi-xvii; Hanson, 1978, 142–3), estimates ranging from approximately 15 acres (6 ha) to as much as 25 acres (10 ha). Even more recently it has been questioned (Maxwell, 1982) whether the basic *pedatura* of 120 ft by 30 ft which Hyginus assigned to a legionary *centuria* should really be accepted as the invariable module it has been deemed in all previous calculations; but this leads on to closer consideration of the archaeological evidence and more rigorous definitions of the term 'temporary camp' (cf. Pitts & St Joseph, 1985, 223–44).

It will be realised that campaigning works such as those described above are by their very nature ephemeral, or virtually so, and the chances of their survival into succeeding ages are very slim indeed. Moreover, since most campaigns would have been directed into areas of dense native occu-pation and along the natural corridors presented by fertile river valleys, it follows that the sites of many of these temporary works will now lie within cultivated ground, where the erosive effects of arable farming may have long since obscured the above-ground traces of earthwork defences. Indeed, that there are now far fewer upstanding Roman temporary camps in Scotland than were visible just a couple of centuries ago we know from the exploits of such early fieldworkers as Captain, later General, Robert

Melville, who in the space of a single summer in 1754 discovered no fewer than four − Kirkbuddo, Keithock, Battledykes, Oathlaw, and Lintrose (Stuart, 1868). Although short stretches of the perimeter of Kirkbuddo can still be recognised on the ground (Fig. **3.2**), too little now survives to permit its identification as Roman on the grounds of superficial

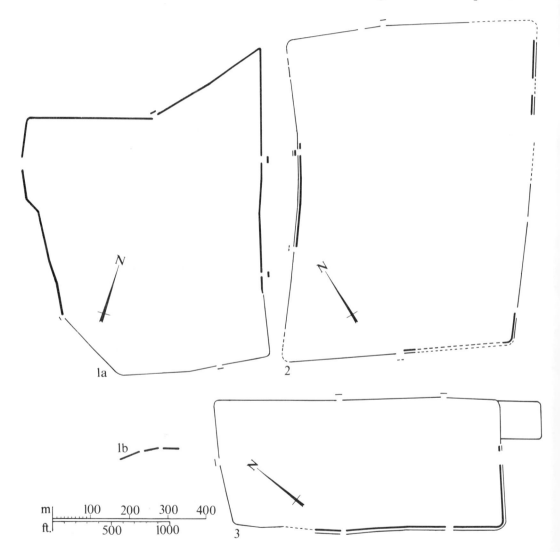

Fig. **3.2**   Roman marching-camps in northern Scotland
1a, b. Raedykes
2. Ardoch 125 acres/50 ha
3. Kirkbuddo.

appearances alone, while the others are no longer to be seen, save from the air. Yet these examples belong to some of the largest classes of temporary work in North Britain, the most massive having a perimeter in excess of 9000 ft. (2740 m).

Melville had only time to sketch these, but he communicated his interest to Roy, who planned the new sites and entered them in the Government Map of Scotland then being undertaken in the aftermath of the Jacobite Rising; Roy found or planned more sites, Raedykes to the north-east of Stonehaven, Grassy Walls near Scone, on the left bank of the Tay, and Ardoch by Greenloaning; a comparison of the present state of the latter site with that in which Roy found it in 1759 is highly instructive (Fig. **3.2,** see below p. 63), especially if one remembers that, for various reasons, the Ardoch area has been protected from the worst ravages of arable husbandry. With few exceptions, however, almost nothing visible now remains of the great camps that were then discovered and measured, or of those located subsequently by the trained eyes of such military surveyors as Shand (the camp of Glenmailen in 1785 – 6) or Courtney (Kintore, as late as 1867). Only where the forms of land-use remain unchanged, where grouse-moor and upland pasture have not yet given way to forestry plantation or plough, can one still gain an impression of the size or appearance of this category of monument: Raedykes (Fig. **3.2**), although much overgrown with heather and gorse may still be traced for much of its circuit; its interest lies as much in its curiously irregular plan as in the fact of its survival. The camp, which encloses 93 acres (37 ha), was last examined in detail by Sir George Macdonald (1916), who found that the ditch varied in width, measuring 17 ft. (5.1 m) at maximum – coincidentally, the upper limit mentioned by Vegetius.

Paradoxically, the majority of well-preserved camps are to be found in the south of the country. They include : Cleghorn (Fig. **3.3**), a 46-acre (19 ha) site to the north-east of Lanark, the northern half of whose parallelogram-shaped perimeter survives above ground, although somewhat obscured, in a forestry plantation; close inspection of the alignment of each side reveals that what appears at first sight to be a single straight line is in fact composed of several short sectors exhibiting minor deviations – the combined result of slight imprecision in the setting-out stage and the subdivision of the construction between different work-parties. The irregularity of plan already noticed at Raedykes represents an accentuated form of the distortions such factors may produce, particularly in conjunction with the need to accommodate defences to awkward terrain. That it was not always thought necessary to compromise in this way is shown by the contrastingly regular lines of the 32-acre (12 ha) camp at Little Clyde (Fig. 3.3) immediately to the north of Beattock Summit; in this example, the rectangular playing-card symmetry of the outline has been maintained, even though both the north and east sides are transected by the rocky gullies of two streams which must also have presented obstacles to communication within the interior. Little Clyde lies sandwiched between what is now extensively afforested upland and long-cultivated low-lying arable; in the latter area its defences are only intermittently visible.

Much farther to the south, at Gilnockie (Fig. 3.3) a little way to the south of Langholm, another camp of regular plan, but only 25 acres (10 ha) in area, has survived within an established hardwood plantation; its south-west side has been destroyed by yet another form of modern land-development, a railway-line (itself now disused and by way of becoming an ancient monument in its own right). Much of the long south-east side may be

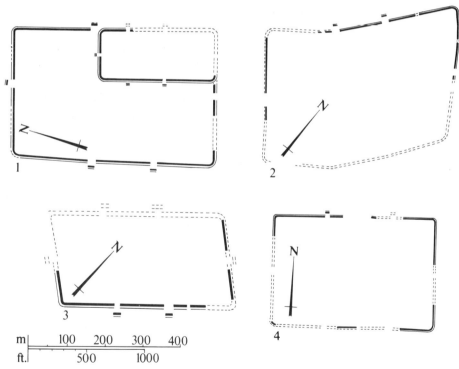

Fig. 3.3   Roman marching-camps in southern Scotland:
1. Pennymuir
2. Cleghorn
3. Gilnockie
4. Little Clyde.

traced beneath the leafy canopy, the rampart in this sector attaining a maximum thickness of nearly 22 ft. (6.5 m), while the position of the defences on the north-east and north-west is indicated respectively by a slight hollow running through rig-and-furrow pasture and by a minor road. The course of this road is a clear indication that in the not-too-distant past the ditch and rampart of the camp presented an obstacle large enough to prevent traffic traversing the camp-site at will; Roman archaeology in Scotland can furnish numerous similar instances where the former existence of some now-vanished military installation is betrayed by features of the modern landscape. However, perhaps the best-preserved examples, the camps at Pennymuir on the northern fringe of the Cheviots in Roxburghshire owe their survival to their remoteness. Dere Street, the main north-south axis of communication in Roman and later times between Corbridge and south-east Scotland, lies only a stone's throw away to the east, but the busy traffic which it once carried over the Border hills has long since dwindled, and modern travellers have chosen an easier route several miles to the west, preferring the gentler, less direct approach by way of Carter Bar. In consequence, Pennymuir has become a 'backwater' site, relatively little affected even by cultivation, dedicated in the main to nothing more harmful than grazing; but in Roman times it provided an ideal camping-ground where troops on the march might bivouac just before or after negotiating the steep north-western slopes of the Woden Law escarpment. The largest of the Pennymuir camps occupied an area of 43 acres (17.5 ha), its ramparts still rising to a height of 4 ft. (1.2 m) above the interior; a smaller camp of approximately 9 acres (3.65 ha) has been constructed in its south-eastern portion, re-using the existing defences, and portions of two other camps may be seen close by, on the opposite side of Dere Street — an indication that good camp-sites might be used not once, but on several occasions, possibly during the same series of operations, probably in the campaigns of other centuries. Indeed, major bases at important cross-roads, (e.g.Newstead, Camelon, Castledykes and Birrens) are now known to be surrounded by large numbers of temporary camps (see below, pp. 53, 69).

Even a brief inspection of the sites described above, which represent the best of the upstanding camps, will reveal that they have certain features in common: most are rectangles or regular parallelograms in plan, with a tendency to tertiate appearance, that is to say, the long sides are half as big again as the short; furthermore, the entrances are, in the main, protected by a short stretch of rampart and ditch set forward from the line of the main defence. This device, which was known to the Romans as a *titulum* — the precise etymology is uncertain — guarded the entrances against a direct assault, for in temporary works there was, of course, no door or gate; the Romans appear to have used it in temporary camps from Republican times, for examples are known at Renieblas in Spain at sites attributed to the Pompeian campaigns against Sertorius (Schulten, 1929).

The uniformity of plan and gate defence, in these examples (not to mention the disposition of the gates themselves) is largely coincidental, and it should not be thought that they display the whole range of temporary works. However, to examine the rest, which far outnumber the upstanding examples, recourse must be made to the discoveries of air photography and excavation. The reasons why this means of prospection has been pre-eminently successful in locating such monuments are simply told. First of all, although the low rampart of turf and earth would soon have succumbed to the onslaughts of weather and cultivation, the ditch was more durable; even if it was filled to the brim with silt or deliberate packing, its profile remained, cut deep into the subsoil (Fig. **3.4**), the anomaly it represented in terms of colour, texture, and moisture-retentive capacity making it directly

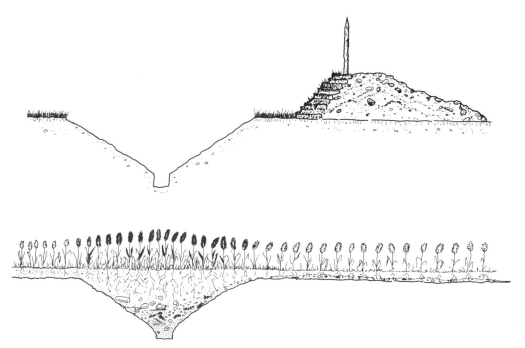

Fig. 3.4   Comparative sections of a camp ditch: as originally dug (above), and as present-day source of cropmarking (below); scale *c.* 1:60.

visible as a soil-mark, or indirectly detectible through the vegetation growing above it. In times of drought, and when bearing a suitably sensitive crop — barley gives the best results — the course of the ditch will be visible from above as a band of vegetation displaying different characteristics from that growing elsewhere in the field : in early spring, the seed within this band will be the first to shoot; in early summer it may 'head' first; and as the crop ripens around it, the band will tend to grow higher and stay green longer, sometimes betraying the below-ground feature with amazing fidelity (cf. Plate 5, *a*); at last, just before harvesting, the cropmark as it is known may appear lighter yellow when the rest of the field is rusty brown, at which stage it is said to have 'reversed'. There are, in fact, numerous states of crop or vegetational discolouration, or markings in bare soil, which can indicate the presence of buried sites, and these are accessible to the aerial observer because of the peculiar advantage of his viewpoint, giving him the perspective denied to the fieldworker on the ground; it is not unlike the advantage experienced by football spectators in the grandstand over those on the touchline. This ability to distance oneself from the object of research is particularly useful in the case of temporary camps, whose vast extent frequently makes it difficult to appreciate their form at close quarters.

The contribution which aerial survey has made to the study of Roman temporary camps in Britain may be judged from the extent to which our quantitative knowledge of the subject has increased over the period of four decades during which it has been consistently practised. The second edition of the Ordnance Survey map of Roman Britain, published in 1928, displayed the sites of no more than a few dozen camps in Britain as a whole; by 1982 the number of camps identified in Scotland alone was at least 185, and the total now (1989) exceeds 200. By far the greater part of these were located as a result of the survey programmes of the Cambridge University Committee for Aerial Photography, directed by Professor J.K.S. St Joseph. Moreover, the intensive reconnaissance carried out since 1976 by the Royal Commission on the Ancient and Historical Monuments of Scotland has shown that the extra concentration of effort and flexibility of application afforded by sorties operating out of a home base (Turnhouse) are capable of maintaining and even increasing this staggering rate of discovery.

If it be asked what qualitative advances have resulted from the use of aerial reconnaissance, the answer must be that they are fully in proportion to the quantitative. For not only can we now distinguish with greater certainty the different types of temporary work, the labour camps used by construction units (see below, p. 51) or practice camps occupied during field exercises (pp. 40–1), but even in that most numerous class, the marching-camp, it is now possible to assign examples to specific periods or even particular campaigns. In consequence, it is now practical to discuss, however tentatively, the tactical objectives of many of the commanders whose roles in history were considered briefly in the last chapter.

First among these is Gn. Julius Agricola, governor of Britain from AD 77–83, almost indubitably the first Roman to lead the legions northward into Scotland (see above, pp. 29–31). It should be admitted at the outset, however, that there is no way of *proving* the connection between any particular camp and Agricola – or any other governor; the most that can be done is to indicate a general date and hence infer the connection. For example, the most distinctive type of camp likely to have been used during the Agricolan campaigns is that named after the example discovered at Stracathro, near Edzell (Fig. **3,5,***1*); the rather squarish plan and unusual gateway defence set it apart from the camps which were examined earlier. In this case, the gate was defended externally by a combination of an oblique traverse-ditch at one side and a quarter-circle extension of ditch and rampart (known as a *clavicula*) on the other; on the inside of the gate there

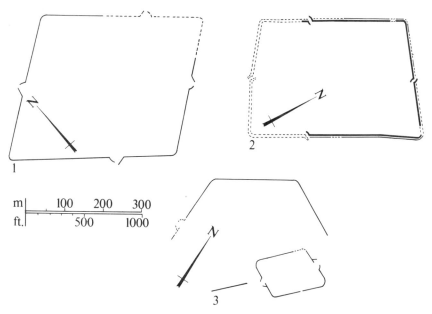

Fig. 3.5   Temporary camps with claviculae:
　　　　　1. Stracathro
　　　　　2. Oakwood
　　　　　3. Woodhead.

was probably a corresponding internal *clavicula* of the rampart, but as it is only the course of the ditch that shows as a cropmark, no visible trace of the internal portion now survives. Occasionally the main ditch appears to have been continued past the root of the oblique traverse to increase the security of the gateway (Fig. **3.5**,*3*). As with the *titulum*, the purpose of this elaborate defence-work was to deny direct access to the camp entrance, but the *clavicula* served the additional purpose of diverting an assailant so that his right-hand side, unprotected by the shield, was exposed to the defenders on the camp rampart.

The plain double *clavicula*, without the oblique traverse, is found at Oakwood (fig. **3.5,** *2*) in the valley of the Ettrick some way to the south of Selkirk. This is the only indubitably Flavian camp in Scotland whose defences may be traced, albeit faintly and in places with difficulty, as an upstanding earthwork for most of the perimeter; some 40 acres (16 ha) in area, it could have accommodated a field force at least 15,000, possibly as much as 20,000 strong, and was presumably used during mopping-up operations in the course of Agricola's third or fourth campaign. An additional interest attaches to it as there are only three *clavicula*-gated marching-camps known in eastern Scotland, south of the Forth, all the other examples exhibiting *titula*. The reason for this almost exclusive distribution can only be guessed; it may indicate that the south-east was a zone of operations assigned to one particular legion, with the result that all camps within its area were designed in accordance with the whim or predilection of a single *praefectus castrorum* (the legionary officer responsible for military works). There is in fact, a sole example of the Stracathro-gated type in the south-east, at Woodhead (Fig. **3.5,**3) just to the north of Pathhead, Midlothian. This is the smallest member of the group, being only 3.6 acres (1.5 ha) in area, and somewhat of a curiosity, for it lies within what appears to be a contemporary polygonal work, also provided with a Stracathro gate. It has been suggested (Maxwell, 1983a, pp. 178–81) that this bipartite site may be a labour camp, possibly housing a legionary work-party felling timber for the building of permanent forts in the area; the site would therefore belong, strictly speaking, to a later stage than the campaigning phase, but as we have already noted, Agricola's first penetration into Scotland was met by so little opposition, that there was even time for fort building before the end of the season (Tacitus, *Agricola*, 22.1).

Extremely large marching-camps with clavicular gates of Stracathro type have been revealed by cropmarks at Dalswinton on the River Nith and Castledykes on the Clyde near Carstairs (Fig. **3.6**). Both occupy an area of some 60 acres (25 ha), are relatively square in plan, and lie adjacent to an important permanent base on the banks of a major river. The former intersects the defences of a second, smaller Stracathro-gated camp and is

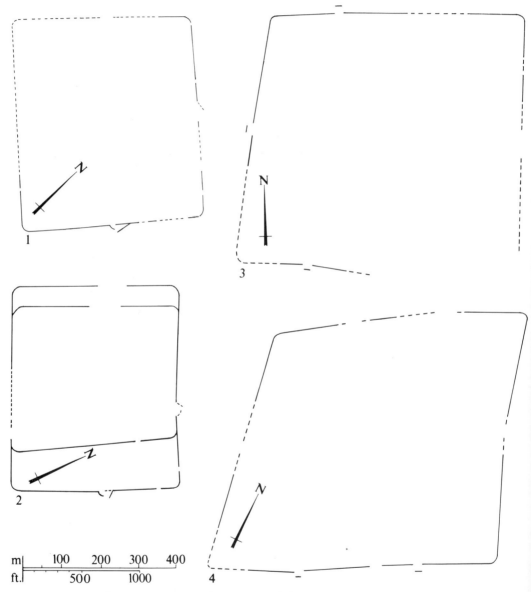

Fig. 3.6   Large marching-camps of the Flavian period:
1. Dalswinton   2. Castledykes
3. Dunning   4. Abernethy.

presumably later than it; the latter appears to have been reduced in a secondary phase to roughly 40 acres (16 ha). In cases like these it would seem that the remains represent evidence of re-use of a strategically significant site in successive campaigns, but the precise identification of the specific campaign is a task which at present lies beyond our capabilities. The similarity of the two large camps at Castledykes and Dalswinton might lead one to suggest that they indicate the route of a large Flavian force, possibly 30,000 strong, proceeding northwards through western Scotland by way of Nith and Clyde, as the left 'prong' of a twin-headed drive from bases at Carlisle and Corbridge. The course of the right-hand column would then be indicated by camps like those of about 40-50 acres (16-20 ha) which lie beneath (and are therefore earlier than) the eastern annexe and adjacent military road at Newstead beside the crossing of the River Tweed. As we have already learned (p. 30, above) that the first thrust into Scotland may have penetrated as far as the Tay, one or both of these columns could have continued beyond the Forth-Clyde isthmus in AD 80. Indeed, the identification of two large camps dated by pottery to the late first century AD, situated 9 miles (15 km) apart at Dunning and Abernethy, near the eastern end of Strathearn (Fig. **3.6**; St Joseph, 1973, 218-21) could be used to argue that on reaching the Forth-Clyde isthmus, the two columns had linked up, for the average area of the camps − about 115 acres (45 ha) − roughly equals the combined capacity of the largest camps of either 'prong' in southern Scotland. The discovery of a Flavian fort at Doune (Maxwell, 1984a), guarding a crossing of the Teith, has led to the suggestion that at this stage Agricola did not advance beyond the Forth Valley, the 115-acre camps belonging to a subsequent campaign.

Moreover, it could be suggested with equal propriety that any of the more southerly camps could have housed troops participating in the consolidation programme of the succeeding season, (Tacitus, *Agricola*, 23); and indeed one might argue that, for the direct drive to the isthmus which a pincer-movement would have almost inevitably entailed, the route through Nithsdale presented a less attractive alternative to the more straightforward passage up Annandale. The presence of a 40 acre (16 ha) Stracathro-gated camp at Beattock could be taken to support this view. Moreover, since it is quite conceivable that the theatre of operations in the fifth season (AD 82) was the entire south-west of Scotland, either Castledykes or Dalswinton, or both, could possibly have served as the bases for the campaign force of that year: from Castledykes a natural corridor leads westwards through Avondale and the valley of the Irvine to the shores of the Firth of Clyde; from Dalswinton two avenues of penetration presented themselves — one by way of upper Nithsdale and the valley of the Ayr towards the same coastal stretch, the other southwestwards to the crossing of the Dee north of Castle Douglas, and hence into Galloway. Agricola's objective in either case was the control of tribes living in the coastal regions, in 'that part of Britain that looked across to Ireland' (Tacitus, *Agricola*, 24,1), and it was presumably fear of being outflanked by them during the northern campaigns proposed for the following seasons that made it worthwhile penetrating the barren, and even then inhospitable, moorlands of the south-west.

Scholars have long debated the meaning of a phrase used by Tacitus to describe the opening stage of this campaign : 'In the fifth season, crossing in the first ship (*nave prima*), he (Agricola) subdued tribes unknown till this time ...' Some have argued that the body of water crossed was the Solway (Postgate, 1930) or the Clyde (cf. Reed, 1971), while Sir Ian Richmond suggested that the Annan (Roman *Anava*) was more likely, being palaeographically similar to the word '*nave*'. All that can be said is that no single solution commands universal acceptance and the text is very probably corrupt. It could be suggested, however, that, if these naval manoeuvres were indeed the object of Tacitus's particular attention, as the word order of *nave prima* has been held to imply, it is curious that he did not choose that occasion to give more specific praise to Agricola's use of the fleet in combined operations; instead, he chose to give it prominence as a tactical innovation in connection with the east coast campaign of the following year. It may therefore fairly be asked whether the word *navis* ever appeared in the original text; given the rough country to be traversed before coming to grips with the coastal tribes, one wonders whether some phrase like *in avia primum transgressus*, 'crossing into trackless wastes', might not better serve the case in terms of both text and context; the phrase would thus echo *in avia ... deferrent* already used by Tacitus (*Agricola* 19,2; cf. also *Historiae* ii, 85; and iv, 70). At any rate, the recent discovery of two Roman temporary camps at Girvan, one of them approximately 30 acres (12 ha) in area and square in plan (St Joseph, 1978) suggests very strongly that, however he succeeded in getting there, Agricola did indeed campaign in strength in the Scottish coastal regions opposite Ireland.

The operations in Caledonia which occupied Agricola's attention in the penultimate season (AD 83) are almost impossible to identify archaeologically. The enemy territory occupied to the north of the Forth (Tacitus, *Agricola* 25,1) probably means the area between the Forth-Clyde isthmus, guarded by a chain of posts built in AD 81 (see below, p. 118–21) and a line drawn from Callander to Perth, the peninsula of Fife possibly, but not necessarily, being included. The Roman forts attacked by hostile Caledonians presumably lay within this area, possibly deep within it, and when Agricola eventually moved out to meet the impending assault of several enemy warbands, we are told he was compelled to divide his command into three separate units. But splitting one's forces in the face of a numerically superior enemy is not a policy to be recommended unless the situation is so dangerous as to leave no alternative, and we may therefore be justified in presuming that at this juncture Agricola was not so much moving to the attack as positioning his troops for defence. On this analysis, the camps used in 83 should be sought somewhere between Strathearn and the Tay, and, if they each accommodated a third part of the field forces available to Agricola, could have been some 30–40 acres (12–16 ha) in extent. Considerable interest thus attaches to the camps at Dunblane, Ardoch, Strageath, and Dornock, about 30 acres in average size, which lie at suitable marching intervals between the Forth and the valley of the Earn; the examples at Ardoch and Dunblane (Fig. **3.7**) were respectively enlarged from, and reduced to, enclosures of about 14 acres (5.7 ha). It must be

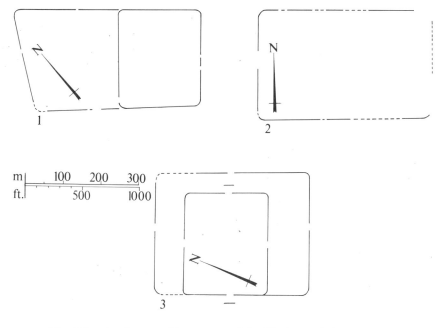

Fig. 3.7　Smaller marching-camps of the Flavian period:
1. Ardoch 33 acres/13 ha
2. Strageath
3. Dunblane.

repeated, however, that there is nothing to prove beyond a shadow of a doubt which of the many frontier-offensives were the occasion for their construction. As regards the close of this season's fighting, the grandiloquent terms used by Tacitus should not be allowed to conceal the fact that a Roman military disaster had been narrowly avoided, and with the Caledonian foe fragmented but still very much in the field, it would have been unwise to extend operations beyond the immediate vicinity of the successful conflict. That is to say, of course, that if the hard-won victory was in any way associated with the 30 acre camps just mentioned, Agricola probably did not campaign much beyond the Tay, if indeed he ever reached that river, which would have serious implications for our understanding of the context of the final campaign.

It may be appropriate at this stage to consider the evidence of the other Stracathro-gated camps and their bearing on the campaigns conducted by Agricola north of the Forth-Clyde isthmus. At the time of writing some nine examples are known (Fig. **3.8**). The most southerly is situated at Lochlands, at the crossing of the river Carron, to the north-west of Falkirk; with an area in excess of 35 acres (14 ha), it occupies what is probably the most advantageous position on the great sand-and-gravel plateau which seems to have served as the marshalling-ground of all the Roman field armies that ever marched north into Caledonia; at least ten camps have been detected there by aerial reconnaissance. In size, the Lochlands camp compares reasonably closely with examples at Glenmailen in Aberdeenshire, at Auchintore, near Huntly, and with Stracathro itself (Fig. **3.5,***1*), but it is significantly smaller than the camp at Callander (59 acres; 20 ha), and considerably larger than the examples at Malling on the Lake of Menteith (26 acres; 10.4 ha), and Dalginross near Comrie (23.5 acres; 9.5 ha). The variation in size, together with the erratic distribution, would seem to be enough to preclude their identification as marching-camps used by a single unit proceeding along a continuous line of march. Moreover, the relationship of some of the camps, (Callander, Dalginross, Malling 1 and 2, and Stracathro) to the sites of permanent Flavian forts has already inspired the suggestion (Maxwell, 1981, 34–5) that their purpose was to provide accommodation for a force quartered in a specific location for more than just a night or two. It is thus possible that only Auchinhove and Glenmailen (and probably Lochlands) fall into the category of marching-camps proper, the first pair presumably representing the start and finish of a single day's march. The small example recently discovered at Inverquharity (*c.* 6 acres; 2.4 ha), immediately to the south-east of the Flavian fortlet (p. 110), invites comparison with

Woodhead and probably served a similar purpose, housing a legionary work-party.

The only other possible candidates for inclusion in the category of

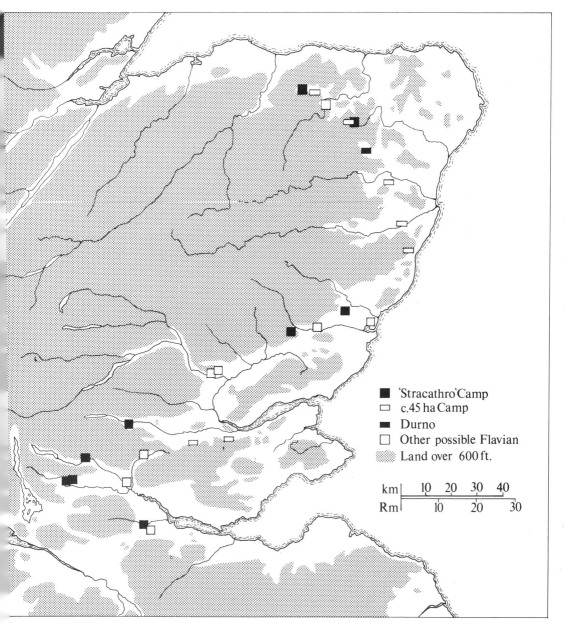

Fig. 3.8 Distribution of probable Flavian temporary camps N of the Forth.

Agricolan camps are Finavon, some 37 acres (15 ha) in extent, at the crossing of the South Esk west of Brechin, and a series of six very large camps arranged in a great arc from a point immediately to the north-west of Stonehaven as far as the Pass of Grange near Huntly; the camps range in size from about 93 to 144 acres (37.4 -58.3 ha), but four closely approach 110 acres (44.6 ha), thus begging comparison with the camps of Dunning and Abernethy mentioned above (p. 53). One (Glenmailen) overlies the Stracathro camp already described, while a second (Muiryfold) lies only 1.3 miles (c.2 km) distant from the Stracathro-gated camp of Auchinhove. At one time it was thought that the large camps which are, for the most part, separated by a day's march, indicated the course of the emperor Septimius Severus in his Caledonian campaigns of AD 209-11, but more recently it has been suggested (St Joseph, 1973, 228-33) that they belong to the Flavian period and were in fact constructed by troops of Agricola on his last campaign. Furthermore, it has been argued (St Joseph, 1978a) that the exceptional size and position of the largest, Durno (Fig. **3.9**) may be explained by identifying it as the camp of Agricola's army before the battle of *Mons Graupius*. This ingenious and attractive hypothesis has more to commend it than any other put forward in recent years by those seeking the site of the famous battle. In full view of Durno to the south-west stands the conspicuous massif of Bennachie, its lofty, peaked summit crowned by a hill fort, with a smaller defensive enclosure on the lower slopes. If, as has been suggested, *Graupius* is a latinised form of a Celtic name descended from Old Welsh *crup*, meaning 'bump' (cf. Rivet and Smith, 1979, 370-1), Bennachie might indeed be an apt identification. Further support is provided by the exceptional size of the camp at Durno, which would certainly have required to be larger than the other members of the series if Agricola had combined his forces to meet the threat of the massed British levies; in fact, the sum of the areas of the Stracathro-type camp and its larger neighbour at Glenmailen approximates very closely to that of the single camp opposite Bennachie.

Nevertheless, there are a number of objections to the hypothesis: firstly excavation of the intersection of the two camps at Glenmailen had earlier been interpreted by St Joseph as showing that at least a century had passed between the two periods of occupation, and secondly, the proportions of the Raedykes-Muiryfold series of camps are much more elongated than one would expect of Flavian works − in this they differ, for example, from the securely dated camps of comparable size at Dunning and Abernethy (Fig. **3.6**). One might also ponder why the northernmost camps are so very large. The forces under Agricola's command at *Mons Graupius* are unlikely to have exceeded 30,000, including both legionaries and auxiliaries, for which one would have thought 144 acres too large a space, especially if they were travelling *expedito exercitu* (without heavy baggage), as Tacitus reports (*Agricola*, 29.2). It is perhaps permissible to wonder, therefore, whether the large camps north of the Mounth may not after all be post-Flavian, perhaps even several decades later than Agricola. In fact, in view of the possibilities expressed earlier that the campaigns of AD 83 did not range much beyond the Tay, there is no reason why even the Stracathro-gated sites at Glenmailen and Auchinhove, or the unconfirmed camp near Fochabers at the mouth of the Spey, should not also be post-Agricolan; but that is another story (cf. Maxwell, 1989 forthcoming).

As with the literary sources, when we turn to the archaeological evidence for campaigning in the second century, we are struck by the contrasting poverty of information. Although attempts have been made (e.g.

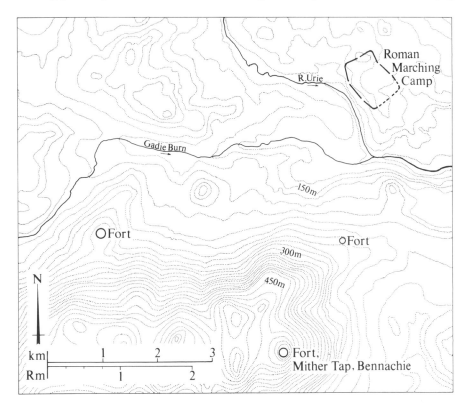

Fig. 3.9 The battlefield of Mons Graupius? The large camp at Logie Durno and the adjacent native sites on Bennachie (after St Joseph).

Hanson & Maxwell, 1983, pp. 64-8) to recognise Antonine marching-camps in certain examples of the size-range 27-56 acres (11-22.5 ha) — mostly located beside the major track routes of Southern Scotland and of regular tertiate (2:3) proportions — we are still very far from understanding where and how intensively the legions fought in the early 140s before establishing the new frontier. There are, however, a number of Antonine labour-camps which aerial survey has revealed beside the Antonine Wall, but it has been thought more appropriate to postpone description of their form and purpose until the second-century frontier is discussed in a later chapter (pp. 154–5).

Paradoxically, the episode of campaigning best illustrated by archaeological data is one of the latest, the expedition of Severus and his sons. Once more, largely as a result of the sorties of the Cambridge University Committee for Aerial Photography, it has been possible to fill out the various series of large camps first identified in fragmentary form by early soldier-antiquaries like Melville and Roy. We now know that there are three main groups: those of 65, 130, and 165 acres respectively (23, 55, and 67 ha). In each case, the series includes sufficient examples to permit a relatively accurate estimate to be made of the relevant line of march. The southernmost group comprises the four largest camps, which are separated by marching intervals of about 6.5–8 miles (10.5–13 km); they extend from Newstead northwards to Pathhead by way of Lauderdale (Fig. 3.10), their proximity to one another being a clear indication of the time it must have taken on each stage to marshal in column of route a field-force numbered in so many tens of thousands. As no such camps have been found to the south of Newstead, we must assume that it was on their arrival at the Tweed-crossing that the various units, including legionary and auxiliary drafts from overseas, were brigaded together for the first time, having marched up individually from Corbridge; conceivably, some of the supplies may have been brought up river from Berwick and stockpiled on the rising ground to the south of the permanent fort, where there was sufficient free space for men and materials. In fact, it is the location of the camp in this area, well to the south of the fort with its surrounding annexes, and clear of the ground used by the Flavian temporary camps, that is adduced as the main indication of its date, there being no absolute dating evidence. However, it is a reasonably safe assumption that the post-Agricolan campaigns most likely to have been the occasion for building camps of this size are those mounted by Severus.

We may therefore envisage the imperial army in AD 209 making its way by easy stages along the Roman road from Newstead to St Leonard's

Hill in upper Lauderdale (Fig. **3.11,** *1*), and thence to Channelkirk at the very head of the valley, where there was insufficient reasonably level ground beside the road to allow a camp of regular plan to be laid out (Fig. **3.11,** *2*); the next stage brought the column over Soutra Hill and down to the crossing of the Tyne Water at Pathhead, at which point the trail at present goes cold. It used to be thought that the army's next staging-point was at Inveresk on the shores of the Forth, but the camp once believed to be the bivouac in question is now known to be too small to have held the entire army. Moreover, since a permanent fort of Severan date is known to have existed at the coastal site of Cramond, on the north-western outskirts of Edinburgh, it is not impossible that the expedition may have held to the inland route along Dere Street, and after two days' journeying, made

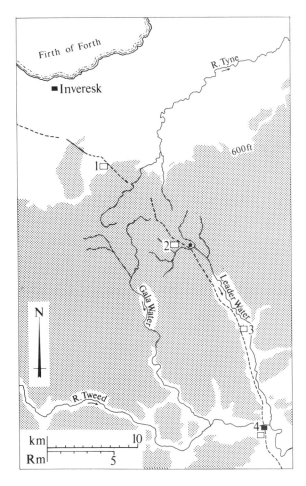

Fig. 3.10 Large Severan marching-camps in Lauderdale

1. Pathhead

2. Channelkirk

3. St Leonards

4. Newstead.

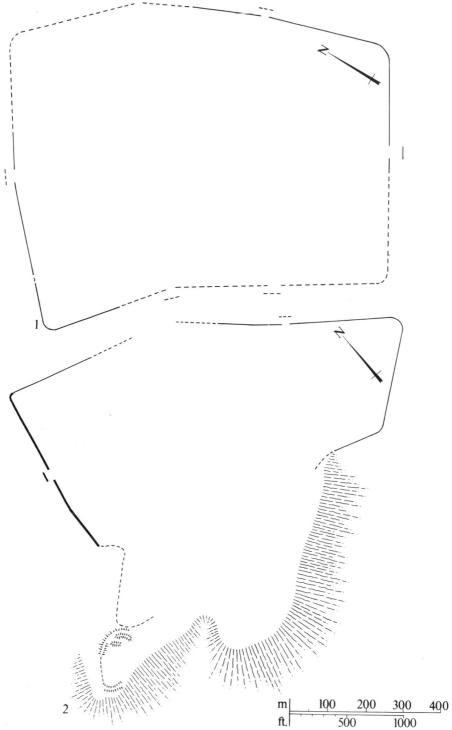

Fig. 3.11 Severan marching-camps at St Leonards (1), and Channelkirk (2).

contact with the fleet at the safe harbourage afforded by the mouth of the River Almond.

Beyond this we may not go, even in conjecture, but since the main targets for this punitive campaign were the Maeatae and the Caledonii, who lived beyond the Forth (see above, pp. 34–6), it would be reasonable to assume that Severus, wishing to come to grips with them as soon as possible, would have pushed on beyond the isthmus without undue delay. That he would have left behind a portion of his forces to secure southern Scotland from attack, and so protect his extended supply line, is another reasonable assumption, and this would explain why neither of the two series of camps located in Scotland north of the Forth is as large as that just examined.

The relationship between members of these two northern groups has been tested by excavation at Ardoch, where it was shown (St Joseph, 1970, 163-8; Hanson, 1978) that the smaller camp preceded the larger, but only by a short interval; it is, in fact, conceivable that they belong to consecutive seasons of campaigning. What is more, the east side of the larger overlies a watch-tower of the Flavian period, while the southern end of the smaller also overlies a third camp of presumed Flavian date, the interval between the two structures in the latter case being evidently longer than that separating the two large camps. From evidence such as this one could argue, as at Newstead, that no period of campaigning after the Agricolan is as likely as the Severan to have left traces on so vast a scale, while the apparently near-contemporary use of the two larger camps would be most apposite in bivouacs of that period.

Some fifteen examples of the 63-acre group have so far been identified north of the Forth (Fig. **3.12**). Separated by intervals that range from about 4.5 miles to 15 miles (7.3-24.3 km), the camps seem to indicate the course of an army, or armies, advancing from the crossing of the River Teith at Craigarnhall near Stirling, and operating in Strathearn, Fife, the Carse of Gowrie, and the coastal districts of Angus, as well as the valley of the Tay and Strathmore. They resemble each other not only in size, but usually also in their proportions (2:3), and in the possession of a small external annexe about 2 or 3 acres (c. 1 ha) in average size. The presence of the latter feature has not yet been explained; it is possible that it was intended to accommodate personnel who could not be conveniently housed in the large enclosure, perhaps native scouts or even hostages and prisoners. Equally possibly, it may have been used by a detachment left behind the main party to fulfil a care-and-maintenance role against the subsequent re-use of the defence-works. It was for just such a purpose that, as Tacitus records

(*Historiae* iv, 35), small parties were left behind by Vocula to guard transit camps from enemy attack during the Batavian revolt in AD 69.

The second explanation may derive some support from both the situations of the individual camps and a consideration of the tactics that Severus needed to employ. If the entire expeditionary force originally required camps of 165 acres for its accommodation, it seems unlikely that operations north of the Forth would have been entrusted to a unit that required no more than 65 acres; in other words, at least two smaller battle-groups were probably engaged simultaneously. Nevertheless, it has

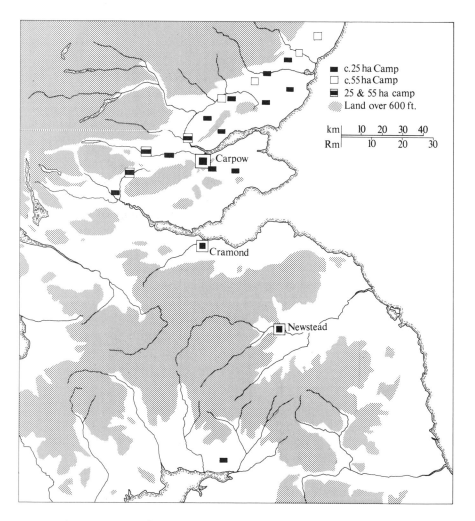

Fig. 3.12   Distribution of Severan marching-camps N of the Forth.

previously been suggested (St Joseph, 1965) that the entire series may represent the route of a single force, making as it were a Grand Tour of eastern Caledonia, from the Forth via Strathearn to a crossing of the Tay estuary near Newburgh, and thence along the coast, round the north-east end of the Sidlaw Hills, returning south to the Tay through the length of Strathmore. That there was indeed a crossing of the Tay may be made more probable by the identification of a small bridge-head camp on the north shore at St Madoes opposite a polygonal enclosure equivalent in size to a 63-acre camp, lying to the south of the Severan permanent base at Carpow; it has also been argued that the event was commemorated by the striking in AD 209 of a bronze coin or medallion depicting a bridge of boats and bearing on its reverse side the legend 'traiectus' (crossing) (cf. Robertson, 1980).

The above interpretation is an attractive one, but not entirely suscep-tible of proof, one way or the other. It may, however, be worth remarking that on the itinerary outlined above the positions of camp-sites relative to river-crossings appear to change on the return journey. Thus at Craigarnhall, Ardoch, Innerpeffray, Forteviot, Edenwood, and Kinnell (i.e. at six out of the seven sites adjacent to major river crossings on the outward route), the camp lies on the far side of the river, whereas at Marcus and Scone, the army would appear to have bivouacked *before* crossing. In conclusion, one might anticipate part of the discussion of the 130-acre camps by pointing out that in every single case – at Ardoch, Innerpeffray, Scone, Cardean, Balmakewan, and Kair House – the camp was constructed after the crossing. One would therefore be justified in suggesting that, say, two battle-groups were active on the earliest Severan expedition, a fifth of the total force (perhaps a legion strong) having been left on the isthmus, and the rest divided into two equal units; one unit proceeded eastwards down the Earn into Fife and, eventually crossing the Tay (not necessarily at Carpow), marched as far north as Keithock; having reached that point, it either retraced its steps or returned (by way of Strathmore, using the camps which had been constructed by its comrades in the other party, and maintained by holding units in the small external annexes; the second battle-group would have done the same in reverse, both parties wintering somewhere south of the Forth. As we know that Septimius Severus was present at York in May 210 and died there in February 211, we may presume that headquarters staff retired there every winter, but a sizeable portion of the army must have remained north of Cheviot.

The second expedition, mounted initially against the rebellious

Maeatae — the Caledonians' southern neighbours, must presumably have been the occasion for the construction of the last category of camps to be described, those of 130 acres (55 ha) in average area. Seven examples have so far been identified as a result of terrestrial or aerial survey; twice as large as the camps of the 63-acre class, they were doubtless intended to hold both the battle-groups of the previous year's operations, for a single direct hammer-blow aimed at the very heart of enemy territory. The surviving members indicate a line of march which followed quite closely the movements of what we may term the left-hand column in 209 (Fig. **3.12**); the imperial army probably crossed the Forth north-west of Stirling, following the Roman road past Ardoch and Innerpeffray to cross the Tay at Scone. The march from thence to Cardean across the Dean Water was probably broken into two stages, an intermediate camp still awaiting discovery near Coupar Angus. Then, skirting the low marshy ground to the southwest of Forfar, the army would have had a relatively easy stage to Battledykes Oathlaw; but between it and Balmakewan, the next known site, lay two river-crossings, at the North and South Esk, and it is possible that this 15 mile (23 km) stage may also have required an intermediate halting place. The final push to Kair House on the Bervie Water, however, could have been made in one determined move; at this point, astride a vital boundary between the lowlands of Strathmore and the Mearns and the rolling terrain of Buchan, the conquering army might well consider that they had come far enough to have neutralised the danger to the Romanised province and its northern frontier. An advance beyond the Mounth might conceivably embroil them in a more protracted campaign against the tribes of north-east Scotland generally, with all the problems of operating so far from base acutely heightened by the need to maintain supply-lines along the narrow corridor where the Grampians march down to the sea.

If this was indeed the appreciation of the military situation made by Severus's son Caracalla, then probably in sole command of the field-army, it is interesting to see how closely it may have followed the decision taken by the Flavian commander more than a century earlier. For if we are right in seeing the northernmost 100-acre camps from Raedykes to Muiryfold (see above, pp. 58–9) as evidence of a separate operation, whether leading up to or immediately post-dating the battle of *Mons Graupius*, it must always have made good tactical sense not to operate north of the Mounth until Strathmore and the Mearns were securely held. On the other hand, once a sure base of operation was established near the Mounth itself, it could have been at least inexpedient not to show the flag amongst tribal groups living immediately to the north. Accordingly, it may have been

Caracalla's failure to do this in 211, on the death of Severus, that gave ill-disposed historians grounds for the accusation that he directly gave up the struggle and abandoned his father's conquests. Nevertheless, whatever the circumstances of this alleged policy reversal, there can be no doubt that the hard-fought Severan campaigns led to almost a century of peace on the northern frontier.

The purpose of this chapter has been to show, as far as possible, how the Roman army, on successive occasions, overcame the native forces in the field and overran their territory. Yet these relatively brief episodes of marching and manoeuvering were just the prelude to a much longer process, in which the Roman military machine attempted to hold what it had won by force of arms and thus turn former enemies into the passive, if not loyal, subjects of a Romanised province. It is with this much sterner task that the following chapters are concerned.

4

The First Occupation:
Watch and ward in the south

HE MILITARY VIRTUES which in open warfare enabled the Roman army to overwhelm even the most spirited native opposition were complemented by an equally wide range of talents that came into play during the less eventful years of occupation. In this the Romans were extremely fortunate, for once the enemy had been beaten in the field, the more daunting problem of preserving the peace presented itself. From the very beginning of their occupation of Britain the method employed by the Romans was to station units of varying size at intervals throughout the countryside, locating them at particularly sensitive points in appropriate strength. The legions represented the backbone of the garrison, as they had of the fighting force, and their fortresses, the legionary *castra*, about 50 acres (20 ha) in area, were the largest permanent fortified sites constructed by the army of occupation. In the early days, however, between AD 43 and c. 75 elements of legionary troops comprising from one to five cohorts were brigaded together with auxiliary troops in what are known to archaeologists as vexillation fortresses (*vexillatio* being the Latin word for a legionary detachment). About a dozen of these are now known, largely through aerial survey, particularly in the Welsh Marches and in the northern Midlands of England (cf. Todd, 1981, 78-89); they differed widely in size, most falling within the range 15-25 acres (6-19 ha.). In a later period it became less usual to detach large units of legionaries on separate garrison duty, although individual officers, as we shall see (below, pp. 173–4) continued to be seconded to the command of auxiliary regiments, whenever a suitable candidate could not be found by the normal procedures. In the Flavian period it would seem that such legionary detachments as were employed did not exceed one or two cohorts, and even these were probably used sparingly (cf. Maxfield, 1986), the policy being rather to station the legions at full strength in the forward areas of the frontier zone, with outlying screens of smaller forts each holding one or two auxiliary regiments.

The only exceptions in Scotland to this deployment pattern appear to be Newstead, which is very much a special case (see below, pp. 90–1), and Dalswinton, but the campaign base at Red House, near Corbridge in Northumberland (Hanson *et al.*, 1979) represents a comparable site in the area campaigned over by Agricolan forces. At Dalswinton (Fig. **4.1**) a double-ditched enclosure of at least two periods is situated on the alluvial plain below the gravel terrace occupied by the two-period Flavian fort. It has been argued that this relationship indicates that the Flavian fort is later than the enclosure (St Joseph, 1976, 10-11), which itself must surely be later than the *clavicula*-gated camp within whose interior it lies. As we have already seen that camps with *claviculae* most probably belong to the

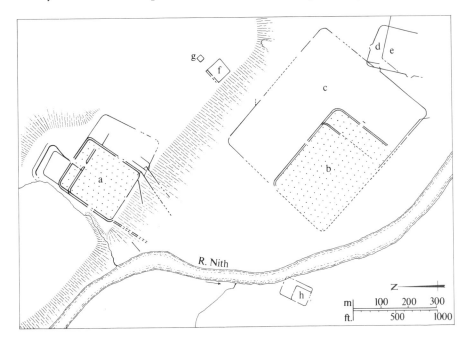

Fig. 4.1 Roman works at Dalswinton: *a*) permanent forts, Bankhead, *b*) possible vexillation fortress, Bankfoot, *c*) – *e*), marching-camps, *f*) – *g*) possible native enclosures, *h*) temporary camp, Ellisland.

Agricolan phase of campaigning, it would seem necessary to assume that the double-ditched enclosure was also the work of the Agricolan army. Its size in its first form almost certainly approaches 21 acres (8.4 ha), although it is impossible to be absolutely sure, as only part of the perimeter has yet been recorded. That the enclosure was intended to serve a more than temporary purpose seems to be indicated by its double-ditch system, yet the cropmarks which reveal its presence are appreciably narrower than for example those of the ditches enclosing the later forts on the adjacent higher ground. To identify it as a semi-permanent campaign base, perhaps housing units left behind once the main party had departed on operations in the south-west, would not be inappropriate. The garrison in this case might well have been some 2000 strong, comprising both legionary and auxiliary troops; in other words, this may be the nearest approximation in Scotland to a vexillation fortress. Yet, its position on ground that could be overlooked from close at hand and was also liable to flooding strongly suggests that no lengthy occupation was ever intended; indeed, it is conceivable that the choice of ground was influenced by the knowledge that the higher terrace site would shortly be required for the permanent forts.

Accordingly, we must imagine that when plans were being drawn up for the stage-by-stage occupation of North Britain, from Brigantia northwards into Scotland, it was believed that the majority of garrison posts would be occupied by individual auxiliary regiments or, occasionally, parts of regiments. The density of deployment was conditioned by two basic factors: the level of military security appropriate to a given area, and the available resources of manpower; both factors would naturally have required to be assessed in the light of the overall strategy as well as local needs. These points having been decided, the individual siting of each fortification would then have been considered. Tacitus makes great play of the happy knack possessed by Agricola in this respect: 'the experts noted that no other general made a wiser choice of site' (*Agricola*, 22, 2). Yet, every Roman commander worth his salt must have possessed and exercised the same degree of skill, and, in any case, the selection of many fort positions would probably have been made by the legionary *praefectus castrorum* in whose area they chanced to lie, rather than by the commander-in-chief himself. Moreover, even a superficial examination of the forts of Roman Scotland will reveal that a comparable ability to read the lie of the ground informed the fort-builders of the second and third century; Agricola's expertise was by no means unique.

There was, however, more to be done than placing forts advantageously. Their ability to withstand siege through the strength of their fortifications and the supply of corn within their granaries was only part of the scheme; just as important, and of more positive effect, was the fact that they were linked by a communications network, the like of which was not seen again in this country until after the Industrial Revolution. It comprised three basic elements: roads, surveillance- and signalling-posts, and regular patrols. Of the last element there are no archaeological traces, but without such positive action it would have been difficult, if not impossible, for the occupying power to have kept its finger on the pulse of native sentiment; were there also, one wonders, the equivalent of the political officers who kept the military abreast of popular feelings on the North-West Frontier of India in the nineteenth century? At any rate, the combined garrison and patrolling duties would have been most appropriately discharged by the part-mounted regiments that were stationed from time to time at such forts as Birrens, Crawford, and Lyne (see below, pp. 85–9).

The most enduring traces of this system are the roads, which, together with the frontier Walls, constitute perhaps the best memorial to the aspirations and achievements of the Roman army in North Britain. Various accounts of their location and appearance in Scotland have been written in recent years (St Joseph, 1952; Davidson, 1952; Margary, 1973; Maxwell, 1984b), but not even the most detailed description could adequately convey the sublime sense of purpose with which the best preserved sectors of these grass-shrouded causeways stride across the rounded hills of the Southern Uplands. Although only intermittent fragments can now be seen above ground, enough survives to reconstruct the main skeleton of the original system (Fig. 4.2) and to furnish even in its decay, numerous examples of the painstaking professionalism and ingenuity of the Roman road-engineer. Moreover, even those sectors where the plough has long since levelled the Roman road-mound may still respond to aerial survey, the lines of buried side-ditches and the rows of silted quarry-pits showing clearly as cropmarks in favourable seasons (Plate 5, b).

The basic geography of Scotland and the strategic requirements of the occupying army dictated that the road system should take the form of an irregular grid. The main longitudinal members (running north-south) were, firstly, the relatively direct route, known as Dere Street, which connected Corbridge on the Tyne with the forts on the Forth-Clyde isthmus, by way of Redesdale and Lauderdale; and secondly, the road that was driven north from Carlisle by a more circuitous route through Annandale and upper Clydesdale, and thence cut obliquely through the Biggar Gap along the south-eastern side of the Pentland Hills to make contact with the first route, possibly somewhere near the bridgehead fort of Elginhaugh on the North Esk. From this junction a single route led north-westwards, its course approximating to the line of the modern A7 as far as Nether Liberton, as though its immediate objective was the fort at Cramond.

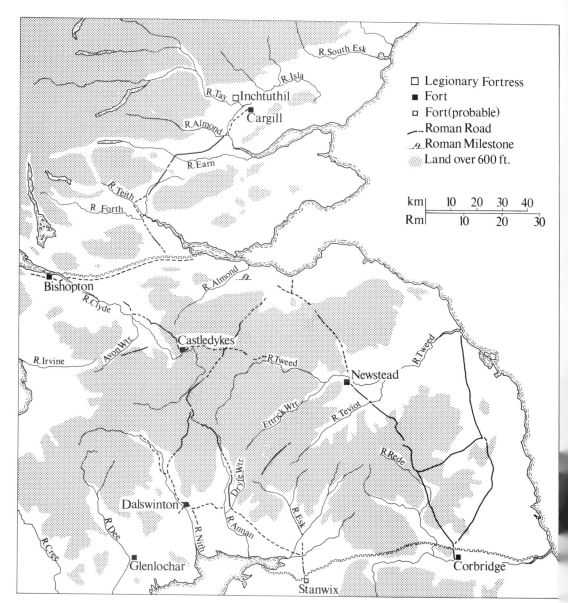

Fig. 4.2   The Roman Road-system in Scotland (all periods).

However, it is possible that somewhere to the west of Edinburgh Castle it altered course to the west and passed through Corstorphine, heading towards a crossing of the River Almond at or near Newbridge. Although no traces of the road itself survive to the west of Edinburgh, the discovery from the air of two Roman camps at Gogar, a little way to the south of Edinburgh Airport and not far from the recorded find-spot of the Ingliston milestone, supports the belief that the continuation of Dere Street proceeded by way of Linlithgow, where Roman pottery of the first century has been found, to Camelon, on the western outskirts of Falkirk; hereabout, by tradition, the Roman road crossed the River Carron, heading north-westwards in the direction of the Tor Wood beyond Larbert, where its course has been verified by excavation. Thence it appears to have led through Bannockburn – its causeway possibly being used as a position of strength during the battle of 1314 (cf. Christison, 1957) but apart from a short sector proved in the western suburbs of Stirling, to the south of the King's Knot, its precise course is not known until it reappears on the northern side of Dunblane (see above, pp. 55–6). From this point, however, its route may be followed almost the entire way to the east end of the Gask Ridge on the north side of the River Earn; in the final portion of this sector its remains are well worth visiting, (see below, pp. 118–21), but elsewhere our knowledge of its course depends largely on the reports of early fieldworkers or the indications of cropmarks recorded from the air.

From the Gask Ridge the road led down to the crossing of the River Tay at Bertha, the sector where it traverses the sand-and-gravel deposits around Huntingtower producing some of the most clearly-defined cropmark evidence of the double row of quarry-pits that flanked the carriageway (Plate 5, b). It may be significant that such cropmark indications of quarry-pits are so consistent a feature of the known archaeological traces of the road between the Forth and the Tay – and one that was strikingly manifested by the extreme, localised drought of the summer of 1982. It is possible that this uniformity may indicate that supervision of the construction of the sector lay in the hands of a single unit, but whether it represents work undertaken in the Flavian period or in any of the subsequent occupations cannot be determined. It is, however, remarkable that no such traces can be found beyond the Tay. Although lengths of road have been recorded as issuing from the gates of forts in the outer frontier area generally, there is as yet no evidence either that outlying forts were connected to the route just described, or that the main artery of communication was ever continued beyond the banks of the Tay; the often-cited example of a metalled road in Caddam Wood a little to the north of Kirriemuir cannot be accepted as Roman without more corroborative evidence than its present isolated position seems likely to afford. Conceivably, the alteration in frontier policy, which necessitated the abandonment of so many of the northernmost forts *c.* AD 86−7 (see below, pp. 122−4) occurred at a time when the road system was still incomplete. When the Roman army again advanced its frontier in the Antonine period, the occupation did not extend beyond the Tay, so that there was no later occasion for road building in Strathmore; in the Severan period, (see above, pp. 33−6) the character as well as the length of the occupation appears to have precluded such military works.

As well as these two main arteries, there were alternative north-south routes. One branched off the western trunk in lower Annandale and drove west by Lochmaben into Nithsdale, which it ascended as far as Thornhill before branching, one route climbing north-east over the watershed into the valley of the Potrail Water; from here a direct route along the Daer Water brought it down into Clydesdale and reunion with the main trunk at Crawford. From Thornhill a second branch crossed the Nith below the newly discovered fort at Drumlanrig (Maxwell & Wilson, 1987, 19-20), thus avoiding the precipitous lower slopes of Dalpeddar Hill, a little farther up the left bank; doubtless the way then led westwards into Ayrshire finally linking up with a coastal road that served the garrisons on the shore of the Firth of Clyde. An alternative route to the isthmus was available − in the second if not the first century 5 − through the lower part of Clydesdale; it diverged from the main east-west lateral road (to be described presently) in the neighbourhood of Castledykes, but, while it is possible that at one time it could have been approached along the valley of Clyde by way of a branch that sprang from the main north-south artery near Biggar, the suggested direct link with Clydesdale across the shoulder of Tinto Hill must be rejected for lack of conclusive evidence. At this point, it may be appropriate to mention the Devil's Causeway, which, although not actually situated in Scotland, relates to the more northerly part of the communications system insofar as it provides a direct route from Corbridge to the mouth of the River Tweed. No structural evidence of Roman occupation has ever been recovered from the vicinity of Berwick or Tweedmouth, but it seems most unlikely that such a spur road would have been constructed unless it served some sort of installation, presumably a harbour site.

We have already learned that supplies or men may have been carried up the Tweed to an assembly point at Newstead for the initial Severan thrust into Scotland. The discovery of a wooden steering-oar during the 1905−10 excavations (Curle, 1911, 313) may possibly indicate that river transport could have played a part in provisioning the fort in normal times, too. If it did, the run of 36 miles (55 km) would have formed the easternmost portion of a lateral route linking the North Sea with the Firth of Clyde. From Newstead a road appears to have led upstream on the left bank of the Tweed, as far as its confluence with the Lyne Water, and then struck north-westwards over the watershed into mid-Clydesdale, passing through the great fort of Castledyke near Carstairs and crossing the Clyde immediately above Lanark. From here the road climbed westwards over the prominent ridge of Stonebyres Hill, crossed the Nethan Water and continued through Avondale, making for the natural 'gateway' to the West below Loudoun Hill, where the covenanters triumphed at Drumclog and in separate en-counters both Bruce and Wallace gained the upper hand over English invaders. The course of the road has not been identified farther west than this, but there can be little doubt that it followed the River Irvine to its mouth, where, beneath some part of the old burgh of Irvine, above the right bank of the river, there must surely have been a fort and harbour.

Lateral communication was also provided, although perhaps not until the Antonine period, by a cross route that probably sprang from the main north-south artery in Annandale near its junction with the Dryfe Water and proceeded north-eastwards up the valley of the Dryfe; it then crossed the Black and White Esks, the latter near Eskdalemuir, and climbed purposefully into the waste of Craik Moor and the Ettrick hills, its destination presumably being Newstead, although since the north-eastern portion of the road has not yet been traced, this is not absolutely certain. Communication with garrisons in the extreme south-west of the country was probably provided by another minor branch which may have crossed the Nith opposite Dalswinton and then driven south-west to ford the Dee at the south end of Loch Ken; excavation and air survey have shown that the road continued to the Water of Fleet and it may even have reached as far as Luce Bay or Loch Ryan. One imagines that at one stage of the Flavian occupation there would have been an intention to link the westernmost parts of Galloway with the presumed station at Irvine by the coastal route already mentioned; the temporary camps at Girvan Mains suggest that the prerequisite reconnaissance had been undertaken, and an intermediate fort at Girvan itself is by no means an impossibility.

The final cross-bar of the road system was provided by a route spanning the Forth-Clyde isthmus, which, as the Romans were well aware, was the narrowest part of the British mainland. It is doubtful whether the chain of *praesidia* constructed by Agricola in his third campaign would ever have been provided with a road, but certainly in the Antonine period, when there was a need to link the garrisons of forts on the Antonine Wall, the so-called Military Way served such a purpose. Moreover, on the west flank of the Wall, a road probably extended from the shallows at Dumbuck along the south shore of the Clyde estuary. On the east flank it seems possible that the new coastal forts at Carriden, Cramond, and Inveresk were served not only by spurs branching off the old inland line of Dere Street, but also by a new road running along the south shore of the Forth, which, like its equivalent on the Clyde coast, would have afforded better facilities for patrols guarding against infiltration from the further shore.

The absence of traces of a road system in certain parts of Roman Scotland north of the Forth has already been noted, but there are some significant gaps or anomalies in southern Scotland which also deserve comment. The line of a road directly connecting Castledykes in Clydesdale with garrisons on the Forth has long been sought, particularly in the vicinity of the small fort of Castle Greg on Camilty Moor to the south-east of West Calder; the lack of success that has attended this search suggests that Castle Greg was an early Flavian site which was evacuated in the troop reductions of AD 86–7 before the road construction programme had started on this part of the system – an indication, therefore, that the sector in question was a minor element in the overall plan. Moreover, the discovery in 1984 of a fortlet, similar in size to Castle Greg, at Bankhead on the north bank of the Clyde a little way to the east of Castledykes (Maxwell & Wilson, 1987, 19) may indicate where it was intended that this route should join the Tweeddale-Clydesdale road. Not being a major link, there was perhaps less urgency for its construction. Another reason for its low priority may be the apparent absence or scarcity of native settlement sites in the area. A similar factor can hardly be advanced to explain the absence of a road in the upper part of Tweeddale, where the archaeological record in the late Bronze Age and early Iron Age is particularly full (cf. RCAMS 1967, *passim*); it is possible that these inmost fastnesses of the tribe known to the Romans as the Selgovae were simply too dangerous an area through which to construct a major communication-line; otherwise one would have thought that the natural corridor which the river valley offered between Newstead and garrisons in Annandale was too convenient to ignore. That it was passed over in favour of the upland road through Craik Moor on the one side and the circuitous route by way of Clydesdale, on the other, speaks volumes for the hostile attitude of the Selgovan tribesmen.

The opposite reason must, however, be sought for the absence of a road in the coastal parts of East Lothian and Berwickshire, the northern territories of the Votadini. The philo-Roman policy practised by Votadinian leaders from the earliest days of the occupation, (and possibly before, for their lands extended southwards to the Northumbrian Tyne) is illustrated most conspicuously by the continuity of occupation of the hill-fort on Traprain Law, the tribal 'capital', which appears to have retained its defences throughout the period of Roman presence in Scotland; the excavation of Traprain produced abundant evidence of Roman trading-contacts with the inhabitants of the hillfort from the 1st to the 4th century. The absence of any traces of Roman marching camps in the coastal districts of Votadinian domains between the Tweed and the Lothian Esk provides further confirmation that this pacific attitude was adopted at an early stage.

It may be appropriate at this point to offer a brief description of the appearance and original form of the various roads that composed this comprehensive system. At the outset the illusion must be banished that Roman road-building was a steryotyped procedure. By no means all sectors of Roman road extend ruler-straight towards the distant horizon; nor are all easily recognised as symmetrically-cambered mounds with flanking side-ditches, which excavation eventually shows to have been built in carefully graded layers, from a foundation bottoming of heavy boulders to a gravel-bound, or cobbled running-surface. For the Roman road-engineer was a practical fellow, with more than enough sense to see that in the widely differing terrain of Southern Scotland a flexible approach was inevitably the best. Consequently, inspection of the course and construction of different sectors of Roman road, as illustrated by excavation or examination of superficial remains, will reveal an almost limitless variety of conditions. More disturbing, however, is the fact that the characteristics commonly assigned to a Roman road are also displayed by roads of much later periods; add to this the occasional confusion of cropmarks of Roman quarry-pits with double pit-alignments of prehistoric date, or, again in cropmark form, of road side-ditches with the double parallel ditches of the prehistorical ritual monument known as a *cursus*, and it will be realised that the identification and hence description of a typical Roman road is far from straightforward.

The first objective of the road-builder was to provide a relatively smooth well-drained running-surface on a course that led as directly as possible towards the required destination, without, however, introducing unacceptable gradients, for the road-system was designed with wheeled traffic in mind, as well as pedestrians and mounted travellers; a final requirement was that of military security, with the result that routes which were feasible in engineering terms may have had to be avoided because, for example, they were vulnerable to ambush. When these criteria had been satisfied the road-engineer might build as he thought best. As we have seen, in the sector between Forth and Tay, his design style might be stamped quite clearly on the finished construction. Dere Street affords numerous examples of the Romans building on a grand scale, as one might expect of what was probably the most important artery of communication in Scotland. Throughout its surviving stretches it exhibits a width that rarely falls below 30 ft. (9m), and where the country permits, for example, on either side of the Teviot crossing, maintains point-to-point alignment over great distances (Plate 6); in the upland areas the road line was still surveyed from point-to-point, but the individual points were relatively close and, at first sight, the course appears to be curvilinear. For much of the way in the southern sector of Dere Street the Roman line has been used as a land-boundary, drove-road, or farm track — a circumstance which has preserved the line but probably destroyed the upper metalling of the road beneath the wheels and feet, or hooves, of later generations. On Soutra Hill, however, just north of the Lothian-Berwickshire border, although mediaeval traffic has followed the general line across the watershed from Lauderdale, the Roman route has survived in excellent condition for considerable stretches. Here one may study the various elements at their best. The mound that carried the road surface (the *agger*) appears as a grass-covered stony bank up to 35 ft (10.5 m) wide; it is centrally placed on a wide artificial terrace with a broad ditch on the downhill side, the latter feature presumably intended to demarcate the road-zone as well as providing a means of drainage. The overall width of the entire complex, more than 100 ft (30 m), gives some indication of the importance which the army assigned to communication.

In contrast, the western half of the road system provides more examples of Roman road-building in difficult country. The difference in climate — then, as now, the western side of the country received more than its fair share of rain-fall — doubtless combined with different vegetational and geological conditions to necessitate the use of other techniques for dealing with excess surface-water and soft ground. On the Craik Moor route, culverts were provided beneath the road to save it from being washed out in periods of heavy rain, and doubtless, as has been suggested at Air Cleuch on the Daer Water branch, some minor streams were crossed by a timber bridge rather than relying on a ford, as might have been acceptable in drier areas. Naturally in such conditions it would have also been more common to have trouble in finding a sure foundation for the road-bed, whether the cause was the presence of a clay subsoil making it more difficult to shed accumulated rainfall, or the depth of peat bog, across which a road might have to be 'floated' on a raft of lighter material. Alternatively, it might be easier to cut down through the peat until the underlying subsoil was reached, although in this case peculiar problems of drainage presented themselves, not to mention those relating to the disposal of such a vast amount of spoil. Not surprisingly, in sectors like these it is uncommon for the running-surface to exceed 20 ft. (6 m), and a similar width was generally the most that could be undertaken in those upland sectors where the road had to be carried on extensive terracing.

A good example of the lengths to which the road-engineer could go in seeking a solution to the problems presented by such terrain may be seen near the fort of Crawford in upper Clydesdale (Fig. 4.3). At this point the main road approaching from the south used the level ground on the right bank of the river to make a relatively direct line for the fort, crossing two minor tributaries without undue change of alignment. On the northern side of the second it probably threw off a spur to give access to the east gate of the fort, but the main route, clearly indicated in 1977 by a broad strip of parched pasture, inclined sharply to the east and began a carefully engineered ascent of the south-east side of Castle Hill. Using a series of zigzag terraces to reduce the gradient to a maximum of 1 in 6, the road gained the summit of the Raggengill Pass some 350 ft (107m) above the valley floor. From here it gradually descended by a curvilinear course towards the valley of the Clyde on the north side of Castle Hill, resuming its linear point-to-point progress as it approached more level ground south of Coldchapel. The reason for this remarkable diversion, involving an apparently unnecessary climb and descent of many hundreds of feet, becomes clear when one follows the alternative route by way of the modern minor road down river from Crawford; at a point just over a mile from the fort, the road passes along a narrow strip of level ground between the face of a steep rocky scarp on one side and an almost equally steep descent to the river Clyde on the other — an ideal place for ambush or blockade. The selection of the tortuous upland diversion in preference to this vulnerable valley-bottom route provides as eloquent an indication of the military character of the Roman road-system as many chapters of text.

Situated at intervals along the network, and in some cases as we have seen occupied well in advance of the road-building programme, there were garrison-posts of various sizes. During the different phases of the Flavian period, between AD 80 and 105, there were a total of at least 32 forts in Scotland, as well as a legionary base. They lay within easy marching distance of each other, rarely more than 20 miles (32 km) apart, often much less, with the result that in time of need one unit might come swiftly to the

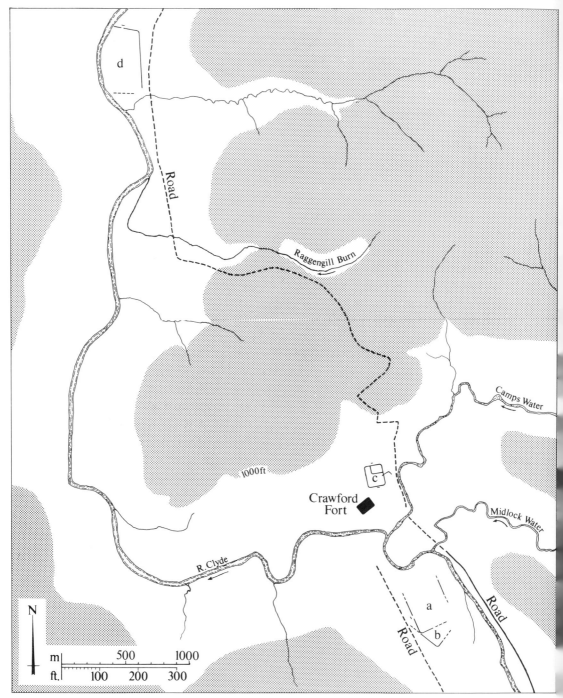

Fig. 4.3 A sector of the road-system near Crawford in upper Clydesdale; a) – d) temporary camps.

assistance of its neighbour, while in more stable times patrol parties were never farther than half a day's march from food and shelter. The actual distance between garrisons in any given area would have been determined by the circumstances — the density of the local native population and its attitude towards the occupying power, and the strategic or tactical importance of the area in the wider context of frontier security. In general, the strength of the garrison would have been determined by similar considerations, but comparison of the troop dispositions in Scotland north and south of the Forth-Clyde isthmus reveals that from the very earliest phase of the occupation, it may have been decided that different methods of deployment would be observed in the two areas. South of the Forth there appears to have been a much greater variety in the size of garrison, and hence size of fort (Fig. **4.4**).

At Newstead and Dalswinton, for example, both of which were sites that appear to have served as campaign bases or marshalling-grounds, extremely large forts 10 – 13 acres (4 – 5.3 ha) in area, * were built at some time in the Flavian period — in both cases as the conclusion of a complicated structural sequence. Their purpose was doubtless to serve as command centres of the south-east and south-west of Scotland respectively, and they may both have accommodated units of legionary troops, as well as auxiliaries. But as well as these extremely large forts, which are probably descended as a type from the vexillation fortresses mentioned above, there were at least three sites — Glenlochar, Tassiesholm, and Castledykes — where forts of 5 – 6.5 acres (2.0 – 2.6 ha) were built. These too could easily have accommodated more than one unit, although it is theoretically possible that they were intended to hold single cavalry regiments. In combination with the largest works they ensured, regardless of the precise composition of their garrison, that each of the major river valleys of southern Scotland contained at least one military force capable of taking the field against even the strongest levies that the local tribes might muster.

It would appear, however, that this practice of massing the frontier garrisons exerted a strain on the resources of manpower that were allotted to the task, for the intervals between these major posts were, on occasion, guarded by units of less than regimental strength. Only four sites capable of serving as the bases of full cohorts are known, two of them in the territory of the Selgovae: one on the Tweeddale road at Easter Happrew, roughly intermediate between Newstead and Castledykes, another at

---

*Except where specifically stated, fort areas represent the space within the ramparts; in unexcavated examples the rampart width has been estimated.

Oakwood in the valley of the Ettrick. A third guards the east-west route at Loudoun Hill, while the fourth, Elginhaugh, stands sentinel where Dere Street crosses the North Esk at Dalkeith. Elsewhere, even smaller units were employed, the two main types being known as small forts, ranging in size from 1.5 – 2.5 acres (0.6m – 1.0 ha) and fortlets, never more than an acre (0.4 ha) in size. The distinction is not necessarily one which the Romans themselves made but derives rather from the needs of archaeologists to categorise their material. Nevertheless, those of the larger type probably housed the greater part of a cohort and therefore contained, as at Cappuck and Crawford, the principal buildings associated with the running of the unit. The fortlets being themselves capable of division into subgroups, are

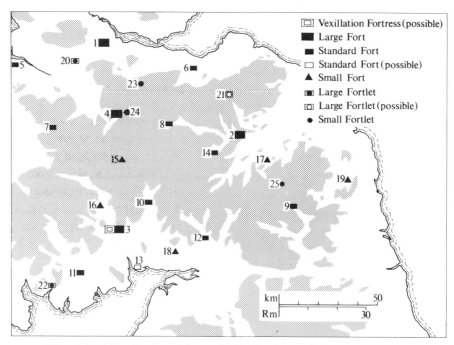

Fig. 4.4   Distribution of forts of S Scotland occupied at some time in the Flavian period:

1 Camelon	9 High Rochester	17 Cappuck
2 Newstead	10 Tassiesholm	18 Birrens
3 Dalswinton	11 Glenlochar	19 Learchild
4 Castledykes	12 Broomholm	20 Mollins
5 Barochan	13 Ward Law	21 Oxton
6 Elginhaugh	14 Oakwood	22 Gatehouse
7 Loudoun Hill	15 Crawford	23 Castle Greg
8 Easter Happrew	16 Drumlanrig	24 Bankhead
		25 Chew Green

unlikely to have held more than a single century of infantry (eighty men); to provide the living and storage space for even this exiguous force, the standard buildings of the cohort—fort had occasionally to be tailored to size. At Gatehouse of Fleet, one of the larger fortlets, two half-size barracks were built, one on either side of the central street — a structural solution which was also adopted in building the minor installations of the Antonine period (see below, pp. 176–8).

While it may be presumed that such small garrisons would have been used only in those areas where it was felt that the local population presented no threat to security, it is remarkable that a couple of hundred troopers or infantrymen, were deemed sufficient to maintain the peace in the heavily populated thirty-five mile (56 km) sector of the western route between Carlisle and Tassiesholm, or in the shorter, but more vulnerable, upland portions on each side of Crawford. Even on Dere Street, where the presence of the philo-Roman Votadini to the north-east would have guaranteed a lower incidence of unrest, one would have thought that the importance of the communications link itself justified a greater density of troop deployment than minor garrisons every 12 or 13 miles (c. 20 km). In short, the contrast with the distribution and strength of garrisons in the northern part of occupied Scotland is such as to suggest very strongly that south of the Forth-Clyde isthmus resources were being husbanded for the intensive campaigning and occupation that lay ahead. If, therefore, we may assume that the pattern of forts in southern Scotland was laid down by Agricola himself, and if, as we shall see, that pattern endured without significant alteration until the withdrawal of troops from the northern frontier in c. AD 86/7, it is not inconceivable that the form of that outermost *limes* was also in great part the work of Agricola.

It will be recalled, however, that before launching his Caledonian offensive Agricola drew a military cordon across the waist of Scotland. Traces of this operation have long been sought, but with equivocal results. The reason for this is that it has generally been assumed that the chain of Agricolan posts would have followed the line adopted by the builders of the Antonine Wall. Some justification for this belief was provided by the discovery of small rectangular enclosures below two of the 2nd century wall-forts (see below, pp. 129–49), but subsequent examination of both of these has conclusively disproved their Flavian origin. Moreover, recent aerial reconnaissance located a large fortlet at Mollins (Fig. **4.5**) to the south-west of Cumbernauld and 2.3 miles (3.7 km) south of the Antonine Wall, and excavation has shown that it was built, occupied, and deliberately demolished at some time before AD 90 (Hanson & Maxwell,

1980). There is thus a strong likelihood that it formed part of a system of posts which may have extended from Barochan on the south bank of the Clyde north-west of Glasgow to the southern shore of the Firth of Forth, incorporating at least two of the positions later occupied by Antonine wall-forts — Cadder and Castlecary (Hanson, 1981). Although not enough is known of this system, it seems not improbable that here, too, alternating small and large garrisons may have been employed, the intervening distance averaging about 6.5 miles (10.5 km). Such density of fort-development, about half as close again as, for example, on Dere Street, represents the earliest approach in the archaeology of Roman Britain to a linear frontier, and hence it would be reasonable to suppose that communication between forts may have been provided, as on later frontiers, by signal towers that doubled as watchposts. No examples of these have yet been observed on the isthmus, but they were extensively used on the greater part of the road between Forth and Tay. The recent discovery of a Flavian fort at Doune (Maxwell, 1984a) has made it appear possible, however, that there was also a chain of posts on the northern skirts of the Forth-Clyde isthmus, and

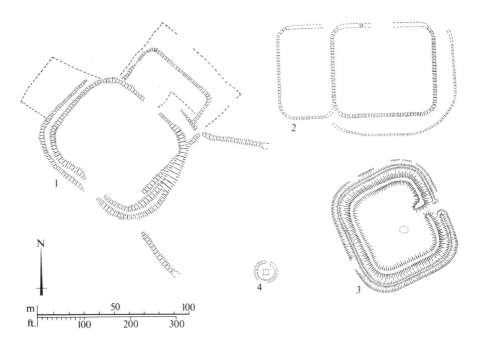

Fig. 4.5   The fortlets of Oxton (1), Mollins (2), and Castle Greg (3); the signal-station on the summit of Eildon Hill North (4).

Plate 9

Air photograph of the two-period temporary camp at Inchtuthil as revealed by finely-detailed cropmarks, with rows of rubbish-disposal pits in the interior showing the emplacement of legionaries' tent-lines. (Royal Commission on the Ancient Monuments of Scotland)

Plate 10

Air photograph of Steedstalls camp; cropmarks reveal the line of the enclosing ditch as well as sites of the curious elongated hollows once thought to be stables; the latter appear as cropmarks and surface-features. (Royal Commission on the Ancient Monuments of Scotland)

Plate 11

Cargill fort as revealed by air photographs, the external ditch-system and even the internal streets being visible as cropmarks. (Royal Commission on the Ancient Monuments of Scotland)

Plate 12a   Cardean fort as revealed by air photographs.

Plate 12b   Air photograph of Stracathro fort (left) with its annexe ditch apparently cutting earlier temporary camp (right).

Plate 13

The fortlet of Inverquharity, near Kirriemuir, discovered from the air in 1983;
on the far (north) side the defences run along the crest of a river terrace. The
clavicula of a temporary camp is visible on the extreme right. (Royal Commission on the Ancient Monuments of Scotland)

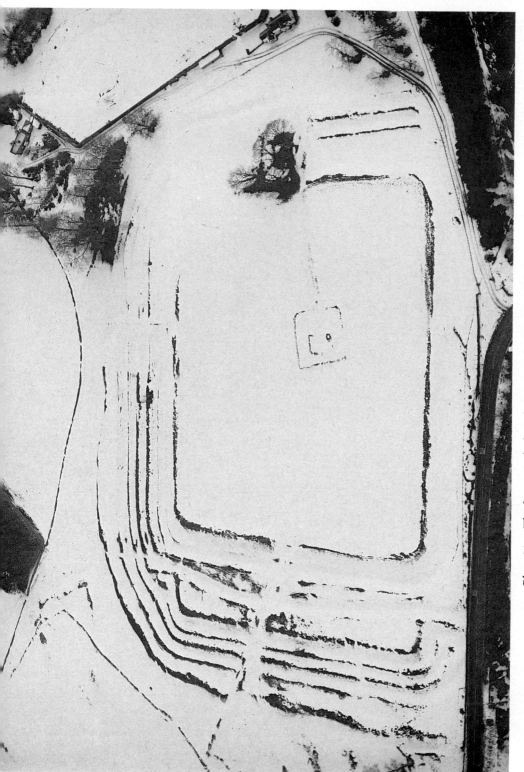

Plate 14 The fort at Ardoch under snow, only the crest of the rampart and the spines between the ditches remaining uncovered.

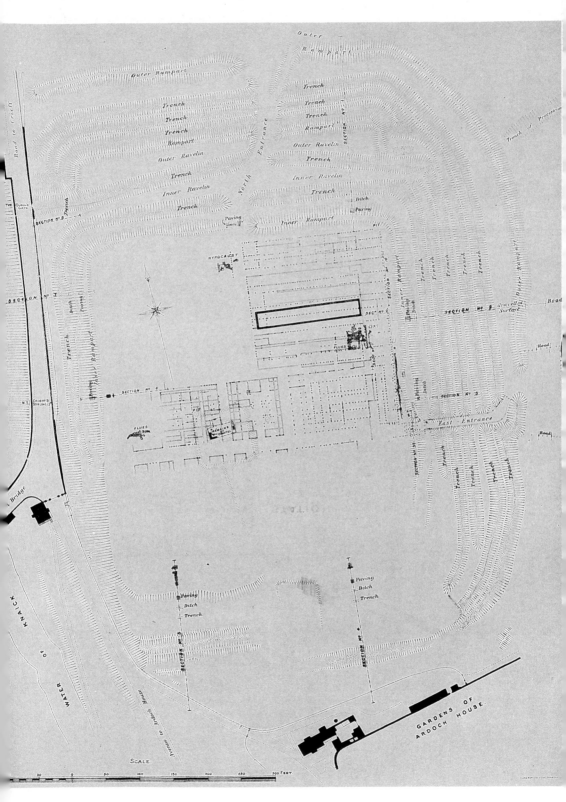

Plate 15   The plan of the 1896–7 excavations at Ardoch.

Plate 16

Air photograph of the Roman fort at Strageath, showing the dark cropmarks of the ditch-systems defining the complicated pattern of defences and external, irregularly-shaped annexes of the Flavian and Antonine periods; light-toned marks indicate the pattern of internal streets and the approach road. (Royal Commission on the Ancient Monuments of Scotland) conceivably it was this system to which Tacitus alluded in *Agricola*, 23; here, too, watchtowers may have provided additional security.

It would therefore be appropriate to commence the final portion of this chapter, which comprises summary descriptions of individual examples of the various types of site used in southern Scotland during the Flavian period, with an account of the signal-tower on Eildon Hill North (Fig. **4.5**). Although it is not absolutely certain that this particular structure was built during the Flavian period — despite the structural analogies advanced by the excavator (Steer, 1952) — there can be little doubt that a series of sites like this would have been required throughout the area to provide facilities for long-range communications. For this purpose its position atop the summit immediately overlooking the strategically important base at Newstead would have been ideal. Set at an altitude of 1327 ft (404 m), it can be seen from as far away as Berwick to the east, the Cheviots to the south, the heights of Soutra to the north, and the tumbled ranges above Clydesdale to the west. It survives at present as a circular ditched enclosure 35 ft (10.7m) in internal diameter, but excavation revealed that the ditch had been a shallow affair, intended mainly for drainage and not for defence; the interior, which was covered with stone pitching, had originally contained a rectangular timber tower measuring 11ft 4in by 10ft 6in (3.45m x 3.2m) in ground plan and supported on a framework of six massive timber uprights; it was observed by the excavator that these dimensions were identical with those of a gate-tower at the Agricolan fort of Oakwood. The appearance of the tower may only be guessed at, but it was evidently a robustly-built structure, as would have been necessary to withstand the extreme wind-forces prevalent in such an exposed position. For the same reason it was provided with a heavy tile-roof and its walls were probably clad with weather-boarding to protect the troops who manned it. Nothing survives of the means by which messages were transmitted, but we may presume that for long-range communication, as in this instance, smoke or beacon would have had to suffice, with semaphore possibly being used in towers situated in much closer proximity to one another.

Castle Greg (Fig. **4.5**) makes a particularly appropriate example of the fortlet group, being one of the best preserved Roman earthworks in Scotland, and, in addition, the first Roman site to be examined by excavation (see above, p. 10). It measures about 190 feet by 165 feet (38 m x 50 m) over a rampart some 15 ft (5 m) thick that rises at least 3 ft (0.9 m) above the level of the interior and about 6 ft (1.8 m) above the bottom of the innermost of the two enclosing ditches. On the north side of the entrance the rampart returns for a distance of 20 feet (6 m) towards the interior, a feature which may represent the position of an *ascensus*, an inclined ramp or staircase giving access to the wallhead. The circular hollow near the centre of the fort presumably indicates the position of the well which Sir Daniel Wilson excavated to a depth of 11 ft (3.4 m), without, however, finding anything of significance. Before afforestation of the surrounding area, the position occupied by the fortlet afforded singularly bleak moorland prospects, and it is difficult to imagine that the air of desolation was markedly different in Roman times. There are few traces of prehistoric sites in the vicinity, and the majority of these are isolated cairns or cairnfields, probably dating to a much more remote period of antiquity (cf. RCAMS 1978, 8-10). Consequently it is not surprising that the causeway which issues confidently from the fortlet gate was never connected to a major road, the abandonment of the site probably coinciding with the general reduction of Scottish garrison strength in AD 86–7, before the road-building programme had turned to such minor routes as this. When Scotland was re-occupied in the second century, an altered perception of military priorities evidently dictated that the situation did not warrant the expenditure of men and resources in re-occupying the site.

The case of Crawford in upper Clydesdale is somewhat similar, for it appears to have been abandoned at the same time as Castle Greg; the Flavian coins found in the demolition layer that covered the ruins of the first-period buildings included an *As* of Domitian, dated to AD 86, which was in almost mint condition when lost; it invites comparison with identical coins in a similar state of wear which have been found in terminal deposits in Flavian forts both north and south of the Forth (Robertson, 1968, 61–3; 1975, 9). But at Crawford this was not the end of the story, for more than half a century later a new fort was raised on the foundations of the old. The reason for this differential treatment may be sought in the strategic and tactical importance of the position occupied by Crawford : its situation at a road junction and bridgehead in the vulnerable upland sector of the major Clydesdale-Annandale trunk-route has already been mentioned, but it should also be noted that it guards the 'back door' by way of the Camps Water into upper Tweeddale, where there was no Roman garrison.

Crawford, measuring 345 ft by 190 ft (105 m x 58 m) within the rampart, belongs to the group of sites known as small forts, which could not accommodate an entire regiment. Its plan in the Agricolan period, which has been tentatively reconstructed from evidence gathered in excavation between 1961 and 1966 (Maxwell, 1972), exhibits an unusual deviation from the standard layout in that the main street (*via principalis*) was drawn parallel to the long axis of the fort instead of at right angles to it, as was more normal in forts of elongated form. As a result, the standard tripartite division of the interior — *praetentura*, *retentura*, and central (or principal) range — is lacking, the barracks which would customarily have lain to the rear of the principal buildings being disposed on either side. The arrangement resembles that of earlier first-century forts in the south of Britain and on the Rhine frontier, and may indicate a conservative streak in the military engineer responsible for its adoption; the Flavian cohort fort at Loudoun Hill was apparently constructed on a similar plan.

All the buildings within the interior of Crawford were timber-framed, their uprights securely set in continuous post-trenches and their walls clad with either wattle-and-daub panels or, in the case of the more important buildings, with weather-boarding. Of the latter, which occupy the customary position fronting on to the main street, only the headquarters building (*principia*) and the granary (*horreum*) have been identified (1 and 2 respectively on Fig. **4.6**). These are particularly noteworthy, because, although of standard plan, they have been scaled down to approximately a quarter of the normal size (Fig. **4.7**). On either side of the principal range there was space for two buildings (nos. 3-6) measuring a little over 100 ft

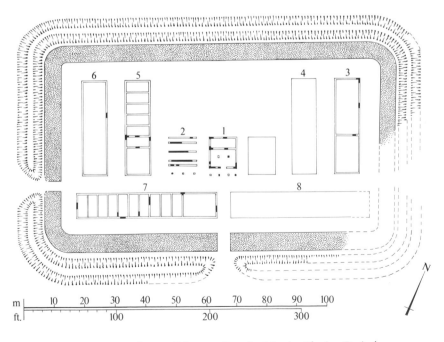

Fig. 4.6 The small fort at Crawford in the Flavian Period.

(30 m) by 27 ft (8.2 m); the limited amount of available evidence suggests that at least some of these were barracks; the greater part of each was divided into individual rooms, 11ft 6ins (3.4 m) deep, occupying the entire width of the building — a suitable area for a single *contubernium*, or messing-unit. It is possible that each of these buildings contained six such *contubernia*, the remaining space being taken up with the suite of rooms or offices allocated to the senior NCO of the unit. The longer building in the south-western half of the forward area of the fort (no. 7) was evidently divided into rooms of similar size; a maximum of thirteen could be fitted into its 150 ft (45 m) length. It has been argued elsewhere that each of the smaller buildings could have housed a single cavalry troop (*turma*) of 32 men, the longer buildings believed to lie on the other side of the main street being large enough to have held their mounts. The garrison would thus have totalled about 130 men. On the other hand, building 7 is of an appropriate size for a full infantry *centuria* of eighty men; 10 *contubernia* and a centurion's suite, as hypothetically reconstructed in Fig **4.6**, also fitting exactly within its presumed area; a slightly smaller centurial barrack

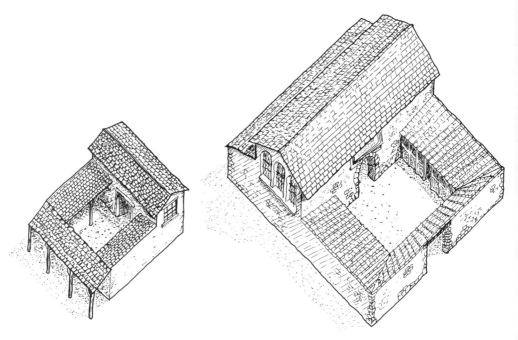

Fig. 4.7   Reconstruction of the headquarters building of
Crawford in the Flavian (*left*) and Antonine periods;
scale *c.* 1:480.

(no. 8) could be accommodated in the other half of the *praetentura*. In this case we would have to assume that two of the smaller buildings were stables, housing the mounts of two cavalry troops, for which purpose their size is not inappropriate. On this analysis, the total garrison strength would have been about 225, consisting of 160 infantry and 64 cavalry, and the parent unit would thus have almost certainly been a *cohors equitata*, or part-mounted regiment.

The second solution is perhaps the more attractive since it allows a combination of horse and foot — which is perhaps more acceptable as a vexillation of a composite unit — and more important, appreciably increases the strength of the garrison. It must be admitted, however, that the establishment and organisation of regiments of this kind are too imperfectly known to permit the above reconstruction to be other than conjectural. The general picture is nevertheless clear: Flavian, and especially Agricolan, garrisons and installations display a considerable variety of form and size. Even those few that were garrisoned by a complete regiment and display no gross irregularities of shape or internal plan may possess features which are characteristic of the 'Agricolan' type of fort. Thus at Oakwood on the Ettrick Water, to the south-west of Selkirk, the gateways are protected by being set at the inner end of a short tunnel formed by an inturn of the rampart terminals on either side (Fig. **4.8,***1*); the same treatment was accorded to gates in certain forts north of the isthmus, though not at many other sites in southern Scotland, as far as is known at present. We have already seen that various devices were adopted to protect the entrances of temporary camps (p. 50 – 1); the same concern lay behind the quirks of planning observed in permanent sites.

This is seen equally in examples at the upper end of the scale. The early fort of 5 acres (2 ha) at Tassiesholm, for example, (Fig. **4.8,***2*) is T-shaped on plan, the purpose doubtless being to provide flanking fire at two of the gateways. However, this would have had less effect at the northern gate, where attackers would have been able to oppose the left-hand side, normally protected by the shield, to any missiles fired from the projecting rampart. This point was evidently appreciated when the fort was reconstructed and enlarged to 5.7 acres (2.3 ha) in the second Flavian period, presumably in AD 86/7. The technique was correctly applied at Newstead, however; the earliest fort on that site, surely the work of Agricola, presents one of the most curious plans found anywhere in the Roman Empire, with half of each side projecting at every gate in such a way as to threaten the unshielded side of prospective assailants (Fig. **4.8,***3*).

For our knowledge of the structural development of the fort at

Newstead we are indebted to Professor Sir Ian Richmond, whose extraordinary trenching in the years following World War II significantly amplified the pioneering work of James Curle (Richmond, 1950). With an area of some 10.5 acres (4.2 ha), Newstead 1 was capable of holding an exceptionally strong garrison, probably two separate units, but the limited information relating to the timber structures of the earliest period makes it impossible to be certain about their identity, or, indeed, about the internal plan of the fort itself. The depth of the area available for barrack buildings in the south-eastern sector of the fort suggests that the unit in this portion of the interior was of auxiliary status, while the splendid cavalry parade-

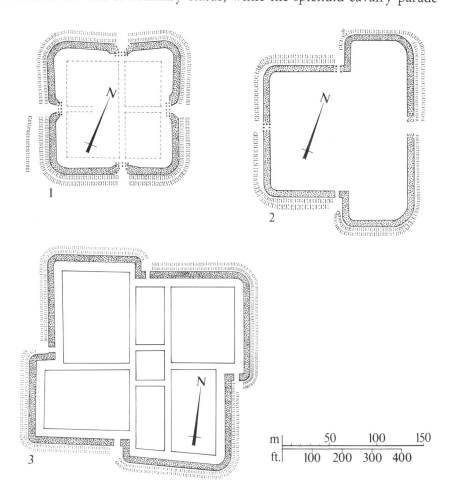

Fig. 4.8   Flavian forts in S Scotland:
1. Oakwood   2. Tassiesholm   3. Newstead

helmets associated with the early occupation indicated that at least one of the regiments stationed here was mounted.

Shortly after AD 86, as mentioned earlier, the first-period fort was demolished to make way for a fort that was of regular plan but appreciably greater capacity, being approximately 13 acres (5.3 ha) within a rampart now as much as 45 ft (13.7 m) thick. The identity of the garrison at this stage is indicated by the material tidied up and shovelled into demolition-pits after the destruction of the fort c. AD 100; it includes equipment of both legionary and auxiliary troops abandoned in the hasty evacuation of the site — whether as a result of policy decisions or because of enemy assault cannot be determined. If the stone-founded building measuring some 220 ft by 60 ft (67 m x 18 m), which was discovered in the south-east corner of the fort, can be safely assigned to this phase of occupation, it would confirm the presence of legionary troops. For the size of the building thus delimited is far too big for an auxiliary unit, but entirely appropriate for a double-barrack housing two legionary centuries. That the adjacent area of the interior (probably the *retentura*, as the fort seems to have faced west in this phase) is capable of containing six such barracks not only confirms the nature of the building, but also shows that twelve centuries, or two complete cohorts, of the legion were present. The eight blocks which Sir Ian Richmond presumed to have occupied the *praetentura* could then have been conveniently allotted to the troopers and horses of the sixteen *turmae* composing a quingenary *ala*. In that case the garrison of Newstead at the end of the 1st century would have been some 1500 men strong — a suitably powerful force with which to guard the frontiers of the province at whose northernmost extremity it now stood.

5

The First Occupation:
The outer frontier

ESPITE THE REMARKABLE EVIDENCE for the painstaking care and ingenuity of Agricola's conquest and occupation of southern Scotland, it is perhaps with the area to the north of the Forth-Clyde isthmus that his name is most closely associated. And yet, paradoxically, this is the part of Scotland where modern scholarship is most starkly divided in assigning an Agricolan origin to permanent sites. The extreme view is that the northernmost forts which Agricola built, or caused to be built, were those belonging to the chain of *praesidia* on the isthmus itself (Breeze & Dobson, 1976, 128), while other scholars, unwilling to believe that Agricola had either troops or time to spare for building forts beyond the Forth, would nevertheless accept that certain sites in Caledonia may have been selected for occupation by him and were thus at least Agricolan in conception. Others again would maintain the traditional view that all 1st-century forts and permanent installations were produced directly by the operation of Agricola, and it was his hand that moulded the form of an outer frontier whose limits were never to be passed by any subsequent commander. Indeed, they would claim that it was Agricola's intention to push on beyond even these and set the boundaries of the province on the further side of the Grampians (cf. Frere, 1981). The problem is unfortunately not one that may easily be solved one way or the other, for the solution depends upon an accuracy of dating that at present is beyond the capacity of the modern archaeologist. Even the testimony of coins is not sufficiently unequivocal to provide the necessary distinction between an Agricolan fort constructed in AD 83–4 and one built in 85–6 at the behest of Agricola's successor.

Accordingly, it may be best to begin by reviewing the general distribution of known Flavian sites in Scotland north of the Forth, and then examine the various ways in which they may have been related.

It is obvious at the outset that the forts of that area differ significantly from those in the south in respect of both size and distribution (Fig. **5.1**). To begin with, there are few garrisons of less than regimental strength, the smaller fortlets at Kaims Castle and Glenbank and the larger fortlets at Cargill and Inverquharity, being the only members of this category to have so far been identified. On the other hand, there are no forts, except perhaps Bertha, to match the exceptionally large composite garrison sites like Newstead and Dalswinton, the reason possible being that the presence of

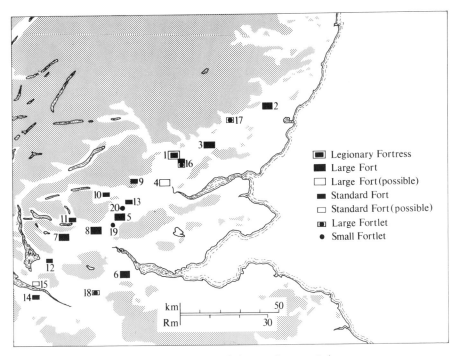

Fig. 5.1   Distribution of forts N of the Forth occupied at some
time in the Flavian period:

1. Inchtuthil	8. Doune	15. Dumbarton
2. Stracathro	9. Fendoch	16. Cargill
3. Cardean	10. Dalginross	17. Inverquharity
4. Bertha	11. Bochastle	18. Mollins
5. Ardoch	12. Drumquhassle	19. Glenbank
6. Camelon	13. Strageath	20. Kaims Castle
7. Malling	14. Barochan	

the legionary fortress at Inchtuthil, on the left bank of the River Tay to the south of Blairgowrie, provided a reserve of offensive or defensive strength that was adequate for the whole outer frontier. Nevertheless, the mere proximity of the highland massif, with its misty glens and passes that frowned like the sally ports of some enemy stronghold upon the invading hosts of Rome, was enough to ensure that five out of the ten forts that flanked the fortress at Inchtuthil were at least of above-average size i.e. 5.1–6.5 acres (2.1–2.6 ha), thus closely matching the sites at Tassieholm, Castledykes, and Glenlochar in southern Scotland. The remaining five posts at first sight appear to be standard cohort-forts, averaging 3.5 acres (1.4 ha) in area. Two of these, however, have been shown by excavation to have accommodated garrisons approaching milliary strength: Fendoch housed a 1000-man infantry regiment, while Strageath in its later phase contained two separate units, one a quingenary part-mounted cohort, the other an infantry unit about 400 strong.

Although none of the larger forts has been more than partially ex-cavated, the discovery that the easternmost portion of Cardean may have contained as many as ten rows of infantry barracks – the complement required for a milliary regiment – suggests that the potential capacity of posts of this size was in the neighbourhood of 1500 men; at Cardean, as at Strageath, it is probable that at least one unit was part-mounted. In addition to more than 5500 legionary troops at Inchtuthil, therefore, it is theoretically possible that the forts so far identified north of the Forth contained as many as 11,000 men. Assuming that at least two more forts await discovery – one somewhere near Dumbarton, at the south-west end of the chain, and one to the north-east of Stracathro at the north-east end of Strathmore – the total garrison of the outer *limes*, had all the posts been occupied simultaneously, could thus have exceeded 18,000. This enormous weight of manpower, the equivalent of three entire legions, was also con-centrated to a degree not approached in southern Scotland, save possibly on the Forth-Clyde isthmus: the average interval between forts on the very outermost line, to the south-west of Inchtuthil, was about 9 miles (14.5 km), the shortest only 5.5 miles (9 km); the spacing of forts to the north-east of Inchtuthil was probably of a similar order.

A closer examination of the Flavian frontier in Caledonia, in the Tacitean definition of the name, will be facilitated by concentrating in turn on the four basic elements of which it was composed: the glen-blocking forts, the legionary base at Inchtuthil, the forts of Strathmore, and the Forth-Tay roadside posts (Pitts & St Joseph 1985, 263-81).

The descriptive title 'glen-blocking' applies strictly only to those forts lying south-west of Inchtuthil, although it is occasionally extended to cover the entire line of outer frontier positions from Loch Lomond to the Mearns. Consideration of the terrain will, however, reveal that the restricted use is much more apposite (Fig. **5.1**): Drumquhassle stands sentinel at a veritable crossroads of natural corridors, controlling movement along Strathblane and the valley of the Endrick, as well as guarding the approaches to the Pass of Balmaha on the east side of Loch Lomond; Malling blocks the route issuing eastwards from the pass of Aberfoyle round the northern edge of the Flanders Moss; Bochastle guards both the Pass of Leny and the eastern exit from the Trossachs along Loch Venachar; Dalginross controls the upper Earn, and Fendoch, situated in the narrows of Glen Almond at the southern end of the Sma' Glen, guards the side door, as it were, that leads into Upper Strathtay. Although all five might have served at a pinch as suitable springboards for invasion of the Highland massif, it is reasonably certain that their main purpose was defensive. This is undoubtedly true of the fortlet of Inverquharity, discovered from the air in 1984 (Plate **13**), which kept watch at the mouth of Glen Clova, its tiny garrison incapable of doing more than alerting major forces stationed in the heart of Strathmore.

The best known member of this group is Fendoch, which was excavated in 1938 (Richmond & McIntyre, 1939), selective trenching being used for the first time in Scotland to facilitate the hypothetical reconstruction of the internal plan (Fig. **5.2**). Comparatively little now survives of the rampart, which was turf-built, but the rectangular plateau of

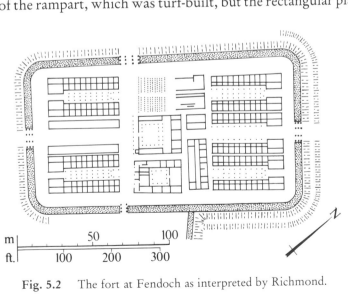

Fig. 5.2 The fort at Fendoch as interpreted by Richmond.

the fort site is readily recognisable. As the buildings of the interior and the gates were of timber, nothing of them can now be seen above ground. During excavation, however, the post-holes and trenches in which the uprights had originally stood were readily recognisable, and knowledge of the symmetry and regularity customarily displayed by Roman military sites allowed the excavator, Sir Ian Richmond, to fill out the partial evidence of the trenches; the fact that Fendoch had been occupied only once allowed this reconstruction to be undertaken with confidence, but it is only fair to point out that modern scholarly opinion would now advise caution in accepting the fine detail of Richmond's plan. Nevertheless, it presents, in general, a trustworthy picture of the layout of an Agricolan cohort fort.

Most of the space is taken up by ten long L-shaped barracks which housed the ten centuries of the milliary cohort occupying Fendoch. In each barrack the narrower part, fronted by a verandah, was sub-divided into ten separate rooms, one for each *contubernium*, or messing-unit, of eight soldiers; the longer space at the end served as the offices and quarters of the centurion in charge. Situated between the barrack areas, and fronting on to the main street, was the range of principal buildings. These comprised the headquarters building (*principia*) in the centre, with a double granary on one side and the commandant's residence (*praetorium*) on the other. The plans of all three structures are of standard appearance: the *principia* was composed of three elements, a colonnaded courtyard at the front, a suite of offices, including the unit's chapel and strongroom, at the rear, and a cross-hall (*basilica*) in between. The *praetorium*, which consisted of four ranges of rooms, looking inward on to a pillared courtyard, was in fact a scaled-down model of the typical Italian townhouse; as a type, it offered the commandant a modest degree of privacy and seclusion amid the hurly-burly of camp life, and occasionally some compensating luxuries; the granaries may be recognised by the singular appearance of their foundations – a series of parallel construction trenches, closely set to provide the exceptional strength of foundation which these heavy-roofed, raised-floor storage buildings demanded.

The nature and purpose of the structures lying immediately behind the principal range cannot be precisely identified, although Richmond suggested that the largest, with a central corridor and cubicles ranged along one side, served as the unit hospital; the others, together with the two longer narrow buildings in the forward area of the fort, may well have provided extra storage capacity, which – together with the workshops, stabling, and minor offices – would have been inevitably required by a unit of this size. The Roman talent for practical organisation and painstaking attention to detail, which such an orderly plan aptly illustrates, is further exemplified by related structures outside the fort. On the lower slopes of the rising ground to the south there are intermittent traces of an artificial terrace, all that remains of the aqueduct by which fresh water was led into the very heart of the fort. The quantity which would have been needed for consumption, ablutions, and sanitation in so large a garrison must have been considerable, more than enough to justify the labour involved in providing a permanent supply. Security of a different kind was afforded by an installation on high ground some 1100 yards (1000 m) to the north-west of the fort — a timber watch-tower. All that now remains to be seen is the eroded rampart within a shallow circular ditch, but originally a square or rectangular timber tower would have stood within the interior, commanding extensive views down the throat of the Sma' Glen, and so placed as to signal advance warning of any hostile movement to the fort in the valley below. The provision of a lookout post was not unique on the frontier, as we shall see (pp. 120 – 1), but this is the only example so far discovered in close association with a fort.

Apart from these structural details and the evidence of artefacts pointing to a late 1st century date, Richmond's pioneering excavation of Fendoch produced a singularly important item of information which earlier excavators in Scottish sites had failed to note. It was observed that at the end of the occupation the timber buildings of the interior had been carefully demolished, the wooden framing of which they were composed being dug out of their foundation trenches. Although the precise method by which this was carried out at Fendoch might now be debated, the discovery was of considerable importance, and it heralded, as we shall see, a completely different perception of the closing days of Roman occupation in the North. No longer was it necessary, or even possible, to think of the frontier sinking in red ruin before the onslaught of Caledonian hordes. Instead, the picture which began to form, as similar tokens were identified on successive sites both north and south of the isthmus, was one of orderly withdrawal after careful dismantling of military installations. What had previously been adduced as evidence of an orgy of destruction — fire-reddened clay and carbonised wood from buildings — was later inspected more closely, with specific questions in mind; hence it was realised that the bent nails scattered through such debris layers had been twisted out of shape by the use of a claw-hammer, and the materials whose burned remains covered so many sites were the lesser timbers and wattle-and-daub panels that could not be used again; the major timbers had been previously removed. Clearly this was not the work of native warbands but of the Roman garrison themselves, and, in most cases, apparently without undue haste.

None of the other 'glen-blocking' forts has been examined as thoroughly as Fendoch. Excavation which took place at Bochastle in the 1950s (Anderson, 1956) indicated that the fort was of the larger class (5.1 acres, 2.1 ha in area) but little of the interior was then explored and even the location of the defences was not precisely determined, although it is evident that the rampart terminals were sharply inturned on either side each entrance, as at Oakwood (Fig. **5.3,**1). The excavator notes various anomalies of structural levels in the interior, but whether these denote a plurality of occupation periods is uncertain. The north-east corner of the defences had been affected by flooding of the River Leny, on whose right bank the fort lies, and it is possible that some of the observed anomalies may be the result of such riverine transgression, whose operation is clearly recorded on air photographs (Plate 7).

Similar erosion has totally destroyed the north-eastern corner of the fort at Dalginross, whose outline plan has been known to archaeologists since the time of General Roy. For long it was believed that there were two forts at Dalginross, a standard cohort fort of about 3.8 acres (1.5 ha) sitting entirely within a larger rectangular work roughly twice as large (Fig. **5.3,**2). Trial excavation, however (Robertson, 1963, 196-8) indicated that the outer portion of the larger enclosure had probably not undergone permanent occupation, while inspection of air photographs suggests very strongly that the outer line of defences defines an annexe associated with the inner fort. The same air photographs, which confirm that there are no permanent structures within the presumed annexe, also reveal by means of crop-markings something of the internal layout of the fort itself. The latter appears to have faced west, the granary, which is indicated by a block of parallel post-trenches, being situated on the south side of the headquarters-building; the parching of the crop above the *intervallum* street seems to bend inwards on either side of at least one of the fort gates, which suggests that here, too, the rampart terminals were inturned.

The three remaining sites, Malling, Drumquhassle and Doune, owe to air photography not just their interpretation, but their identification, all having been found as a result of aerial reconnaissance. The first, discovered by Professor St Joseph in 1968, has an internal area of 5.8 acres (2.3 ha). It lies at the western end of the Lake of Menteith, its double ditch system extending on the east towards the very shore of the lake to enclose a roughly rectangular annexe (Fig. **5.3,**3). Although lines of pits may be seen as faint cropmarkings within the interior, not enough detail is visible to provide even a tentative reconstruction of its building plan. However, the defences stand out with sufficient clarity to show that the enclosing ditches curve in

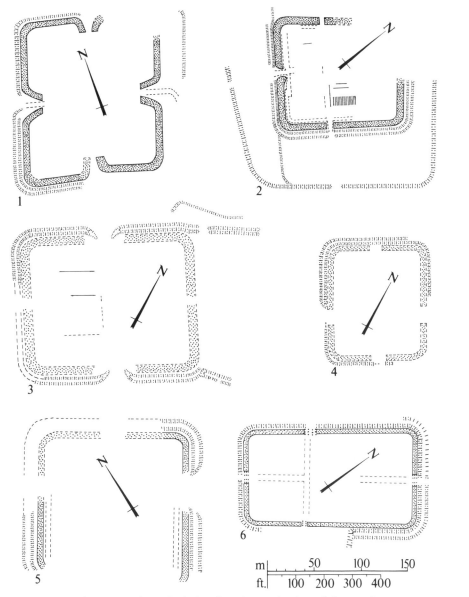

Fig. 5.3   Plans of Flavian forts in Scotland N of the Forth:

1. Bochastle	3. Malling	5. Doune
2. Dalginross	4. Drumquhassle	6. Fendoch

to unite on either side of the north-west and south-east entrances; from this feature it would not be unreasonable to presume that at least some of the gates at Malling were of Oakwood-type. Air photography offers one further clue, in the form of a detached linear cropmark lying some way to the north of the lakeside annexe: while it is impossible to be certain, a conceivable explanation may be that the mark represents a ditch forming the northern side of a slightly larger annexe – the merest hint that the fort could have undergone more than one structural phase.

Drumquhassle occupies the lower southern end of a broad ridge of sand and gravel on the south-eastern outskirts of Drymen. Ever since the discovery of Malling it was realised that an intermediate fort must have existed in this area to guard the interval between headwaters of the Forth and the estuary of the Clyde. The name itself (meaning 'the fort on the ridge') had even drawn the attention of fieldworkers as a possible clue to its location, but it was not until the severe drought of the summer of 1977 that the permanent pasture in which it lay began to betray its existence through differential growth patterns. Even then, the area of the fort itself remained largely invisible, and it was from the angular outline of the fort's annexe ditches that the Roman origin of the site first suggested itself to the aerial observer. Subsequent examination on the ground and trial-excavation were necessary (Maxwell, 1983a, 167–72) before the size of the fort – *c*. 3.1 acres (1.2 ha) – and the course of its defences became clear (Fig. **5.3,4**). However, despite the limited extent of the exploration, it was observed that the fort had been occupied only once, while the defences and internal buildings appeared to have been respectively slighted and dismantled before the evacuation.

The third fort, Doune (Fig. **5.3,5**), is a route-blocker, sitting astride an important and long-used crossing of the marshy middle reaches of the Forth Valley. It faces south-west towards the Fords of Frew, whose significance in prehistoric times is indicated by such native structures as the adjacent brochs of Leckie and Coldoch. The discovery of Doune in recent aerial survey (Maxwell, 1984a) has necessitated the reconsideration of evidence relating to Flavian strategic intentions on the northern *limes* (cf. Jarret 1985). Being still at an early stage of examination, it cannot yet be assigned confidently to a precise category, but it probably resembles Bochastle and Malling in respect of size and plan.

The legionary fortress at Inchtuthil on the left bank of the Tay, which appears to represent the hub of the entire outer frontier system, has long been known as an ancient site (Fig. **5.4**). The gravel plateau some 200 acres (80 ha) in extent, was known to Hector Boece in the early sixteenth century

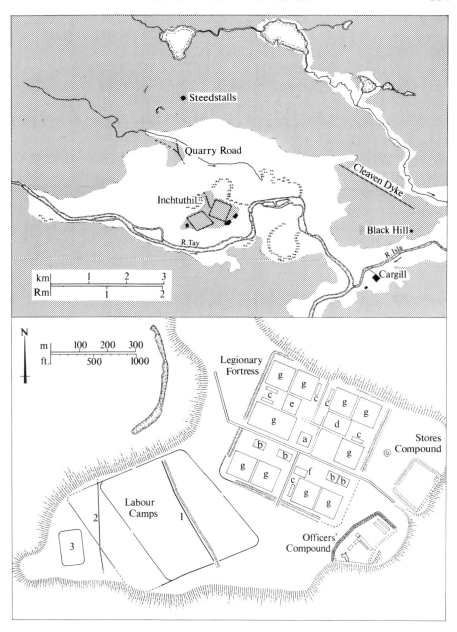

Fig. 5.4 Inchtuthil and its environs
Key to lower plan:

a) *Principia*, b) tribunes' houses, c) granaries, d) hospital, e) main workshop,
f) workshop/store, g) cohort barrack-blocks; Nos. 1) and 2) outer earthworks
overlying two–period temporary labour camp, no. 3) small temporary camp.

as the site of a fortified settlement of the Picts, burned to the ground on the approach of Agricola; its name, meaning 'Tuathal's inch or island', possibly contains a reference to this fanciful tradition, and it is beyond doubt that the Roman works at Inchtuthil are not the only ancient structures to have been recognised : a multivallate promontory fort occupies the tip of the south-western salient, and excavation has confirmed the indications of air photography that a long enclosure of prehistoric date but unknown purpose underlies the barracks in the southern angle of the fortress; that the plateau continued to attract settlers in post-Roman times, as might have been expected of so advantageous a position, is proved by the presence of burial mounds constructed on top of the counterscarp bank of the south-eastern defences.

The location and nature of the Roman military structures at Inchtuthil were realised by General Roy, who identified three elements: the fortress itself, a small rectangular redoubt lying to the south-east, and a linear earthwork (known as the western vallum) cutting across the plateau to the south-west. Excavation by the Society of Antiquaries of Scotland in 1901 (Abercromby *et al.*, 1902) showed that the rampart of the fortress had been revetted externally with ashlar masonry, while the catalogue of structures was extended by the discovery of a stone-built bath-house and timber barrack-like building in a third enclosure, immediately outside the southern angle of the fortress. There matters rested until the application of aerial reconniassance brought to light a further series of structures; first of all, a small camp 3.5 acres (1.4 ha) in size was discovered on the east side of Gourdie Hill, the source of the conglomerate stone with which the fortress wall was built; within the camp lay the dozen or so elongated quarries which popular tradition had explained as the stables of some mythical hero – hence the feature's name, Steedstalls.

A little later, during an exceptionally prolonged summer drought, the air camera of Dr St Joseph recorded the intricate pattern of crop anomalies within the fortress, which persuaded him and Professor Richmond that trenching of the Fendoch type, but on a vastly enlarged scale, could recover the complete plan of a single-period timber-built legionary base. Such a prize amply merited the dedicated attention with which, over the fourteen years from 1952 till 1965, Richmond and St Joseph gradually explored and recorded the defences and internal buildings of the 53.5 acre (21.7 ha) site and its associated works (Pitts & St Joseph, 1985). Aerial reconnaissance which has continued to be conducted in the Inchtuthil area has further added to our knowledge: to the south-west of the fortress and straddled by the western vallum there lies a large two-period temporary camp, its interior containing rows and settings of pits (Plate 9) marking the tent-lines of legionary troops briefly stationed here on campaign, or else engaged in building the permanent fortress (cf. Maxwell, 1982); a small camp only 1.7 acres (0.7 ha) in area was also found between the large camps and the native promontory fort, and a second linear barrier, resembling the western vallum, was seen to transect the south-western portion of the large camp, presumably providing the same kind of protection to the reduced area of temporary encampment that the vallum would later have afforded to the fortress. It would be idle to believe that the process of discovery is yet at an end, as recent developments have shown (see below, p. 107).

The task of building so elaborate and important an installation as a fortress for nearly 6000 troops was not achieved overnight, and not the least interesting of the discoveries made during the modern excavations was that the polygonal enclosure to the south of the fortress had probably contained the temporary residence and headquarters of the senior officers (the *praefectus castrorum* and *praefectus fabrum*) charged with the construction of the permanent base. In its earliest phase, the enclosure had been protected by a single rampart and ditch, and had evidently contained a long timber-framed building of elaborate plan which incorporated two masonry-built rooms heated by hypocausts. The scale and furnishings of this handsome structure, which was only the temporary quarters of the two officers mentioned above, provide as clear a picture as one could wish of the importance which was attached to the permanent fortress and the time which the Roman army was willing to expend on its construction. Even the temporary compound can be seen to have undergone at least two phases of development, in the earlier of which the garrison consisted of a single century accommodated in a block 205 ft (62.5 m) long comprising 15 *contubernia*; at a later stage, possibly when elements of the legion began to take up occupation in the fortress itself, the rampart of the compound was demolished and the officers' guard was increased to two centuries housed in a matching pair of barracks. The arrival on the scene of more troops which this event appears to signal was also marked by the commencement of work on the stone-built bath-suite discovered in 1901 (Plate 3); the magnificence of this building suggests that it was intended for use by the legion's officers. The fact that it overlay not only the compound defences, but also the remains of a timber-revetted rampart and ditch which were earlier than the compound, may give some idea of the complicated and lengthy timetable required for the undertaking. Even more remarkable is the fact that the bath-house, when systematically demolished on the evacuation of Inchtuthil, had apparently never been put into use, because its heating system was still incomplete!

Although similar deficiencies were noted in the fortress, the plan re-vealed by excavation is so remarkably full in comparison with what is known about nearly every other legionary base in Britain, that it provides an unrivalled illustration of the life and conditions of service of a Roman legionary in the late first century AD. Roughly 1500 ft (457 m) square (Fig. 5.4), the fortress contains, on an extended scale, all the types of building that were noted in the auxiliary fort of Fendoch. But, where the Fendoch barracks were about 150 ft (45 m) long and ten in number, the legionary barracks extended to over 275 ft (84 m) and totalled sixty-four; they are disposed in nine groups of six, one group for each of the six-century strong quingenary cohorts, together with a single group of ten which housed the ten centuries of the first cohort. Each century block was sub-divided into a maximum of fifteen *contubernia*, while the average centurion's quarters measured as much as 70 ft by 40 ft (21 m by 12 m). The centurions of the first cohort, however, by virtue of their superior rank, were assigned much more spacious quarters, those of the *primipilus*, the senior centurion, almost rivalling in size and style the elegant courtyard-houses of the six tribunes. These latter were the officers of staff rank who supported the legion's commandant, the *legatus*; that only four tribunes' houses were built at Inchtuthil shows again that the legion had not been brought up to full establishment by the time of the evacuation. The absence of the commandant's residence, which should have stood in the area to the east of the headquarters building, further suggests that the nucleus of headquarters staff continued to be stationed at some more southerly base. Presumably it was intended that their move to the north would be the final phase of the relocation programme. In fact, in anticipation of that event most of the major building works appear to have been nearing or to have reached completion: the *principia* (although of smaller than normal size), a hospital, legionary workshop, drill-hall, and series of colonnaded store-rooms lining the major streets, were all ready; all but possibly two of the legion's granaries were built, and may even have been partly filled, for some of the ovens set in the rear of the rampart had already been fired for baking the soldier's meals.

However, the evidence is quite clear that, before the final touches could be put to this monumental work of military engineering, the entire site was systematically and deliberately dismantled. In addition to the kind of demolition traces already encountered at other sites, the excavators of Inchtuthil found that the external revetting-wall of the fortress had been taken down stone by stone, the slabs covering internal drains had been removed and the conduits packed with gravel; gutters had been choked with the pounded fragments of glass and pottery vessels taken from adjacent stores, and even the stone walls of the buildings in the temporary compound had been uprooted from their very foundations. Materials that could not be destroyed were hidden in vast disposal pits, the outstanding example being the million iron nails which were discovered, most of them still in pristine condition, buried beneath the floor of the workshop. When the legions left Inchtuthil, it was intended that there would be nothing of use to fall into enemy hands. To the archaeologist, however, such scenes of deliberate devastation are not unwelcome, as they often more effectively seal ancient occupation levels than the normal processes of gradual decay. At Inchtuthil, in addition to this, the demolition layers contained a number of bronze coins, *Asses* of the Emperor Domitian, struck in AD 86 or 87 and in mint condition when lost. As mentioned before, in connection with similar losses, they pinpoint to within a year the precise time when Inchtuthil and so many other military sites throughout North Britain were either abandoned or drastically reconstructed.

Before leaving Inchtuthil it is necessary to draw attention to two related structures. The first, known as the Cleaven Dyke, consists of a pair of parallel ditches set at an average distance of about 175 ft (53 m) apart, with a medial bank about 62 ft (18.9 m) in maximum thickness. Extending in a nearly straight line for a distance of at least 1.9 miles (3 km), the Cleaven Dyke traverses the level ground between the right bank of the River Isla and the rising ground to the north of Inchtuthil (Fig. **5.4**); it may be traced for a considerable distance on the ground as an earthwork, but unfortunately much of this sector has been obscured by recent afforestation; in open country it has been reduced by ploughing and is visible solely as a cropmark or soilmark. Its antiquity has never really been in doubt, but the relationship to Inchtuthil, from which it lies some 2.3 miles (3.5 km) distant, was not explicitly argued until its examination in 1939. Excavation showed (Richmond, 1940) that the central bank had consisted of upcast, revetted on either side with blocks of turf. This constructional technique, combined with both its rectilinearity and relationship to the fortress at Inchtuthil, suggested to Richmond that it was of Roman origin, possibly marking the limit of the legionary *territorium*.

The small earthwork of somewhat irregular plan on the Black Hill, which lies 550 yds (500 m) to the south-west of the Dyke not far from its south-eastern end, was also excavated at this time, when it was found to be a Roman watch-tower – a discovery that lent further support to Richmond's interpretation of the linear work. More recent investigation

(Adamson, 1979) has tended to confirm the opinion derived from superficial observation of the remains, that the Cleaven Dyke, if intended to be
a Roman boundary-mark, was not completed; the parallel that this finding
would provide with the fate of legionary fortress has not gone unnoticed.
On the other hand, it must be said that the line followed by the Dyke is not
entirely what one would expect either of a defensive frontier that was
perhaps intended to cut across the full width of Strathmore, like a *fossatum*
on the North African frontier (cf. Jones, 1978, 130-3), or of a boundary
designed to enclose ground that might be agriculturally or otherwise
profitable to the legionary garrison. Furthermore, the appearance of the
work, as seen in cropmark form through the eye of the aerial camera (Plate
8), is so very much less regular than has previously been realised that one
wonders whether a prehistoric origin may not also be possible. In that case,
it would be appropriate to see the Cleaven Dyke as some kind of *cursus*, a
ritual monument of the Neolithic period consisting of two wide parallel
ditches, extending for considerable distances and occasionally enclosing
such features as pits or, as at Scorton in Lincolnshire, a medial bank.

The second site related to the Inchtuthil complex is really a group of
structures (Fig. **5.4**); it comprises Steedstalls, the semi-permanent labour
camp on the eastern slopes of Gourdie Hill, which has already been
mentioned (p. 102, Plate **10**), a pattern of cropmarks indicating the course
of a Roman road at Wester Drumatherty roughly a mile (1.6 km) to the
south, and a vast artificial hollow, high up on the south-east face of the hill
itself. The discovery of the significance of these different features and of
their relationship to each other resulted from the happy conjunction of
several independent avenues of research in a manner not unlike that used
by the authors of detective fiction to produce an exciting and convincing
dénouement to a tangled plot. The discovery of the Roman camp
surrounding the small group of quarries at Steedstalls was the work of Eric
Bradley, an R.A.F. pilot engaged in flying training at nearby Scone during
World War II. When Richmond and St Joseph were later engaged upon the
excavation of Inchtuthil it was realised that the revetment of Strathmore
conglomerate which clad the fortress wall had required the quarrying of
some 300,000 cubic feet (*c.* 8500 cubic metres) of stone; so vast a quantity
could never have been won from the Steedstalls site, which might have
sufficed, however, to provide sufficient material for the suite of baths in the
early compound, or the stone-built hypocausted portions of the adjacent
officers' residence. If, as seemed reasonable, the stone had nevertheless
come from Gourdie Hill, it was argued that the quarry-site should still be
visible on the ground. Eventually, by viewing the area from the air in as

wide as possible a range of conditions of light and crop-growth, Professor St Joseph identified the likeliest site, some 800 yards (730 m) west of the camp at Steedstalls, a huge artificial corrie-like depression facing south-east towards the Inchtuthil plateau, the obvious destination of the road which the early Society of Antiquaries excavation-team had uncovered issuing from the west gate of the fortress. Finally in 1982, routine air survey by the Royal Commission on the Ancient Monuments of Scotland in the upper valley of the River Tay revealed the existence of lines of pits crossing a gravel plateau about one mile (1.6 m) to the north of the fortress; ground inspection, and further aerial reconnaissance confirmed that these were traces of a Roman route linking Inchtuthil with the presumed quarry-site, the *agger* of the road actually being visible as a low stony mound in the recently harrowed barley stubble; the final link of the chain had been discovered, and a unique illustration provided of the thoroughness with which the legionary workforce went about the construction of their new base.

To the north-east of the great bend in the River Tay below Inchtuthil lies the valley of Strathmore; more than thirty miles (53 km) in length and at least 4 miles (6.5 km) in breadth at its narrowest point, it is traversed by several rivers of appreciable size — the Isla and the Dean Water, draining into the Tay, and the various tributaries of the North and South Esks flowing eastwards into the North Sea. Beyond the North Esk the level strath continues as the Howe of the Mearns, which is drained by the Luther Water and its tributaries flowing southwards to join the Esk; but immediately north-east of the turbulent Bervie Water the outlying spurs of the Highland massif link arms with the hills of the coastal range, effectively blocking the broad natural corridor. One may imagine that this part of Scotland presented the Roman army of occupation with peculiar problems. Although the lower-lying portions of Strathmore were probably too poorly drained to be habitable, recent archaeological fieldwork has recovered enough evidence of probable Iron Age dwelling-sites to suggest that the valley as a whole supported a population of some size. It would clearly have been in the Roman interest, therefore, to deploy garrisons in sufficient strength to overawe the local tribesmen as well as guard the mouths of river valleys that presented so many gateways through the south-east wall of the Grampians. In addition to these considerations, there were also the inhabitants of the coastal plain — not less numerous than their inland compatriots, if we are to judge from the distribution of Iron Age monuments discovered in recent programmes of aerial survey. It was presumably to deal with this twofold problem that Agricola called upon his fleet in the final campaign, the naval force patrolling and harrying the coastal regions, while the infantry column made its way north-eastwards through Strathmore.

Only five garrison posts have so far been identified in the whole of this area to the north of the Tay; what proportion they represented of the total planned and built will be considered later (p. 123). The second smallest and southernmost is the large fortlet at Cargill Mains, which was first seen from the air by Eric Bradley, the discoverer of Steedstalls, during his wartime duties (Richmond, 1943, 47). Only 1.1 acre (0.4 ha) in size, it lies immediately to the east of the confluence of the Isla and the Tay, about 2.5 miles (4 km) south-east of Inchtuthil. Comparable with the minor intermediate stations already described in Southern Scotland, Cargill occupies a position roughly half-way between Bertha, at the crossing of the Tay, and the fort at Cardean. When explored by trial-trenching in 1965 (*D.E.S.* 1965, 30) it was found to have been occupied only once, and the evacuation was accompanied by deliberate demolition. Although no definite evidence of date was then discovered, the probability of its being other than Flavian is remote, and indeed the manner in which the ditch terminals can be seen to join in 'parrot's beak' fashion at the entrance is strongly suggestive of late first-century fort-building practices. The purpose served by a relatively small garrison at this point may have been twofold: to provide surveillance on the central sector of the interval between the forts at Bertha and Cardean, and to guard the crossing of the Isla on the most direct route to Inchtuthil along the left bank of the River Tay.

Barely 550 yds (500 m) to the north-east of the fortlet, and immediately overlooking the bridge by which the modern Perth-Blairgowrie road crosses the Isla, there is a full-sized cohort fort (Plate **11**). Its presence was confirmed by Professor St Joseph in the course of aerial survey during 1977, but it is possible that Bradley may have observed the first tell-tale cropmarks during his wartime sorties (Bradley, 1960). Excavation in 1980−1 (St Joseph & Maxwell, 1989) confirmed that the fort, which is about 3.5 acres (1.4 ha) in area, had been occupied in the Flavian period; it faced north towards the presumed river-crossing, a strongly defended annexe enclosing the ground between the fort itself and the river bank. A section through the north-eastern defences revealed evidence of a secondary structure inserted in the space behind the turf-and-earth rampart, while, on the north-west front, it appeared that the outer face of the rampart had been twice repaired; the second reconstruction apparently followed an episode of destruction by fire which affected timber buildings in the adjacent annexe. Despite these unmistakeable signs of alteration, however, there is nothing to indicate that they represent an unduly prolonged occupation rather than a comparatively brief but eventful one.

The next fort to the north-east, Cardean, situated at the confluence of the Isla and the Dean Water, a little way to the north of Meigle, was one of the earliest aerial discoveries in Roman Scotland; it was found by O.G.S. Crawford, the first Archaeology Officer of the Ordnance Survey, during an epoch-making flight in the summer of 1939 (Crawford, 1939, 287), but it was not until 1966 that excavation began to reveal something of its date and character (Robertson, 1979). The fort faced west, looking back down Strathmore in the direction of Cargill, and from the amount of Iron Age pottery found beneath it, would appear to have occupied the site of a native settlement; whether this represents the military requisition of a contemporary 'village' site or merely the re-use of advantageous ground that had also attracted occupation at some previous time cannot be determined. As mentioned earlier (p. 94), the southern half of the eastern, or rear, third of the fort contained five timber barrack blocks; they measured 160 ft (48 m) by 32 ft (9.8 m) and were divided into ten *contubernia* and a centurion's quarters. In the northern half there was space for five similar buildings, and compartments recorded on air photographs (Plate 12a) indicate that this symmetrical arrangement of buildings did in fact exist; the same reasoning and evidence would confirm the partial evidence of excavation that the front third of the fort held a like complement of barrack-type buildings, although the discovery of items of horse-equipment was taken to suggest the presence of cavalry; consequently, some of the structures in the *praetentura* may be stables, the total garrison-strength thus possibly being two separate regiments − one a ten-century infantry cohort, the other a 500-strong part-mounted cohort. However, this estimate is based on the assumption that whole units were present, and it is now becoming clear that, throughout the Roman occupation of Scotland, it may have been rare to find any garrison at full establishment (and even this strength is not absolutely clear for all units). Thus at Cardean, the ten buildings of the *retentura* could theoretically comprise the six infantry barracks, two stables and two barracks for troopers required by a 500-man part-mounted cohort − the same arrangement that has just been argued for the *praetentura*. Similarly, the cavalry presence might conceivably be provided by a vexillation of a full cavalry *ala*, which required as many as sixteen blocks for the accommodation of its men and their mounts. The problem provides an apt illustration of the degree of uncertainty attending any assessments of frontier policy and troop deployment at any period.

What is not open to doubt, however, is the evidence relating to the date and manner of the abandonment of the fort at Cardean. Excavation revealed that the typically looped ends of the ditches on either side of the east and west gates contained a great quantity of Flavian pottery and glass vessels, deliberately deposited there at the end of the occupation and neatly covered with a spread of clay; within the fort, timbers had been carefully extracted from the trenches and post-holes of buildings whose construction levels had contained coins of Vespasian extending in date from AD 70–2 to 77–8. The few possible traces of structural alteration included an apparent anomaly in the ditch-system and an abnormal setting of post-holes in the foundations of the granary – too little to indicate a really prolonged occupation.

It was once generally reckoned that the interval of 24 miles (38.5 km) which separated Cardean from the next known large fort at Stracathro pointed to the existence of an intermediate post situated at some suitable crossing of the South Esk. Despite long and close scrutiny of the most likely point, at Tannadice, beside the temporary camp of Finavon, no traces have so far been detected there. By curious coincidence that delightfully misleading confection of an 18th century forger, the fictitious work of the 14th-century monk Richard of Cirencester, mentions a Roman site at Careston, some way farther down the Esk, but, like most of the other statements of 'Richard', this is pure invention. It was in the course of the search for this crossing, however, that aerial survey by the Royal Commission on the Ancient and Historical Monuments of Scotland in 1983 brought to light the fortlet at Inverquharity (Plate 13), a little way to the north-east of Kirriemuir (Maxwell & Wilson, 1987, 15). Situated some 9 km upstream from Tannadice, the new post closely resembles the smaller work at Cargill and was presumably occupied by a garrison of similar size. It is clearly positioned at the very mouth of Glen Clova in such a way as to maintain extensive surveillance to the north, which leaves open the question of whether an intermediate garrison remains to be found at a crossing lower down the South Esk in Strathmore itself. If there is one, the further question of dating presents itself: would the two sites be contemporary, or, as at Cargill, would they represent successive phases of frontier development?

Stracathro fort is situated on the right bank of the West Water, just short of its confluence with the North Esk and immediately to the north-east of the well-known temporary camp (Plate 12, b). Within its defences, which enclose an area of approximately 6.5 acres (2.5 ha), lies the parish church where Edward I of England received the submission of John Balliol in 1296, and barely 2 miles to the north is the site of the battle of Stracathro

(1130), in which David I defeated the army of Angus, mormaer of Moray
– one of the many conflicts forced upon the mediaeval kings of Scotland
by the need to assert their authority over vassals on the farther side of the
Mounth; both events may serve as an indication of the continuing tactical
and strategic importance of the area, which straddles the approach to the
Cairn o' Mounth pass – the back door into Deeside. Although what we
know of the occupation of Stracathro stems from a rescue excavation in
1969 (Robertson, 1977), that spare account more than suffices, in combination with the aerial record, to demonstrate that its history is in all major
respects comparable with that of Cardean, Cargill, and Inchtuthil. In
particular, an unworn *As* of Domitian dated *c*. AD 86, which was found
inside one of the fort's demolished barrack-blocks, represents terminal
dating-evidence identical to that recovered from the legionary fortress.

No forts have so far been identified beyond Stracathro, but, although
the deployment of garrisons in the northern parts of the Mearns, or on the
coast near Stonehaven, would have exposed those positions to the risk of
being outflanked and assailed from the rear by native warbands using the
Cairn o'Mounth route, the logic of the situation would seem to demand
that at least two more outposts should have been established. One would
expect the first to have been located at some crossing of the Bervie Water,
the second at Stonehaven, where the coastal strip is at its narrowest and a
natural harbour would have facilitated the supply of materials to the northernmost forts, as well as providing shelter for occasional naval patrols.

6

The First Occupation: Questions of strategy

*A*T THE CORE OF THE FRONTIER SYSTEM whose outer screen was described in the previous chapter and forming as it were its spinal column, there lay the forts and installations disposed alongside the road that led from Forth to Tay. The course of this route and its present appearance have already been described, and attention has been drawn to its apparent significance as the only built road north of the Isthmus.* We shall now learn that the steps taken to maintain its security amply confirm that this importance was fully appreciated in Roman times.

The position of the fort which guarded the crossing of the Forth (Fig. 6.1) has long been sought, most antiquaries and scholars presuming that the site would lie not far from Stirling, perhaps almost in the shadow of the castle rock. The length of the interval between the forts at Camelon and Ardoch (some 22 miles; *c.* 35 km), together with the strategic value of the position, persuaded them that a crossing which had warranted so strong a defence in the mediaeval period would not have been left unwatched by a Roman garrison. There was, moreover, a long-established tradition that a fortified structure had formerly been visible at the King's Knot, a sixteenth-

---

*The precise character of the various stretches of road connecting some of the outer *limes* forts which have from time to time been reported in archaeological literature (e.g. *Britannia*, V (1974), 402; vi (1975), 22, viii (1977), 363; xii (1981), 317) is not yet established; whatever their date and origin, the tracks in question do not appear to have been constructed on the same scale, or designed with the same skill, as the Forth-Tay route.

century ornamental garden immediately below the castle on its southern side (RCAMS 1963, 112). Aerial reconnaissance has recently clarified the situation, however. In the first place, photographs of the King's Knot taken during a period of extreme drought have revealed that there is indeed a rectilinear ditched enclosure beneath the later garden, but it is certainly not

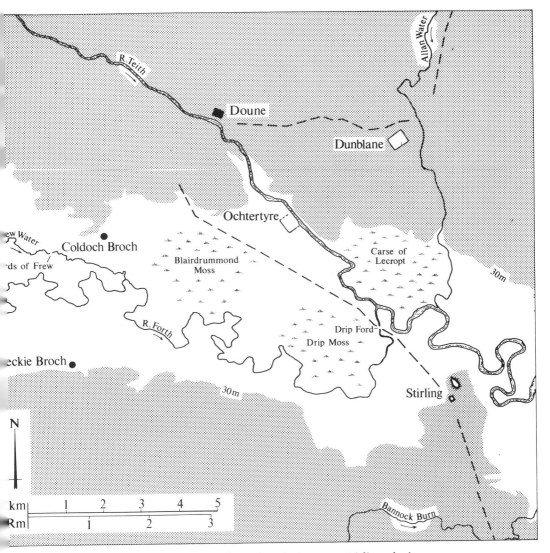

Fig. 6.1 First-century military installations near Stirling: the importance of the crossing at Doune – the S terminal of the Forth-Tay frontier – is underlined by the proximity of two brochs 'guarding' the Fords of Frew passage.

Roman and may even be prehistoric. Secondly, in 1983 an entirely unsuspected Roman fort, possibly as much as 5 acres (2 ha) in area was identified on the level plateau overlooking the River Teith, just to the north-west of the Castle of Doune (Maxwell, 1984a). It is therefore possible that the Roman road from Camelon continued north-westwards beyond Stirling, crossing the Forth at the Drip ford and the Teith at Doune; only then may it have begun to proceed towards Ardoch. In that case, a Roman garrison could also have been stationed at some intermediate point between Doune and Camelon. The crossing of the Bannock Burn would have been a likely spot.

At Ardoch (Plates 14–15), however, we emerge from speculation into a reasonable degree of certainty. Constituting the most impressive remains of any Roman post in Scotland, and rivalled by the sites of few earth-and-timber forts anywhere in the Roman Empire, Ardoch has attracted the attention of the curious from the earliest times. In the eighteenth century, as the pace of antiquarian studies accelerated, it was visited by a veritable procession of travellers, scholars, and enthusiasts, some of whom were so impressed by the evident strength of its surviving defences that they hailed it as the headquarters of Agricola before *Mons Graupius* (e.g. Chalmers, 1807, I, 112). Even before that, popular interest and folktales of buried treasure had led some to examine the ruins in search of relics, occasionally with fatal results (*Stat. Acct.*, viii, 494). Most of the objects thus recovered have long since vanished, but fortunately a grave slab, probably dug out of the fort's cemetery at the end of the seventeenth century, has been preserved (Fig. **6.2**). It records the death of Ammonius, a centurion in the

Fig. 6.2

Tombstone of Ammonius serving in the First Cohort of Hispani, a Flavian garrison of Ardoch.

Cohors I Hispanorum, who were probably stationed at Ardoch during the period with which we are at present concerned. As we shall see, this piece of information may help in elucidating the maze of ramparts and ditches which present themselves to the visitor. Indeed, the splendid state of preservation (which is due to the enclosure of the site by Sir William Stirling in the later eighteenth century, with the express purpose of saving it from the plough) in some ways hinders an appreciation of the site because the sheer complexity of the multiple ditches and banks leads quickly to a feeling of confusion in the visitor (Plate **14**).

The partial excavation of the site on behalf of the Society of Antiquaries of Scotland in 1896–7 has already been mentioned (above, pp. 16–17). At this time most of the central range and the eastern half of the *retentura* were uncovered, and at least two periods of occupation detected, the keys to this discovery being the identification of the plans of timber buildings beneath the foundations of stone successors. Although several sections were cut through the defences, neither the development of these earthworks, nor their relationship to the internal structures was satisfactorily explained. However, the quality of the recording of this early excavation was such that it offered, and continues to offer, a means whereby the excavated data may be re-assessed in conjunction with a new interpretation of the upstanding works. One of the first to see the possibilities of the situation was Professor Ernst Fabricius of the Römisch-Germanisch Limeskommission, whose inspection of the site in 1928 in the company of A. O. Curle and Sir George Macdonald, enabled him to suggest that the extraordinary complex of ditches on the north front was the result of the last period fort having been reduced by 100 ft (30 m) on this side (Macdonald, 1939, 20). This appreciation has been the basis of all subsequent interpretations, including that of O.G.S. Crawford (1949, 30–9). Most have pointed out that the extreme edge of the settings of post-holes in the rear of the fort is too close to the back of the last-period (Antonine II) rampart to be contemporary with it; but as the visible eastern rampart was also the rampart in the previous period (Antonine I), the post-holes in question must be earlier than Antonine I, and hence Flavian. It is also customary to argue that the eastern rampart of the Flavian fort must lie farther out beyond the Antonine, and indeed Crawford has argued that the excessive height of the *spinae*, or upcast banks, between the second and fourth ditches on the eastern front is the result of them following the approximate line of the early rampart, from whose demolished remains they derived most of their extra bulk. Apart from the practical difficulties involved in this process, another solution suggests itself from a closer reading of the section-drawings published by the first excavators.

To begin with, in the platform or 'berm' immediately in front of the final-period rampart, both plans and section indicate the presence of a relatively slight ditch (Fig. **6.3**), which appears to have extended all round the perimeter and to have been covered, in most cases, with a capping of gravel. The proximity of this feature to the outer face of the Antonine I and II ramparts makes it extremely improbable that it was contemporary with them, while the stratification of collapsed material from the ramparts extending over it make it plain that it was not dug subsequently. The only viable explanation is that it was earlier, and its similarity in scale, position, and subsequent infill to the 'berm'–ditches at Crawford (Maxwell, 1972, 151, 154–6, 159) and Castledykes (Robertson, 1964, 14–15, 103–19) gives strong support to the suggestion that it belonged to the defences of a Flavian, probably Agricolan, fort. The average distance between the inner edge of this ditch and the nearest settings of post-holes is more than 38 ft (11.6m), which is just enough for the thickness of a rampart and breadth of an *intervallum* street. Assuming a rampart width of 20 ft (6m) a fort thus defined would have had an internal area of 5.4 acres (2.2 ha), closely comparable with other above-standard forts on the outer frontier. As to the internal structures, although it would be unwise to put too much weight on

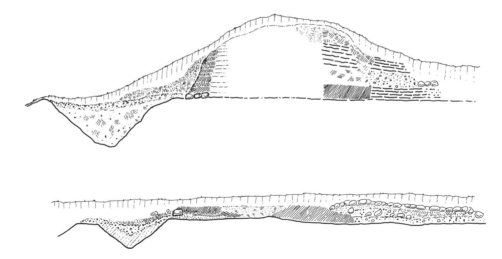

Fig. 6.3   Excavated sections of the Flavian 'berm ditch' at Ardoch (above) and Crawford (below); in each case the early ditch, which lies just to the left of the Antonine rampart, has been deliberately filled and then sealed with gravel; scale *c.* 1:150.

the fine detail of the early plan, since it does not attempt to distinguish between the timber structures of one period and another, it must be admitted that a rudimentary plan can easily be made out. Thus it is possible to distinguish the central range, in which the position of the *principia* is particularly clear, although to which period of the fort it belongs is unclear. If, in one of the Antonine periods, the barracks were built or at least founded in stone, one imagines that the contemporary headquarters building would have been similarly constructed, along with most of the principal structures. The post-hole and post-trench *principia* thus possibly embodies both the early Antonine and Flavian structures; in this case, it seems likely that in both phases the *principia* (and consequently the fort) faced south, the visible alterations of plan and position not being particularly drastic.

The complex pattern of post-holes and construction trenches in the north-east quarter of the fort, which we must presume to be the *retentura*, is less easy to disentangle. There can be little doubt that it represents the remains of successive barrack-buildings, which in the latest phase were replaced by stone-founded blocks of smaller size. Once again, it is possible that one phase of wooden structures belongs to the earlier Antonine period, but the task of distinguishing between traces of these and the remains of the Flavian blocks may not be undertaken without serious reservations. Nevertheless, it has already been observed (e.g. Breeze, 1970, 127–8) that the length of the blocks, if that may be deduced from the predominantly east-west alignment of the structural features, exceeds that of a normal auxiliary barrack, and may therefore indicate the presence of legionaries. To go farther, one might remark that the overall dimensions of the rectangular area defined by these traces are approximately 205 ft by 186 ft (62 m by 57 m), which corresponds very closely to the *pedatura*, or accommodation space, assigned to the *contubernia* of a block of four centurial barracks at Inchtuthil. The separation of the men's rooms from the centurion's suite which this interpretation necessitates is an unusual feature, but as we have seen (above, p. 83) the division of barracks was not unknown in Flavian sites, and a close parallel is provided by the separation of *contubernia* and centurion's offices in the construction compound at Inchtuthil itself. In this case, the four centurions could have been accommodated in the other half of the *retentura*.

As to the disposition of buildings in the *praetentura*, lack of evidence precludes anything more than the suggestion that the structural remains would be appropriate for the presence of five barracks, each about 30 ft (9.1 m) wide, aligned north and south in either half. The depth of the *praetentura*, however, does not appear to have greatly exceeded 170 ft (52 m), and the ten barracks it contained must have held auxiliary troops; as at Cardean, whether these belonged to a milliary regiment of infantry, or a 500-strong composite unit, cannot be determined.

The strategic importance of the route which linked the outer *limes* to the rest of the province is attested not just by the strength of the Ardoch garrison but also by the brevity of the interval between it and the next fort at Strageath – roughly 6 miles (10 km). It may be significant that this corresponds so closely with the intervals separating Mollins from Cadder and Castlecary on the Forth-Clyde 'frontier', for the road between Ardoch and Strageath (as elsewhere along its route), is furnished with the kind of minor installations (Fig. **6.4**) which at about the same time were used to watch over the Roman frontier in Germany (Schönberger 1969, 155–64). At intervals of approximately 1000 yds (910 m) from Ardoch northwards to the watershed between Strathallan and Strathearn there are three timber watch-towers, each enclosed within a slight double ditch; on the watershed itself stands the fortlet of Kaims Castle, which takes the place (and presumably performed the duties) of a fourth tower. Barely one-tenth of an acre (0.05 ha) in internal area, the fortlet was examined on behalf of the Society of Antiquaries at the same time as Ardoch, but unfortunately without revealing its date or purpose; that information was supplied by Professor St Joseph, whose aerial survey detected two of the towers. In brief trial-excavation of all three (St Joseph, 1973, 218; 1977, 135–8) the presence of the rectangular timber tower measuring 8 ft by 10 ft (3 m by 2.5 m) with main uprights 1 ft (0.3 m) square was confirmed, and vital evidence of the nature of their abandonment recovered; at Shielhill North the inner ditch had been deliberately filled with turf and spadefuls of burned debris – some of it evidently derived from the wattle-and-daub panels with which the tower framework had been clad – while the massive timber uprights had been dug out of their post-pits.

About 1.2 miles (2 km) north of Kaims Castle, a fourth tower was discovered from the air and subsequently excavated (Friell & Hanson, 1988) revealing similar structural details, together with possible evidence for a ladder providing access to the upper storeys of the tower. It thus seems possible that it was intended, at least originally, that the remaining distance to Strageath was to be guarded by towers set at similar intervals of about 3000 Roman feet (0.6 Roman miles); in all, ten would have sufficed to provide cover for the 6.6 Roman mile interval.

The interpretation of these patterns of deployment – no easy task at the best of times – is made even more difficult by the pace of archaeological discovery. Recent years have seen the detection from the air of a second fortlet, at Glenbank (Maxwell & Wilson, 1987, 16–17), about six Roman miles to the south-west of Kaims Castle, and yet another double-ditched watch-tower roughly midway between Glenbank and Ardoch. The new fortlet is closely comparable in size and appearance with Kaims

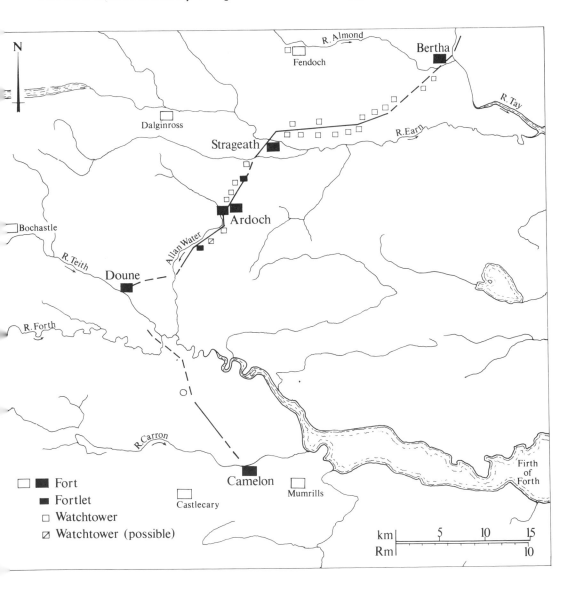

Fig. 6.4   The Flavian Forth-Tay frontier.

Castle, save that the former is set with its long axis at right angles to the road, while that of the latter is nearly parallel. There can be little doubt that the two fortlets, together with the adjacent towers, belong to the same period of frontier development; in view of their close similarity to the recently excavated fortlets at Burlafingen and Nersingen on the Upper Danube (both of the mid-1st century AD) that period can hardly be other than the Flavian (cf. Mackensen, 1987).

Strageath, situated on a plateau on the right bank of the River Earn, demonstrates the dire results of centuries of agriculture which Ardoch happily was spared. The position of the fort is nevertheless still betrayed by the swelling of the ground where the material of successive ramparts has been spread widely by the plough − a process which was already advanced when Roy planned the site in 1754 (Roy, 1793, plate 32). Air photography has demonstrated a complexity of defences, both of the fort and a range of annexes, which rivals and possibly exceeds even that of Ardoch (Plate 15). On the other hand, the operations of the Scottish Field School for Archaeology, under the direction of Professor Frere and latterly Professor Wilkes, have provided so much detailed information about the complicated pattern of occupation at Strageath that we now know not only more about its role in the northern frontier, but also more about the working of the frontier as a whole.

Although only 3.5 acres (1.4 ha) in extent in the Flavian period, Strageath appears to have accommodated the bulk of two separate auxiliary regiments (Frere, 1979). As only the northern halves of both the *praetentura* and *retentura* have so far been excavated, the situation will eventually require re-assessment, but there is clear evidence of major structural alterations in the *praetentura*: a stores-building, apparently of legionary workmanship, was erected on a site later occupied by what may be a stable and a barrack-block, both of auxiliary type, and this, in conjunction with other evidence, has led the excavator to suggest that in the first phase the fort was occupied by a *cohors quingenaria equitata*, with the space unoccupied by stables and barracks serving as a storage-area. Later, but still in the Flavian period, the composite regiment was joined by five centuries of a *cohors peditata*, one cohort being permanently detached from the unit, perhaps on a rota basis, for service in installations outside the fort. Such outposting of troops we may imagine to have been a common occurrence (cf. Fink, 1958; Syme, 1959) and surviving duty-rosters for a legionary vexillation in 1st-century Egypt perhaps identify the sort of tasks which detained the missing century at Strageath − 'road patrol', 'watch' and more enigmatically 'tower' (Watson, 1969, 223−9). In other words, as

Frere has argued, the garrison at Strageath may have been responsible for providing some of the troops who manned the road-side watch-towers. If we may assume that from four to eight men could usefully have been employed in each tower, one century could have serviced a minimum of ten such outposts; hypothetically, it would have been possible, for example, to man the Kaims Castle fortlet and most of the towers between Ardoch and the Earn, even if these had been the maximum of nine or ten suggested above.

There were, however, another eleven watch-towers on the Gask Ridge on the opposite side of the Earn from Strageath. These too are disposed along the Roman road, separated by intervals which, although for the most part much longer than those in the Kaims Castle-Ardoch sector, are nevertheless far shorter than one would expect of a mere signalling-system. Situated on the crest of a ridge, with extensive views to north and south, they are much better placed to carry out surveillance, lateral communication from tower to adjacent tower being easily effected by semaphore or similar device. The Gask Ridge towers, some seven of which survive as visible earthworks (Fig. 6.4), exhibit certain features which distinguish them from those lying between Kaims Castle and Shielhill – single ditches, and internal or external banks for example – but otherwise they seem to fulfil the same purpose. Excavation at Parkneuk, the westernmost member of the Gask Ridge group (Robertson, 1974) produced general confirmation of a Flavian date, without, however, indicating the precise context.

At the north-eastern end of the Gask Ridge the road inclined a little to the north, making for the crossing of the Tay at Bertha. Until recently no watch-towers had been recorded in this sector, even as cropmarks, for the area is intensively cultivated and the drift geology not entirely suitable for the purposes of aerial inspection. In 1985 and 1986, however, the faint traces of a small single-ditched enclosure were recorded from the air immediately to the south-east of the line of the road at North Blackruthven. It would thus appear probable that, in the fulness of time, aerial prospection will identify further elements of this integrated system of forts, fortlets and watch-towers, which could easily have provided effective defence and surveillance from the Forth to the Tay.

The fort at Bertha, which lies on the left bank of the Almond at its confluence with the Tay, thus assumes a greater importance as the northern terminal of what was potentially, at one stage of the Flavian conquest, the outermost frontier of Britannia.

It was first described as a Roman work by Maitland in the eighteenth century (1757, i, 198–9), and examined by fieldworkers from Roy to Callander, the latter defining its area as 9.1 acres (3.7 ha), which would put it on a par with southern bases like Dalswinton (Callander, 1919). Despite this and more recent excavation (Adamson & Gallagher, 1987) we know relatively little about the site, probably just enough to say that it must have been occupied in the Flavian period but without being able to offer even an estimate of its size at that time. However, the probablity is that, as in the Antonine period, its position at the head of the main north road would have justified the presence of a garrison of considerable strength.

Justification is nevertheless an empty word if Flavian reserves of manpower were not adequate to supply the necessary troops. And the same qualification must be applied to discussions of the merits of any position on the northern *Limes*. We have already seen (above, pp. 81–3) that the use of smaller intermediate garrisons in Southern Scotland may point to an appreciation by Agricola himself that manpower had to be used sparingly in the hinterland, if the northern frontier was to be held in appropriate strength. But was it realised at that early stage just how far north the legions would be required to march and occupy? Moreover, how certain could Agricola, or his successor, be of the reserves that would be available to him after the needs of the army on the continent had been taken into account? It must not be forgotten that while Agricola was pushing north into Caledonia, the emperor Domitian was conducting a bitter campaign against the Chatti in Upper Germany, and the legions in Britain had already been depleted to provide troops for the Imperial operations – perhaps by as many as 3,000 legionaries (Dobson, 1981, 9–10), doubtless with an equal number of auxiliaries. Yet it is possible that after Domitian's victory in AD 83 the vexillation returned to Britain, probably not soon enough to take part in the *Mons Graupius* campaign, but not long after – for the barrack accommodation at Inchtuthil is designed for an entire legion.

Yet by AD 87 the Romans had suffered two serious setbacks on the Danube, and once again the army of Britain was laid under tribute, this time losing a whole legion, the *II Adiutrix*, and an appropriate force of auxiliary troops; their departure from the province cannot be dated later than 92, and may have been as early as 86. With these facts in mind, it is possible to accept that until about 86 any governor of Britain could have afforded to entertain expansionist dreams. What Agricola was doing in 83–4 in the context of an under-strength garrison, his successor could have essayed to imitate in years when the vexillations were returning from Germany to their parent-units.

Consequently it is not necessary to believe that, on Agricola's recall in 83–4, the situation had dramatically changed for the worse, or that a process of seemingly irresistible Roman advance must then have ground to a halt. In other words, Agricola's successor could have been the man responsible not only for the construction of the Strathmore forts and the establishment of a legionary base at Inchtuthil, but also for the conduct of aggressive campaigning beyond the Mounth.

It must be admitted, however, that the evidence at our disposal is insufficient to decide the matter one way or the other. Neither the pottery nor the coins admit of such refined dating as to justify assigning the construction of any fort to AD 82–3 rather than 85–86. Not surprisingly, with this degree of uncertainty, various interpretations have been offered. The case for assuming that all the Flavian forts north of the isthmus are Agricolan, at least in conception, has recently been restated with some force (Frere, 1981), and the years following the battle at *Mons Graupius* have been characterised as 'a disastrous pause', with Agricola's successor in the governorship labouring, from the time of his arrival, under the severe restraints of manpower shortage and impending troop withdrawals. Nevertheless, in the past few years the 'anti-Agricolan' view has attracted more support, although in a variety of forms (e.g. Daniels, 1970; Breeze & Dobson, 1976, 124–31; Hanson, 1980, 28–32; Breeze, 1981, 20–3; see now Pitts & St Joseph, 1985, 267–80; Hanson, 1987, esp. 143–88). These include the assumption that Agricola had no time for building any forts at all to the north of the Forth, as well as the suggestion that during his governorship only the line of the Forth-Tay road could have been adequately garrisoned; the screen of glen-blocking forts, according to this theory, was added by Agricola's successor in 85–7 when the garrisons were withdrawn from the Forth-Tay road and a legion was established at Inchtuthil, with outlying forts deployed in Strathmore; the Gask Ridge watch-tower system was not instituted until 86–7, however, on the withdrawal of the legion from Inchtuthil and the abandonment of the Strathmore forts.

It must also be said that none of these theories has proved entirely acceptable. The 'all-Agricolan' case does not account satisfactorily for the manifest contradictions and duplication displayed by the existing pattern of garrisons (and temporary camps). The alternative 'non-Agricolan', or partly 'post-Agricolan', schemes can be faulted in one detail or another: particular attention should be drawn to the apparent improbability of either the 'glen-blocking' forts or the Forth-Tay road forts existing independently of each other. Of more fundamental importance, however, as already remarked in the accounts of individual sites, is that the coins of AD 86 (or at latest 87) are found in mint or unworn condition at so many forts both north and south of the Forth, and in several cases in the very demolition layers which marked their end. What is attested here must surely be an overhaul of the entire garrison of North Britain, not just the strengthening or weakening of one part of it, and all the evidence suggests that it happened — whether at Newstead or Inchtuthil, Crawford or Strageath, Stracathro or Fendoch — in or around AD 87. In the three years which elapsed after the recall of Agricola (or four, if the earlier dating is preferred) there was thus ample opportunity for the succeeding governor to add further lustre to the laurels of the army in Britain.

In the midst of all this uncertainty, is it possible to estimate what Agricola's aspirations may have been? To judge by the words which Tacitus used (*Histories*, 1, 2; *Agricola*, 10, 1), Agricola believed he had broken the last native resistance in Britain; yet, also on the authority of Tacitus, (*Agricola*, 38, 2), if the battle of *Mons Graupius* had been fought earlier in the season, he would have campaigned more widely in the north. It is therefore possible to suggest that Agricola may have been in two minds about both his strategy and tactics for the last campaign: on the one hand he probably knew that there were tribes and territories extending much further north than he could ever hope to advance, and on the other he had probably decided where it would be practicable to draw the eventual frontier of the province, not that this would necessarily have taken the form of a linear barrier. If events had followed their normal course, the frontier or occupied zone would have lain some way behind the limits reached by the field army on campaign; for example, in AD 71–4 Petillius Cerealis had campaigned widely through the territory of the Brigantes — the powerful confederacy controlling most of Northern England — but it was not until Agricola's governorship that Brigantia was garrisoned with Roman troops (Tacitus, *Agricola* 17, 1–2; 20, 2–3).

We have already learned (above, p. 83–5) that Agricola had rejected the Forth-Clyde isthmus as a suitable line for the northernmost limit of Roman rule in Britain, but there is every reason to believe that he may have found another naturally defensible barrier, the River Tay, a much more attractive proposition. There is a growing body of evidence that the valley of the Tay adjoins the southwestern boundary of Iron Age peoples whose typical dwelling-site was of the unenclosed variety, comprising random clusters of round stone or timber houses, often accompanied by underground structures known as souterrains (Fig. **6.5**; Maxwell, 1983; Maxwell, 1987) similar settlements are also found in significant numbers in northern and eastern Fife. From the little that we know of such kinds of habitation it seems likely that they form part of a cultural tradition that flourished in north-eastern Scotland from at least the middle of the first millennium BC to the beginning of the early historic period; they are therefore of utmost relevance to an assessment of Roman strategy, both with Flavian and later periods of occupation.

To Agricola this natural and political boundary would surely have offered an eminently suitable line along which to deploy his forward garrisons, particularly in the aftermath of *Mons Graupius*, when the fighting capability of the tribes living to the north-east had been destroyed in the field; to his successor the same line could have presented a convenient springboard from which to launch the campaigns resulting in the occupation of Strathmore. On this analysis, there may exist a chain of Agricolan posts along the Tay, comparable to the 'glen-blocking' forts and

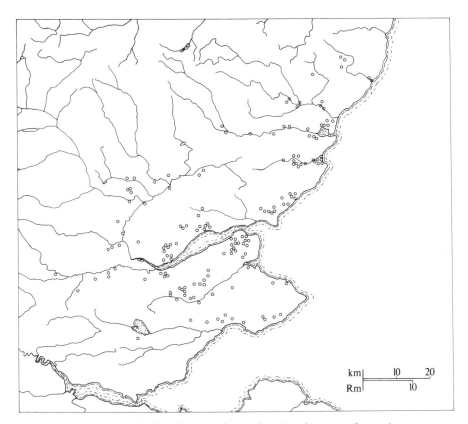

Fig. 6.5   The distribution of unenclosed settlements of round timber houses in eastern Scotland N of the Forth.

presumably contemporary with them; so far only the forts at Cargill and
Bertha could be cited as part of that chain, but the Flavian site known to
Ptolemy as *Horrea Classis* ('granary, or stores-base of the fleet') is as likely
to lie on the bank of the Tay as anywhere, possibly beneath the 3rd-century
fortress at Carpow, while a fort guarding the narrows of the Dunkeld gorge
upstream from Inchtuthil is not inconceivable; indeed the north-west
branch of the Roman road recorded at Wester Drumatherty could be the
signpost which will lead to its discovery.

In such a scheme the road between Forth and Tay would have served
a double purpose, by providing the quickest access to the outer frontier garrisons and serving as a trip-line which no hostile force might cross un-
detected. Although it is usually assumed that the source of enemy penetration would have lain to the north-west, it may be prudent to observe
that the equation of unenclosed settlement with potentially dangerous
native groups would place the major threat to Roman communications on
the east, in the Fife peninsula; furthermore, the area defined by the 'glen-
blocking' forts and the Tay-Forth road appears to be assigned by Ptolemy
to a tribe known as the *Dumnonii*, whose cultural affinities seem to have
lain with the native peoples of Southern Scotland, and who may therefore
have required protection from their Caledonian neighbours.

It may therefore be possible to see the separate stages of Agricola's
conquest of Caledonia as culminating in a series of successive linear
defence-systems. The base-line was the Forth-Clyde isthmus, on which the
chain of forts that ran through Cadder, Mollins and Castlecary (or possibly
Drumquhassle, Malling, Bochcastle and Doune) represents the *praesidia*
mentioned by Tacitus. To the next stage, the penultimate year of the
Agricolan campaigns, may belong the Tay-Forth system, which could also
be viewed as a logical extension of the previous 'frontier', drawing a
military cordon across Scotland from the Clyde to the Tay. What happened next is less easy to conjecture. While the feasibility of a defensive line
on the Tay has been discussed above, a continuation of the strategical
thrust implied by the earlier stages would suggest that the annexation of
Strathmore was already intended to be the final step, whatever the interim
solution may have been. Doubtless an awareness of the relationship
between the various tribal groupings in eastern Scotland would have played
an important role in the formulation of policy.

The activities of Agricola's successor, whether he was initiating a new
forward policy or merely carrying out the final stages of a plan already
approved – and it is important to remember that frontier policy was
determined by the emperor himself – could not have failed to depend on

a similar appreciation of the political situation in Scotland. One of the main features of post-Agricolan dispositions in the north was the move to establish an entire legion at Inchtuthil, a positive step in frontier policy that compares with the decision to base the *Legio IX Hispana* at York in the 70's, before the annexation of Brigantia; those who view Agricola as somewhat conservative in his approach to military matters, may interpret this as evidence of a new broom at work. Whatever may be the explanation, to continue the metaphor, the dust was presently allowed to settle on the northern frontier. By the end of the decade it would appear that shortage of manpower had compelled the Romans to abandon all the forts north of the Forth-Clyde isthmus, and probably many of those to the south. Although the northern limit of territory occupied after AD 87 appears to be indicated by a line joining the forts of Glenlochar, Dalswinton, Tassieholm, and Newstead (Fig. **6.6**) this does not mean that the Roman

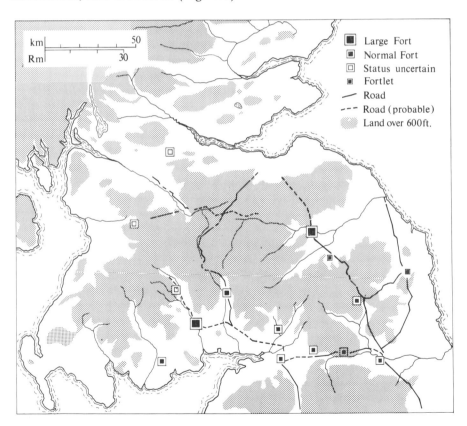

Fig. 6.6   The reduced garrison of Scotland in the late-Flavian
period(*c*.AD 90–100).

high command intended that this line should form the new frontier (cf. Breeze & Dobson, 1976, 131–3; *contra* Frere, 1981, 97). It seems more likely, although there is no evidence to give explicit support, that if a lineal concept was in fact intended, the Tyne-Solway isthmus would have been selected, as it most probably was only a decade later. The remaining forts in Nithsdale, Annandale, and Tweeddale should accordingly be seen as outposts guarding the road-heads of salients extending at right angles from the frontier's main axis, which may be an apt illustration of what Domitian's troops were undertaking to do at about this time on the German frontier (Frontinus, *Strategemata*, I, 3, 10; cf. Schönberger, 1969, 159). The importance of the role played by these outposts is indicated by the presence of a legionary detachment at Newstead, possibly part of the force stationed, during the Agricolan phase, at Corbridge, where a new fort was now built on a different site to accommodate the cavalry regiment *Ala Petriana*.

It is ironical that, although these dispositions were destined to endure for twice as long again as the Agricolan frontier, we know so very little about their organisation. Suffice to say that in the early years of the second century the costs or risks of maintaining the Scottish outposts appear to have exceeded the advantages, and they were abandoned. For nearly forty years thereafter the lower isthmus formed the north-western frontier of the Empire, and the tribes of Scotland were left to pursue their respective ends without the hindrance or help of a resident garrison.

7

The Antonine Occupation: the form of the frontier wall

*I*N THE YEARS FOLLOWING the abandonment of the last
Flavian foothold in Scotland, Roman frontier policy
underwent a fundamental change. The seeds of this trans-
formation had already been sown in the Agricolan period: we have noted
its earliest manifestations in the chain of posts on the Forth-Clyde isthmus
and the integrated system of watch-towers fortlets and forts guarding the
road between Doune and Bertha. The essence of the new policy was the
conversion of a frontier *zone*, which had consisted of a deep but densely-
clustered band of garrison-posts, into a frontier *line*; in its earliest forms,
throughout the Empire, this was physically marked by a road or patrol-
track, along which were ranged towers, fortlets and forts, but finally it was
expressed as a continous barrier, a ditch palisade, or wall. Such obstacles
were not originally intended to serve as defensive platforms from which
the assaults of hostile natives could be driven off by a resident garrison, but
to provide as effective a means of surveillance as the watch-tower system,
with a greater potential for controlling the movement of local tribesmen.
Nevertheless, the creation of a running barrier, by turning the frontier into
a more or less static position, compelled the garrison to concentrate mainly
on defence and removed from the provincial governor the freedom of
action and tactical flexibility that had facilitated the sweeping advances of
the Flavian period.

What persuaded successive emperors of the wisdom of this policy cannot be precisely determined, but the experience of Domitian in Germany
and on the Danube, where both external foes and internal revolt had to be

faced, may have been a vital factor in the early stages of its formulation.* The realisation that reserves of manpower were finite may have led ineluctably to the conclusion that the Empire could not continue to expand indefinitely, since amassing the necessary forces to roll back the frontier in any given sector always entailed weakening the defences on another; the penalties of failure were therefore doubled. Moreover, the destabilising influence of excessive military activity which such expansionist operations promoted, whether in the exploiting of a successful advance or the retrieving of some unlucky reverse, delayed the attainment of that stage which was the goal of all Roman conquest: the establishing of a society whose acceptance of the *pax Romana* would facilitate its admission into the wider circles of the civilised world. However, although by the beginning of the second century it was becoming evident that — almost literally — a line must be drawn somewhere, the career of the Emperor Trajan (AD 97–117) demonstrates that the policy was not uniformly applied; Trajan's military adventures in Dacia and Parthia, whether born of realistic appraisal or incipient dementia (cf. Lepper, 1948, 198–201), represent a last episode of what may be termed aggressive imperialism.

Events in Britain, however, appear to have been unpropitious for such undertakings, frontier policy there being allowed to follow the course mapped for it by Domitian and his successor, Nerva. From the limited archaeological and historical evidence available to us it is possible to reconstruct no more than a shadowy outline of the form the northern frontier now took. Although it no longer seems that the precise form of deployment can be confidently identified, a concentration of garrisons on the Tyne–Solway isthmus during the reign of Trajan reinforced the line first selected under Domitian (Fig. **7.1**). The forts at Corbridge, Nether Denton, Chesterholm, and Carlisle, lying at intervals of about a day's march from each other along the lateral road known as the Stanegate, formed the framework of the new system, intermediate cohort-forts being constructed at Newbrough, Carvoran, and Old Church, Brampton, with at least two small forts of less than 1 acre (0.4 ha), at Haltwhistle Burn and Throp, roughly halving the already reduced intervals; in addition to these there were probably also watch-towers providing facilities for surveillance and communications, as on the Gask Ridge. It is uncertain, however, if the

---

*A non-expansionist policy was not an innovation. Augustus himself, influenced by the dire results of reverses in Germany, had enjoined it on his successors (Tacitus, *Annals*, I 11, 4).

intention was to create a uniform system, composed of such elements and extending across the entire width of the isthmus, but one may at least claim that, as far as its effect on the position and form of the subsequent Hadrianic frontier is concerned, the point had been made: by diminishing the size of individual garrison-posts and reducing the intervals between them it was technically possible to construct a military cordon across the country which could exclude all undesirable influences and prevent them disturbing the process of Romanisation within the province.

Although there is evidence to suggest that the northern frontier under Trajan was never peaceful for long, a major test of the efficiency of these new dispositions did not occur until the end of his reign. To what extent this resulted from the growing strength and belligerence of the tribes living to the north of the isthmus, as opposed to some form of internal unrest, cannot be told; nor can we be certain how much the frontier garrison had been weakened by the despatch of troops to serve in other provinces. Several aspects of the situation may briefly be considered: the first, the fact that a *vexillatio Britannica* is recorded at the legionary base of Nijmegen on the lower Rhine after the departure of the *Legio X Gemina* from that site in 104, and secondly that a major part of the *Legio IX Hispana* which had been stationed at York at least as late as 107–8, was also at Nijmegen at about that time. It was formerly thought that *Legio IX Hispana* had been annihilated in fighting which broke out on the British frontier under Trajan, but it now seems that the unit may not have vanished from the

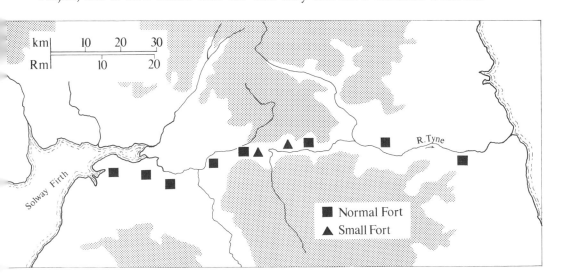

Fig. 7.1   The Tyne-Solway frontier in the Trajanic period (*c*.AD100–118).

army list until the second half of the second century, by which time it had been away from Britain for more than forty years. Warfare of some kind in Britain is strongly suggested by the battle honours *Ulpia Traiana*, which were awarded to the *cohors I Cugernorum* during service in Britain after 103, and by the transfer to the province of the *cohors II Asturum*, but it is unlikely that either event was connected with the disaster that threatened when Hadrian succeeded in AD 117.

The scale of the danger that then threatened is conveyed by the importance assigned to the British troubles in the literary sources. The Augustan History (*Hadrian*, V, 2) listed it as one of the most important tasks facing the emperor on his accession, while the rhetorician Cornelius Fronto compared the troop losses in Britain with those suffered in the bloody Jewish revolt of 132–5, when the *Legio XXII Deiotariana* was probably cut to pieces. It is not surprising therefore, that when Hadrian came in AD 121–2 to view the British frontier in person he set in motion plans for the construction of a more effective barrier; but his purpose was not purely defensive. Like his predecessors, he wished to use it as a demarcation between the Romanised world of the provinces, with all its economic and political benefits, and the disadvantaged realms of the barbarian living literally beyond the pale.

The means he employed was a wall drawn across the Tyne-Solway isthmus from sea to sea, but not in the valleys where the Trajanic Stanegate frontier had lain. The new line ran along the crests of the high ground some way to the north, occasionally perched precariously on the bank of precipices forming the northern face of the Whin Sill outcrop, always choosing the most advantageous position from which to command the approaches to the province. From Newcastle to the River Irthing the wall, from the beginning, was built of stone, varying in thickness from 10 to 6 Roman feet (3.0m – 1.8m); to the west of the river, possibly in the absence of adequate supplies of limestone to make the mortar (used in a stone structure), the wall was built of blocks of turf; in consequence, to permit its construction to the same height as the stone wall, the turf sector was as much as 20 Roman feet (6m) in thickness. In front of the wall, sometimes carved out of the living rock, there was a broad V-shaped ditch, the spoil from which was spread out as a levelled mound to increase the height of the counterscarp, but in such a way as to ensure, wherever possible, that it did not conceal intending assailants from the view of the patrols on top of the 15 ft (4.4m) high wall. In time the stone wall was extended from Newcastle to the north bank of the Tyne at Wallsend, and the western portion was also rebuilt in stone at a narrow gauge, the total length being eighty Roman miles.

On the Solway coast, below the western terminal at Bowness, it has long been known that a series of fortlets and watch-towers extended the system of watch and ward for at least 26 miles (42 km) and possibly even 40 miles (64 km), to terminate at St Bees Head. In recent years, aerial survey has revealed (Jones, 1976, 1982) that the coastal posts were at first enclosed by a pair of parallel ditches, possibly holding palisades or stockades, but, eventually, after a refurbishment of the outermost palisade, the running barrier was removed and not subsequently renewed. Similar fortlets and watch-towers or turrets accommodated the garrison of the Wall in its earliest phase, too. Abutting the south face of the curtain, whether of turf or stone, they were disposed at regular intervals throughout the entire course of the barrier, and the same spatial relationship was maintained on the Solway coast: each fortlet lay one Roman mile (1618 yds; 1480m) distant from its neighbours – hence the traditional names 'milecastle' and 'milefortlet'; between each pair of fortlets, there were two turrets dividing every wall-mile into three equal portions. The remarkably close similarity in size and layout between the 'milecastles' and freestanding fortlets constructed on the German frontier in the time of Trajan (Fig. **7.2**), clearly indicates the common origin of the different methods used in the early second century to solve the frontier questions throughout the Empire.

[handwritten marginal note: NOTE. NOT ENTIRELY CONVINCING.]

The soldiers billeted in such minor installations were little more than sentries and doorkeepers, watching for signs of hostile movement, supervising the peaceful passage of local tribesmen through the frontier as they followed their lawful business – for it must be remembered that the new barrier would have cut across traditional patterns of native life, trade, transhumance, and social intercourse, as surely as it barred the way to raiding bands. To deal with the latter, should they have come in strength, would have required more troops than were initially stationed on the Wall, the main supporting garrisons still being located on the Stanegate. The serious weakness that this represented became evident and before long cohort forts began to be built on the line of the Wall itself. The earliest of these actually straddled the curtain, permitting easier access to the enemy beyond through the entrances placed in each side-wall north of its junction with the barrier. At about the same time as the decision was taken to build these forts, twelve in number, it was also felt necessary to define the rear limit of the entire wall-zone by a broad flat-bottomed ditch (known erroneously as the Vallum); whether this additional feature was intended as a protection for the Wall garrison and its installations from unruly local tribesmen, or merely as a means of indicating the limit of 'Ministry of Defence property', cannot be determined; but its dimensions – ditch and enclosing banks form an obstacle 120 Roman feet in width — suggest very strongly that there was a real threat to Wall security. Despite these disturbing signs of instability to the rear, it was nevertheless still from the north that a major assault was likely to be launched, and as confirmation of this it seems probable that from the very beginning it had been intended to have garrisons outposted in enemy territory. Significantly, all were located on the north-western approaches: at Birrens, Netherby, and Bewcastle; we do not know if this deployment was designed to protect

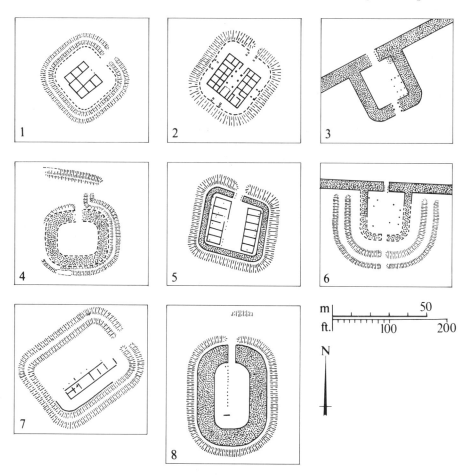

Fig. 7.2 Fortlets in Britain and Upper Germany

1. Kemel, Hessen (earlier)   5. Barburgh Mill
2. Degerfeld, Hessen   6. Wilderness Plantation
3. Hadrian's Wall, Mc.50   7. Kemel (later)
4. Redshaw Burn   8. Durisdeer.

outlying territory of the Brigantes, most of whom lived to the south of Hadrian's Wall, or to guard against attack by the Novantae of south-western Scotland; the fact that the Solway coast defences are not balanced by a similar system on the eastern flank of the Wall suggests that that latter explanation is more applicable.

The distribution of the twelve 'primary' forts on the Wall, displaying a relatively even spacing, with no apparent concern for protecting weak points, has been taken to show that their garrisons were still not intended to act as bases for highly mobile units in a defence force that was capable of long-range operation. Whatever their precise role, there can be no doubt that before too long they required to be supplemented by the addition of further garrisons, which were all added behind the curtain, as were the last of the primary forts — as if in recognition of the dangers lying immediately to the north. This complicated pattern of evolution took place over several years. It has been suggested (e.g. Breeze & Dobson, 1976, 28 – 78) that work may have commenced on building the curtain, milecastles, and turrets in 122, that the decision to locate the forts on the Wall was taken in 124, and that the full implementation of the revised scheme, including the replacement of the Turf Wall in stone, may have continued until Hadrian's death in 138.

Once again the circumstances prevailing in Britain on the accession of a new emperor are only to be deduced from the most meagre of historical evidence. Although it has recently been argued (Birley, 1974, 17; Breeze, 1980, 47) that the Antonine advance into Scotland was practically a walk-over, which was motivated by political considerations and had little to do with the military situation, there is no gainsaying the fact that all the sources (*S.H.A., Pius*, V, 4; Pausanias, *Descriptio Graeciae*, viii, 43, 4; *Pan. Lat. Vet.*, VIII (v), 14) mention a war in Britain during the reign of Antoninus Pius, and the association of the governor Lollius Urbicus with that war makes it clear that it was in the years following 139 that the hostilities took place. Moreover, since the eulogy addressed to Antoninus on the completion of the war was cited with approval in the panegyric dedicated to a later emperor, we must presume that the Antonine victory was deemed no hollow achievement. To argue otherwise would be tant-amount to claiming that the Romans, from the highest to the lowest, practised a most thoroughgoing form of self-deception. For, in addition to the historical accounts, and the evidence of coin types recording victory in Britain, there are the monuments hewn by the very soldiers who took part in the campaign; they show in several cases (see below, p. 154 and Fig. 8.3) the unmistakable face of victorious action, with prostrate foes trampled beneath the hooves of Roman cavalry, headless corpses, and pinioned captives. It is difficult to believe that monuments portraying such scenes could have been raised and dedicated by an army which had not earned the fruits of victory by the sweat of its brow and in the heat of battle.

Nevertheless, granted that there were good military grounds for mounting the campaign, it is difficult to identify the specific source of the danger. A case has been made out (Hanson & Maxwell, 1983, 64–8) for identifying a number of marching camps in Southern Scotland – none of them exceeding 50 acres (20 ha) in area – which may possibly indicate the passage of troops engaged in the reconquest of Scotland under Lollius Urbicus; not surprisingly they are to be found beside the major Roman roads in Annandale, Clydesdale, Tweeddale, and on Dere Street itself, but even if their Antonine date could be confirmed they reveal no significant concentration of military activity. The possibility of the south-western tribes presenting particular problems has already been noted with respect to Hadrianic troop dispositions, and there is a certain amount of evidence to show that in the Antonine period, too, they required to be treated with caution (see below, pp. 177–8). However, this is not likely to have been the only *casus belli*, although it may well have been a contributing factor. Once again, the answer may lie in a plain reading of our main historical source: '[Antoninus] defeated the Britons through the actions of the governor, Lollius Urbicus, and driving off the barbarians, built another Wall of turf' (*S.H.A. Pius,* V, 4). The implication is that, when victory came, the enemy were back where they belonged, beyond the newly-built Wall. It is not inconceivable that the barbarians who had to be driven back were Agricola's old foes, the Caledonians, but it must be repeated that there is little, if any, archaeological evidence to support this. The only traces of intrusion by the peoples of the north at about this time are the southern examples of small drystone-walled forts known as duns and brochs. The structural origin of both types of site lies in the Atlantic Province of Iron Age Scotland, where they appear to have evolved over a period of at least five centuries before the Roman era.

Examples of duns and brochs are scattered over nearly all areas of the southern and eastern lowlands of Scotland, with an appreciable concentration in the central rift valley between the Rivers Carron and Teith. Although it is possible that their distribution represents a gradual process, the evidence recovered from excavation suggests in every case that the broch or dun was built and occupied at some stage of the Roman period. Indeed, at the broch of Leckie in Stirlingshire, where the occupation was brought to a close in a holocaust of sudden destruction, apparently as a result of assault by some form of primitive artillery, it has been suggested that the assailants were elements of the Roman army under Lollius Urbicus (MacKie, 1983). It would be unwise, however, to apply this interpretation to all southern brochs and duns, and it would be equally inappropriate to assume, even were their dates of occupation known, that all, or even any, represent hostile intrusion by tribesmen from the north and west. Nevertheless, as fortified dwellings they are undoubtedly exotic, and while not in themselves substantiating a 'Caledonian' invasion, they may still demonstrate the results of external pressures likely to have disquieted the watchers on the southern wall. Furthermore, as will be seen (below, pp. 165–9), the Antonine province extended far beyond the *murus caespiticius*, or turf wall, raised by Lollius Urbicus and his successor; its outposts lay on the River Tay, echoing in their dispositions the measures possibly taken by Agricola to deal with the northern tribes some sixty years before.

However, beyond doubt it was the building of the northern Wall that gave the Antonine occupation its main justification (Fig. **7.3**). The line it followed may have coincided in part with that chosen by Agricola for his chain of *praesidia* in AD 80–81 (see above, pp. 83–5), but its purpose was quite different; in this relationship it resembled the Hadrianic frontier

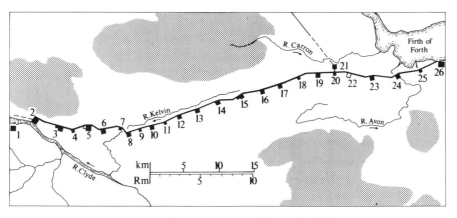

Fig. **7.3**   The Antonine Wall in its final form

1. Bishopton	10. Cadder	19. Rough Castle
2. Old Kilpatrick	11. Glasgow Bridge	20. Watling Lodge
3. Duntocher	12. Kirkintilloch	21. Camelon
4. Cleddans	13. Auchendavy	22. Falkirk
5. Castlehill	14. Bar Hill	23. Mumrills
6. Bearsden	15. Croy Hill	24. Inveravon
7. Summerston	16. Westerwood	25. Kinneil
8. Balmuildy	17. Castlecary	26. Carriden
9. Wilderness plantation	18. Seabegs	

vis-à-vis the Trajanic, representing the substitution of what may be termed active surveillance for passive defence. Thus, instead of depending upon garrisons situated in the river valleys, as at Mollins on the northern isthmus, or Corbridge on the southern, the new frontier drew its strength from the occupation of a tactically dominant position; from east to west, wherever possible, it was drawn along the very crest of the escarpments that immediately overlook the southern side of the central valley. Between Bridgeness and Falkirk it commands an area which in Roman times comprised salt marshes on the shores of the Forth and the low-lying flood plain of the River Carron; from Falkirk westward to the watershed near Kilsyth it looms above the ill-drained upper reaches of the Bonny Water, and then, striding over the basalt massifs of Croy Hill and Bar Hill, descends the left bank of the Kelvin as far as the outskirts of Glasgow; at Balmuildy it crosses the river, commits itself to a winding course across the southern outliers of the Kilpatrick Hills through Bearsden and the northern outskirts of Clydebank, and finally gains the right bank of the River Clyde at Old Kilpatrick. Its total length was thirty-seven miles (59 km), roughly half that of Hadrian's Wall, but, despite its lesser dimensions and less permanent structure, it was by no means of inferior design, nor was it necessarily intended to serve as a temporary expedient.

The Antonine Wall is made up of several distinct elements, each with its own standard form and purpose. Of these the turf wall is naturally the most important. Technically known as the Rampart or Curtain, it was based upon a stone foundation 14-16 ft (4.3-4.9m) wide, consisting of a pitching of boulders contained between two lines of shaped kerb-stones. In this it differed from the turf-built sector of Hadrian's Wall, which was based directly upon the ground; the innovation, presumably adopted as a result of experience gained on the southern frontier, would have afforded a more stable base for the Wall's superstructure and would have greatly improved drainage, both from the body of the rampart itself and beneath it. In addition, to prevent groundwater ponding at the back of the Wall − a serious hazard in the western half of the frontier, where rainfall is generally heavier − stone culverts were incorporated in the base. On steeply-sloping ground care was also exercised to provide as level a foundation as possible, a shallow terrace being excavated to receive the base, where the fall was from the rear to the front, while the base itself was stepped like a staircase where the fall was along the line of the wall. If the situation demanded, more elaborate precautions might be taken; at Cadder, for example, to negotiate a steep descent where the Antonine Wall formed the northern defence of a fort, the Rampart rested upon a stone foundation five courses high.

Although the *Historia Augusta* calls it 'a wall of turf', there are sectors of the Antonine frontier, mostly in the easternmost portion, between Watling Lodge and the Forth, where the bulk of the Rampart is built of earth, revetted with inner and outer skins of turf or clay (cf. Keppie, 1974, 156−7; 1976, 77−8); more recently it has been shown that similar constructional techniques and materials may have been used in more westerly sectors; most probably the reason for this divergence is a lack of suitable turf in the immediate vicinity of the Wall, and this could have been the result of various situations − e.g. the prevalence of arable land, as possibly in the eastern half of the Wall, or of poorly developed turf, as in heathland or forested areas. For the most part, however, the Wall is indeed built of turf, as sections cut through its surviving remains clearly demonstrate, the compacted and leached layers of grass, roots, and topsoil transformed during the passage of centuries into a laminated pattern as richly striped and coloured as the skin of a tiger. The turf was cut in blocks of manageable size − the military manuals recommended a rectangle measuring one by one and a half Roman feet, with a thickness of six inches − and the turves were then stacked on the stone base to the required height. As many as twenty-two separate layers of turf have been observed in sections of really well-preserved stretches of the Wall (Steer, 1957, Fig. **3**), which would support the assumption that the barrier rose to a height of at least 10 ft (3m). The inner and outer face appear to have been battered, the outer rising more steeply than the inner, as might be expected, although the lowest 3 ft or so (1m) of the latter may occasionally have been vertical (Fig. **7.4**).

Despite the fact that reconstructions of the Antonine Wall usually show it surmounted, as here, by a sentry-walk and crenellated breastwork, there is in fact no archaeological evidence to support this interpretation directly. On Hadrian's Wall, the profile of the Ditch and the bank on its outer lip are presumed to have been dictated by the need to afford a direct line of sight for the sentries on top of the Wall, and similar calculations have been applied on the Antonine barrier to show that it too could have incorporated a wall-walk at a height of about 10 ft (3m). On the other hand, neither the Hadrianic nor the Antonine frontier was designed to be defended like mediaeval castle wall, and even on the southern barrier it could be argued that a crenellated breastwork was not in fact provided − at least not on the turf sector. Some slight support for this view may be provided by the stylised representations that appear on two Roman souvenir vessels of bronze, known as the Rudge Cup and the Amiens Skillet (Fig. **7.5**); both bear the names of forts in the western half of Hadrian's Wall in a decorative

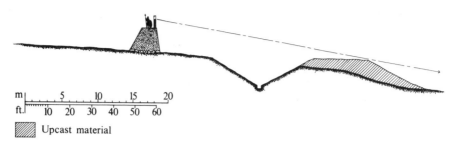

Upcast material

Fig. 7.4   Cross-section of the Antonine Wall at Seabegs
Wood showing 'dead ground' to N of counterscarp bank.

frieze just below the rim, together with a portrayal of the Wall itself.
Though the evidence should not be pressed too strongly, the portrayal
comprises a series of square crenellated towers rising above a curtain with
an uncrenellated wallhead. Moreover, as it is the western half of Hadrian's
Wall which is depicted, the recent suggestion (Breeze & Dobson, 1976, 271)
that a Hadrianic date for the vessels may be preferred could mean that it
was the Turf Wall which the souvenir-makers had taken as their model; it
is thus possible that the form of barrier depicted here in silhouette, with
turrets linked by undefended curtain, could be of relevance to an attempted
reconstruction of the Antonine Wall. It may be observed that neither the
palisade nor the stone wall which at different times formed the linear
barrier on the Rhine and Danube frontiers was provided with a sentry-
walk on the curtain itself.

It is important to remember, however, that the Rampart was only part
of the frontier work. To the north of it, at a distance which varied between
about 20 ft (6m) and 30 ft (9.1m), there lay the Ditch. Roughly V-shaped in
profile, with sides that sloped up at an average angle of 30° to the vertical,
it too varied widely in size. The 'standard' dimensions are approximately
40 ft (12.2m) in width and 12 ft (3.7m) deep, but on occasion it may be as

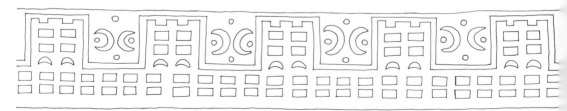

Fig. 7.5   Detail from decoration of the Rudge Cup and Amiens
Skillet showing possible milecastle towers and uncrenellated wall-
head between them.

narrow as 14 ft (4.3m) or as wide as 68 ft (20.7m), the width of the platform between it and the Rampart varying in proportion. To the west of Kirkintilloch the ditch appears to be consistently slighter than the standard width, which may have been adhered to throughout most of the central sector between Kirkintilloch and Falkirk, and it is possible that the narrowing may indicate an attempt to economise in time and labour in the later stages of the Wall-construction programme (see below, pp. 162–3); the apparent correlation between the decrease in the size of the ditch and the increase in width of the berm or platform to the north of the Rampart may indicate that the centre-line to be followed by each element of the frontier had already been marked on the ground before the reduced scale of construction began (cf. Keppie, 1974; 1982).

The vast amount of spoil cast out of the ditch was disposed in a bank, generally known as the Outer Mound, lying immediately beyond the outer lip. Being composed of tipped subsoil and rubble, the Outer Mound frequently overshadows the Rampart with its surviving bulk. Where cultivation has not softened its outlines, the fans of original tipping heaps may still be seen on the northern edge; on Croy Hill, where the ditch seems to have been re-cut, a secondary Mound apparently overlies the primary. The Mound thus served to heighten the counterscarp, and, in localities where the ground fell sharply away in front of the Wall, was heaped up in a pronounced comb or spine. Elsewhere, the Outer Mound was spread out with a more or less level top, but even in these situations it would appear that its profile was not modelled in such a way as to allow watchers on the Wall to see beyond it; indeed, in several instances where the ground slopes down beyond the Mound, there would have been adequate cover for prospective assailants. What is perhaps more remarkable is that in such a situation it would seem to have been open to the military surveyors to have avoided these consequences by setting the Wall a little nearer the crest of the slope. At Seabegs Wood for example (Fig. 7.4), where the Outer Mound is sufficiently well preserved to permit an examination of its relationship to the original ground profile it would almost seem that tactical advantage has been sacrificed to the convenience of the planners or builders; and the sacrifice is even more blatant at Bar Hill, as the sections made almost ninety years ago by the Glasgow Archaeological Society clearly show (Fig. 7.6, *b*), the Rampart being set far enough back to allow the full width of the frontier – wall, berm, ditch and counterscarp bank – to occupy the same shelf of ground. Yet again, the role of the Wall as a defensible frontier may be seen to require revision, although on Croy Hill (Fig. 7.6, *a*) there can be no doubt that the natural strength of the position is such as to require no artificial enhancement.

Nevertheless, the Antonine Wall was maintained and operated by a garrison of considerable size, who served or were accommodated in a wide range of installations which, with one exception, abutted the inner face of the Rampart. The largest of these were the forts, probably eighteen in number, although the precise locations of five presumed sites have still to be identified. They are disposed at relatively regular intervals of between 1.5 and 3 miles (2.4–4.8 km) along the Wall (Fig. **7.3**), and display a wide variety of sizes and internal plans. The five largest – Mumrills, Castlecary, Bar Hill, Balmuildy, and Old Kilpatrick, ranging from 3.2 to 6.5 acres (1.3–2.6 ha) in area – are all likely to have been occupied by auxiliary regiments at full strength. Of the remainder, some may also have accommodated 500-strong infantry units – Cadder, Auchendavy, and Castlehill, for example – but the others are too small to have held anything but vexillations; Rough Castle at 1.1 acre (0.5 ha) and Duntocher at 0.5 acre (0.2 ha) would have been hard pressed to provide sufficient space for a century or so.

There are equally wide variations in plan and construction : Castlecary and Balmuildy were defended by stone walls, and at the latter site the presence of wing-walls, also of stone, at the north-east and north-west corners plainly indicates that the fort was built in advance of the Antonine Wall at a stage when it was believed that the curtain, too, might be constructed in stone, like the eastern half of Hadrian's Wall. The ramparts of

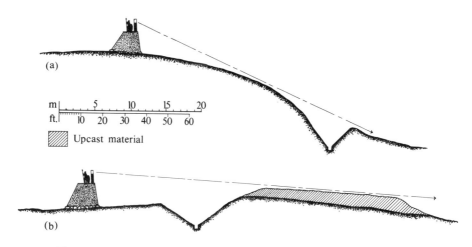

Fig. 7.6   Cross-sections of the Antonine Wall: a) as it traverses the crags on Croy Hill; b) on Bar Hill, showing not only 'dead ground' to the N, but also disadvantageous position of the Rampart below the crest on the S.

all the other forts on the Wall were built of turf or earth on a stone base resembling the Antonine Rampart, and in most cases the Rampart itself was utilised as one side of the defences. At Old Kilpatrick and probably at Mumrills, however, it would appear that the forts were built, like Balmuildy and Castlecary, in advance of the curtain, which was eventually made to butt against the existing defences. Bar Hill, on the other hand, lies some way to the south of the Antonine Wall (Fig. **7.7**, *1*) and its chronological relationship cannot therefore be ascertained. Had it existed before the arrival of the Wall-builders, however, it is strange that the opportunity was not taken to link it to the barrier, even although that might have compelled the latter to abandon a tactically more advantageous line; at Mumrills, for example, where the location of the Wall is determined by the position of the fort, the penalty was evidently thought well worth paying (Fig. **7.7**, *2*). The fort at Carriden, situated on the south shore of the Forth about one mile (1.4 km) east of the presumed terminal of the Wall, should be grouped with the larger wall-forts; its outline is only partly known, but with an area of approximately 4 acres (1.5 ha) it appropriately balances the fort of Old Kilpatrick which guards the western end, and doubtless it served a similar purpose.

The relationship of the smaller forts to the Wall curtain has long been characterised as secondary, although not in an entirely straightforward

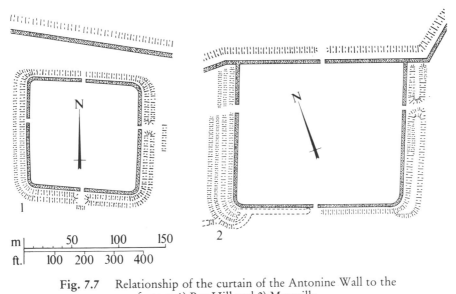

Fig. 7.7 Relationship of the curtain of the Antonine Wall to the forts at 1) Bar Hill and 2) Mumrills.

way. Thus, at Rough Castle, although the ramparts of the fort appear to have been added to the south face of the Wall, the Ditch was interrupted for a crossing opposite the north gate, indicating that an installation at this point was part and parcel of the early construction programme. At Wester-wood (2.0 acres; 0.8 ha) the relationship of the Wall and fort rampart was similar, but there was no evidence of an original gap in the Ditch. Croy Hill fort, on the other hand, at 1.5 acres (0.6 ha) presents a more complicated picture; the Ditch is indeed interrupted just to the east of the fort-site – a welcome relief, no doubt, to the toiling legionary work-gangs, who had hewn it out of the living basalt in this sector – but the fort's east and west ramparts are clearly secondary to the north, which here forms part of the Antonine curtain. Yet at the north-east corner of the fort a conduit leading the overflow from a well constructed for the use of the fort garrison was overlain by, and therefore earlier than, the foundation of the Antonine Wall, a relationship which would appear to be inconsistent with that deduced from the other structural evidence. Similar ambiguity and structural complexity was revealed by excavations at Cadder, which although only 2.8 acres (1.1 ha) in area nevertheless appeared to contain the six century barracks required for a full quingenary infantry regiment. At Bearsden, however, where the denudation of the remains made it impossible to ascertain the nature of the junction between Wall and fort (Breeze, 1984), the garrison consisted of a small vexillation of an unidentified auxiliary unit who occupied only a fraction of the 2.3 acres (0.9 ha) available within the interior. That this may not have been the original intention of the Wall-planners is strongly suggested by, amongst other features, the curious misalignment of the east rampart of the fort, whose relationship to the rest of the defensive system is perhaps best explained as an attempt to subdivide an existing larger enclosure of regular plan (Fig. 7.8); the area of the latter, about 3.7 acres (1.4 ha) would place it amongst the category of larger forts.

The last example about which we have certain information is Duntocher. Paradoxically, although the smallest of the Wall forts so far investigated, (Robertson, 1957), it is the only site among the smaller works to have produced unequivocal evidence of both its relationship to the Rampart and its place in the Antonine scheme of things (Fig. 7.9). As built originally, this tiny fort was a free-standing structure, but, unlike Old Kilpatrick, which also stood alone in its primary form, it had only two rounded angles, the eastern angle apparently being squared in the expectation that the turf curtain would eventually butt against it; it was thus earlier than the Wall. However, the fort was not the first Roman structure

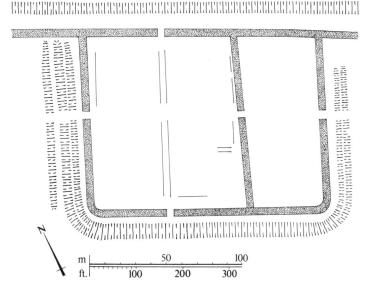

Fig. 7.8   The defences of the Antonine Wall fort at Bearsden
showing misalignment of the E rampart (after Breeze).

at Duntocher; immediately to the north-west lay a fortlet whose south-east
rampart had been incorporated in the defences of the fort, but there had
been a time when the fortlet too had stood alone, for it had originally been
enclosed by a ditch, which was later overlain by the rampart of the fort. As
with the fort, so in the case of the fortlet, the squaring of two of its angles
indicated that its builders knew that it also would sooner or later become
part of the Antonine barrier. After the building of the fort, both structures
were apparently maintained in use, and when the ditch-digging party

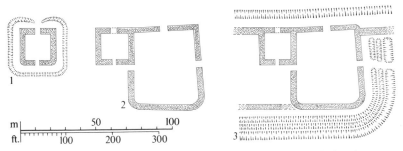

Fig. 7.9   Three stages of construction at Duntocher: 1. isolated
'milefortlet', 2. 'milefortlet' incorporated in W rampart
of freestanding fort, 3. Antonine Wall building-party
reaches Duntocher.

arrived, they used the front of each work as a baseline from which to measure the width of the berm; hence the slight angle of misalignment between fort and fortlet is faithfully reproduced in the course of the ditch – which is here doubled for extra security, a unique feature. However, when the Wall-builders arrived, in order to maintain the berm at a standard width of 30 ft (9.1m), it was necessary to bring the Wall too close to the ditches that were already dug on the south-east side of the fort, and a buttress had to be built at the terminal of the innermost ditch to prevent the Wall from collapsing into it. It can thus be seen that Duntocher illustrates not only the complicated process by which the various elements of the Wall came to be built, but also the changes in plan which it might be reasonable to recognise in other sectors of the frontier.

For example, when the fortlet at Duntocher was first discovered, and for many years after, it was thought that such minor structures had only been used on the Antonine Wall in exceptional circumstances. The existence of a similar work at Watling Lodge to the west of Falkirk had been explained as a guard-house for the break in the Rampart where the road that led to Camelon crossed the frontier. In more recent years, aerial survey revealed the existence of two more fortlets, one at Glasgow Bridge to the west of Kirkintilloch and the other at Wilderness Plantation some way to the east of Balmuildy. Excavation at the latter (Wilkes, 1974) confirmed that these sites were in every way comparable with the fortlets known as milecastles on Hadrian's Wall (Fig. **7.2,6**), measuring approximately 60 ft by 70 ft. (18m by 21m) internally, and in the case of Wilderness Plantation, built as one with the Antonine curtain. Even at that stage there were still those (the present author was one) who believed that the Hadrianic milecastle had been adopted for use on the northern barrier to serve as minor intermediate posts where the interval between Wall-forts was exceptionally long. For those who had been 'brought up' on Hadrian's Wall, however, the implication was clear: the Antonine Wall possessed a series of fortlets at mile intervals throughout its course, (cf. Gillam, 1975). In the past few years further examples have come to light : those at Kinneil, Seabegs and Croy Hill were found to have been bonded with the curtain; the example at Cleddans evidently preceded the building of the Wall, like nearby Duntocher; while at Summerston the fortlet ditch appeared to respect the defences of a temporary camp which probably accommodated a Wall-building party, presumably indicating that the fortlet was constructed at the same time as the curtain (Keppie & Walker, 1981; Hanson, 1979; Hanson & Maxwell, 1985). To these eight confirmed examples should also be added two possible sites, one at Castlehill, where the early antiquaries give reason to believe that a fortlet may have been succeeded by a fort in the same manner as at Duntocher; and the other at Rough Castle, where a small rectangular enclosure, found immediately to the east of the fort by the original excavators in 1903, has been tentatively identified as an earlier fortlet by John Gillam (1975, 54).

The smallest installations known on the Antonine Wall fall into two classes. The first, traditionally called 'expansions', were first identified by the antiquary Alexander Gordon (1726, 58–9). They consisted of a turf platform, some 17–18 ft (5.2-5.5m) square, resting on a stone base which was built against the south face of the Antonine Rampart. At the only fully excavated example, Bonnyside East (Fig. **7.10**,2), about 595 yds (242m) west of Rough Castle fort (Steer, 1957), the turf superstructure was bonded with the curtain and therefore built at the same time as it; a section of another example, on Croy Hill, however, showed that the turfwork of the expansion had been applied to the south face of the Wall, and was therefore secondary, although by what interval of time cannot be determined. Only six expansions have been recognised throughout the entire length of the Wall, and the most that can be said about their location is that they appear to be grouped in pairs: two lie 115 yds (135m) apart on Croy Hill, about

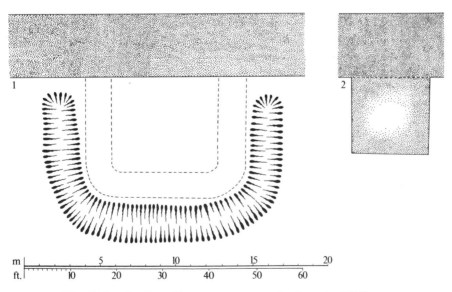

Fig. 7.10   Small ancillary structures on the Antonine Wall:

1. Expansion near Rough Castle
2. Enclosure at Wilderness Plantation.

523 yds (478m) west of the fortlet; a second pair lie 355 yds (325m) apart, 592 yds (542m) west of Rough Castle; and a third pair, lying 645 yds (590m) apart, are situated almost exactly midway between Rough Castle and Watling Lodge. In the absence of more explicit structural evidence it is clearly impossible to understand their function, and the suggestion made first by Macdonald (1934, 354−8) that they were signal-platforms or beacon-stances used in long-range signalling has been generally accepted, *faute de mieux*; the excavation of Bonnyside East identified the extensive traces of burned material found there as evidence of such a use, suggesting further that the signalling operation in question was designed to provide communication with garrisons in the hinterland or beyond the frontier, not solely along the line of the Wall. This might explain why expansions are not found more widely.

Nevertheless, when the possibility of there being a regular series of Antonine Wall milecastles was first discussed, it was realised that a renewed search for the equivalent of the Hadrianic turrets might also be appropriate. Eventually a combination of aerial survey and the inspection of existing air-photograph cover revealed the presence of three ditched enclosures lying just behind the Wall in the Wilderness Plantation sector (RCAHMS, 1978, 113; 159). At an early stage it was hoped that these might represent the sites of timber towers, set at intervals of approximately one-sixth of a Roman mile (half the turret-interval) but excavation (Hanson & Maxwell, 1983a) has shown that the story is at once more complicated and less informative. The average interval can now be seen to approximate to one-fifth of a Roman mile (1000 Roman feet), while the relationship of the enclosures to each other and to the fortlet at Wilderness Plantation may be compared with that of the expansions to adjacent Wall-installations. The form of the enclosures appears to be of the simplest (Fig. **7.10**, *1*); within the ditch a low turf-revetted bank enclosed an area about 20 ft (6m) square which contained no traces of built structures; there was no evidence of burning, or indeed anything but the most transitory occupation, and while it is possible that, like the expansions, they could have served some purpose related to signalling or surveillance, it would perhaps be wiser to admit our ignorance about their function. With regard to their place in the construction programme there can be no argument, however, as excavation at Wilderness West demonstrated that the work-parties engaged in building the adjacent stretch of Rampart forebore to strip the turf from the area to be occupied by the enclosure; we may therefore presume that the relationship between enclosure and curtain was similar to that between the expansion and the curtain at Bonnyside East. Curiously enough, both structures overlay pits which appeared to have been recently dug in quest of building materials; at Wilderness West the material sought may have been stones for the Wall-base, whereas at the other the pit was one of a series of quarry-holes which produced metalling for the adjacent Military Way. This road was a feature which had not been incorporated in the early phases of Hadrian's Wall, although experience gained on the Antonine Wall led to its introduction on the southern frontier at a later stage. With an average width of *c.* 18 ft (5.5m), the Military Way afforded swift and easy communication between the garrisons from one end of the Wall to the other. It normally lay within 50 yds (46m) of the back of the Wall and ran through most of the forts from east to west, bypass loops being provided for traffic which did not wish to call at every post.

The presence of such a link on the Antonine Wall emphasises the importance which its designers assigned to the frontier's role as an integrated system, with each garrison and structural element performing a separate but indispensable task. There is considerable uncertainty, however, as to the process by which this effective barrier was constructed, and the various, often conflicting, items of evidence produced belie its monumentally uniform appearance and deserve a separate chapter for their exposition.

8

The Antonine Wall:
Legionaries at work

ROM THE PREVIOUS CHAPTER it can be seen that the
Antonine Wall was a complex installation, combining
basic strength with tactical flexibility, and exhibiting
several innovatory features. Such complexity, however, does not appear to
have been the result of a single planning decision, but, as in the case of
Hadrian's Wall, of a process which has been described as 'conception and
afterthought'; readers with experience of military planning may suspect
that it could be more appropriately be styled 'order, counter-order, and
disorder'. At any rate, it is no longer possible to accept that the Antonine
Wall was intended, from its origin, to assume the form in which we now
see it. Indeed, much of the research currently being carried out on the Wall
is directed towards the solution of the basic problems concerning this
evolution, in particular the identification of the various stages of structural
development and the reconstruction of the actual building programme. It
must be admitted, however, that we are still a long way from understanding the full picture, and the account which follows is little more than
a tentative sketch, which future excavation and discovery are bound to
modify.

When Antoninus Pius gave the order for the legions to march north
into Scotland it is almost certain that he intended the advance to be followed by the building of a new barrier. It would be reasonable to assume,
and the evidence justifies our belief, that the second barrier was modelled
on Hadrian's Wall; the only question is 'how closely'? One feature which
appears to have been faithfully reproduced is the mile-fortlet system, for,

although only eight examples have so far been identified, all are clearly based upon a Hadrianic milecastle archetype. Moreover, the fact that the interval between the adjacent sites of Cleddans and Duntocher is almost exactly one Roman mile (1618yds; 1480m) or that the distance between Seabegs and Croy Hill so closely approximates to six Roman miles, makes it highly probable that mile-spacing was observed throughout. It must nevertheless be observed that even on Hadrian's Wall there was considerable variation in the Wall-mile (Birley, 1961, 101-3), and there is reason to believe that similar fluctuations may have occurred on the Antonine Wall. Thus, the distance between Kinneil fortlet and the eastern terminus of the Wall at Bridgeness is only 2⅔ Roman miles, and the interval separating the fortlets at Watling Lodge and Seabegs is 3⅔ Roman miles. As far as can be seen, these inequalities approximate to regular fractions of a Roman mile and it is possible that they represent an attempt by the original military surveyors to harmonise the Wall-mile, i.e. the interval separating two adjacent fortlets, with some non-standard feature which might otherwise disrupt the regularity of mensuration.

The difference between 'notional distance' and 'true distance' is a point to which we shall return later, but it is clear that the former had a real significance for the Roman builders. In the Augustan History's reference to the construction of Hadrian's Wall the length is given as eighty miles, which corresponds exactly, not with the measured distance of the Wall from Wallsend to Bowness, but with the eighty milecastle-intervals it occupies. Assessed in these terms, the Antonine Wall probably extended for forty-two Wall-miles (cf. Hanson & Maxwell, 1983, 122), or 41.66 Roman miles in lineal measurement.* The troops who occupied these mile-fortlets provided, as on Hadrian's Wall, the appropriate level of surveillance, while the protection of the new frontier line lay in the hands of garrisons occupying the Wall-forts.

The original estimate of how strong a force would be required to guard the Wall cannot be precisely determined, but the evidence of structural sequence in Wall-forts, as detailed above (pp. 142–7), might lead one to believe that, as first conceived, the garrison was to be housed in six or seven forts, all large enough to hold complete regiments and separated by inter-vals averaging 8.3 Roman miles – a closeness of spacing that matches the

*The lineal measurement exceeds the notional because in certain sectors of the Wall above-average fortlet-intervals appear to have predominated; the fact that, where this occurs, the excess distance often approximates to a third of a Roman mile, may suggest that the Hadrianic tripartite division of Wall-miles was also observed on the Antonine Wall.

deployment on Hadrian's Wall; these primary forts were Carriden (near the eastern end, but not actually on the Wall), Mumrills, Castlecary, Auchendavy or Bar Hill, Balmuildy, and Old Kilpatrick (Fig. **8.1**). The exceptionally long interval between Mumrills and Castlecary was evidently to be covered by the fort at Camelon, but it is odd that a similarly wide gap between Balmuildy and Old Kilpatrick does not appear initially to have given cause for concern, despite the vulnerable situation of this sector on the north side of both Clyde and Kelvin and immediately overlooked by the Kilpatrick Hills. In fact, if this density of deployment had been allowed to stand, the Antonine frontier posts would have been more widely spaced than the Agricolan *praesidia* on the same isthmus (see above p. 83), which would represent a curious reversal of the trend towards ever more intensive manning of defensive systems. In the event, it may have been an appreciation of the potential weakness of so thinly stretched a garrison that persuaded the Roman high command to supplement the primary forts with up to eleven smaller forts, thus reducing the interval between adjacent garrisons to a little over two Roman miles (cf.Fig. **7.3**). It appears likely that a majority of these secondary works were capable of

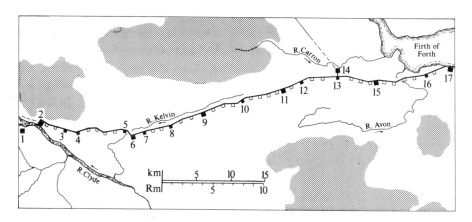

Fig. 8.1   The Antonine Wall in its early phase

1. Bishopton fort	10. Croy Hill fortlet
2. Old Kilpatrick fort	11. Castlecary fort
3. Duntocher fortlet	12. Seabegs Wood fortlet
4. Cleddans fortlet	13. Watling Lodge fortlet
5. Summerston fortlet	14. Camelon fort
6. Balmuildy fort	15. Mumrills fort
7. Wilderness fortlet	16. Kinneil fortlet
8. Glasgow Bridge fortlet	17. Carriden fort
9. Auchendavy fort.	

accommodating only sub-divisions of regiments, although a few, like Cadder, were garrisoned by whole units.

How long a time elapsed before work began on the secondary forts cannot be precisely determined. It has been claimed (Breeze & Dobson, 1976, 98-102) that the change of policy did not occur until the Wall-building programme – which was commenced at the eastern end – had reached as far west as the neighbourhood of Castlehill, midway between Kelvin and Clyde. However, while this assessment accords with the evidence from Duntocher, two miles to the west of Castlehill, where a free-standing fortlet was incorporated in the structure of a minor fort *before* the arrival of the legionary Rampart-builders (see above, p. 144), it conflicts with the evidence at Cadder and Rough Castle, where the Ditch-digging parties were aware of the need to have a causeway of undug ground opposite the north gate of each 'secondary' fort. It would seem likely, therefore, that the decision to increase the strength of the Wall-garrison was taken at a relatively early state, and the disparate evidence relating to such features as the relationship of fort installations to the Antonine Rampart, including the presence or absence of a primary causeway, can be explained as the result of the individual legionary construction-teams adopting different patterns of work with regard to the various structural elements of the Wall; for example, some may have elected to lay the Wall-base and erect the curtain before digging the ditch.

It will not escape notice, however, that once this principle is intro-duced, it becomes very difficult to be sure that the structural sequence outlined above is necessarily an indication of policy change and not merely the result of organisational convenience, the larger forts being built first because they represented the biggest task or because they were needed to house troops to guard the isthmus while construction-work proceeded on the running barrier. Moreover, as mentioned earlier, at Bearsden the original plan may quite possibly have been to construct a fort 3.6 acres (1.4 ha) in area, but at an early stage it was decided to reduce the fort to only 2.4 acres (0.9 ha) by drawing a rampart across the interior, and using the superfluous space as an annexe. If this was indeed the course of events – and it must be stressed that the reconstructed sequence is no more than hypothetical – in its original form Bearsden would have been the largest of the 'secondary' forts, larger even than the primary fort at Castlecary. It is unfortunate, therefore, that excavation failed to produce evidence to demonstrate the nature of the relationship between the fort and the Wall itself. At present the secondary character of the former can only be assumed, and the ghost of a possibility arises that Bearsden, only 3 Roman miles distant from the primary fort at Balmuildy, was also a primary installation; the close proximity of two primary works, it scarcely needs to be pointed out, could seriously weaken the case for the less strongly defended prototype of the Antonine Wall described above.

The reconstruction of the programme according to which the legionary work parties built the Wall itself presents problems which are just as intractable as those related to its planning. Once again the main difficulty lies in the defects of the material evidence. We know, or can deduce from the structural evidence already cited, that the work of building the frontier proceeded from east to west. The main clues to its progress are provided by the temporary camps that accommodated the labour-force and the monumental inscriptions which they erected to commemorate the completion of their work (Fig. **8.2**), but unfortunately neither body of evidence is anything like complete, and rarely do both categories coincide. The troops engaged in this work were drawn from all three legions then stationed in Britain: *legio II Augusta* from Caerleon in Wales, *legio VI Victrix* from York, and *legio XX Valeria Victrix* from Chester. Only the first mentioned was present in anything like full strength, the others being represented by detachments or vexillations.

The clearest guide to their activities is provided by the Distance Slabs, elaborately embellished inscriptions which record the length of barrier completed and the identity of the building party. Altogether nineteen or twenty examples are known, all but three having been found in the western portion of the Wall, between Eastermains (near Kirkintilloch) and Old Kilpatrick. A similar number of legionary labour camps, ranging from 3.5 acres (1.4 ha) to 7.9 acres (3.2 ha) in area, have been detected in the vicinity

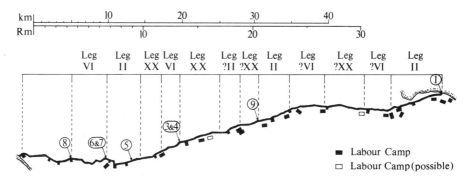

Fig. 8.2   Distribution of Distance Slabs and labour camps on the Antonine Wall with possible legionary building sectors between Castlehill fort and the E terminal.

of the Wall as a result of aerial survey; ironically, all but three of these are located in the eastern portion of the Wall lying between Kirkintilloch and Bridgeness (Fig. **8.2**). Nevertheless, despite the mutually exclusive nature of their distribution patterns, recent research (cf. Hanson & Maxwell, 1983, 104–36) has shown that it is possible to combine their respective testimony to produce alternative allocation of legionary work-sectors.

Of the easternmost stint there can be no doubt, since it is the only one to be confirmed by both labour-camps and Distance Slab. It stretched from Bridgeness, just above the shore of the Firth of Forth, to the River Avon, a distance of 4⅔ Roman miles. The relevant Slab, found at Bridgeness in 1868, is the largest and most handsome of the series; it records the construction of 4652 paces of the frontier (each Roman mile was a thousand paces long), by the troops of the Second Legion, who were housed, it would appear, in four temporary camps, disposed in pairs at either end of the sector. It has therefore been suggested (Maxwell, 1974, 329) that the work parties in each sector commenced at the ends and proceeded towards the middle, the two gangs in each half being allocated different tasks – one digging the ditch, for example, and the other building the Rampart; it cannot be demonstrated beyond doubt, however, that this quadripartite arrangement was actually practised, even in the easternmost Wall-length, and its application throughout the rest of the Wall may be presumed only in the most tentative manner. The two adjacent camps at Little Kerse and Polmonthill may seem to indicate that a similar deployment of work-parties occurred in the next sector to the west, but the pattern has not been detected convincingly elsewhere on the Wall; at Dullatur the two labour camps clearly represent successive and not contemporary operations, while most other camps occur as singletons.

On the other hand, it seems quite probable that every legionary work-length was marked by four Distance Slabs, two being erected at each end, one looking south, the other presumably in the northern face. The presence of clamp-holes in several of the slabs indicates that they were originally set in some form of masonry surround, where they would present a most handsome and imposing appearance (cf. Fig. **8.3**). Indeed, their importance is indicated by the manner in which they were treated at the end of either the first or second Antonine occupation, for it would appear that some, and perhaps all, were laid to rest in specially-dug holes, possibly to protect them from desecration by native hands after the Roman army had left Scotland. The discovery of at least two examples on the *north* side of the Barrier seemingly confirms that some were indeed set into the northern face. The work of building the frontier line which these Slabs record – the inscriptions show us that the Romans called it *opus valli* – was measured, as we have seen, in Roman miles. Within the individual legionary sectors the work would have been divided into smaller lengths allocated to cohorts and centuries; on Hadrian's Wall it is the smaller units' building-records, the centurial stones, that have survived, and their distribution has allowed scholars (e.g. Stevens, 1966) to reconstruct in some detail the internal organisation of the legionary parties. Such evidence is lacking in the Antonine Wall, but it is gradually beginning to appear that the method of allocation within the different vexillations may have approximated to the Hadrianic model. The recognition that there was a regular mile-fortlet system on the northern barrier has been instrumental in persuading scholars of this, for it is clear that on Hadrian's Wall the intervals between the minor installations, that is, the milecastles and turrets, were used as units of measurement, each being one third of a mile long; moreover, as the sites of milecastles and turrets had been selected and marked, and in some cases the actual structures built, before the Wall-building vexillations arrived on the scene, they could readily have served as reference points for the allocation of tasks.

Fig. 8.3 The Distance Slab found at Summerston; the goddess Victory decorates the eagle standard of the Twentieth Legion, flanked by two bound prisoners.

Although no structures corresponding in regularity or form to the Hadrianic turrets have so far been recognised on the Antonine Wall, it is curious that third-of-a-mile measurements, or close approximations thereto, figure in so many of the Distance Slabs; the Bridgeness Slab is a case in point. That the occurrence of these fractions in the recorded Wall-lengths may point to the existence of undiscovered installations is not entirely impossible. Such installations, if they existed, together with the mile-fortlets would have been constructed by some legionary work-party charged with the building of the adjacent length of Wall; and, as it seems probable that the Antonine Wall mile-fortlets, like the Hadrianic mile-castles, belonged to one or the other of two structural types, which may be ascribed to individual legions, our increasing knowledge about the position and plan of mile-fortlets should also help us identify the Wall builders where Distance Slabs are lacking. At present it looks as if the Twentieth Legion built short-axis fortlets, (those in which the axis at right angles to the Wall is shorter than the axis lying parallel to the Wall) and the Second Legion built 'long-axis' fortlets, while the type constructed by the Sixth Legion has still be be determined (cf. Keppie, 1982). Thus the long-axis fortlets at Kinneil, Seabegs Wood, Croy Hill, and Wilderness Plantation indicate that the adjacent stretches of Wall were the work of either the Second or Sixth Legion. In the case of Kinneil and Wilderness Plantation, the evidence of the Distance Slabs confirms that it was indeed the Second Legion, and as the primary fort at Castlecary was probably built by the Second Legion, the sector between it and the fortlet of Seabegs was possibly also that Legion's work.

Using such fragments of evidence it is possible to design hypothetical reconstructions of the proposed and actual Wall-building programme (Fig. 8.2), but the number of variable factors makes it difficult to say how close to reality any of these schemes may come. The existence of a Distance Slab of the Twentieth Legion, for example, recording the completion of three Wall-miles somewhere in the eastern half of the frontier (Macdonald, 1934, 365; Keppie, 1979, no.2) might tempt one to assume that the Second Legion work in the Castlecary area extended between the temporary camps of Tollpark and Dalnair, which are approximately three Wall fortlet - intervals apart, thus balancing an equal sector of the Twentieth Legion on one side or the other of Tamfourhill camp, which lies adjacent to the short-axis fortlet at Watling Lodge. The fact, moreover, that the presumed camp at Langton on the eastern outskirts of Falkirk – corresponding to the 'great fort' mentioned by Pont (Sibbald, 1707, 30) – bisects the six Wall-mile sector between Watling Lodge and the River Avon, might seem to provide cogent support for this proposition. On the other hand, measurement on the 1:2500 map makes it reasonably clear that the distance between the Avon and Watling Lodge is 6.333 Roman miles, while the three Wall-miles between Seabegs and Watling Lodge actually cover 3.666 Roman miles. Do the lengths recorded on the Distance Slabs refer to actual or notional distances? We do not yet know.

Even in the western half of the Wall there is considerable room for doubt. Macdonald's attempt to correlate the findspots of the Slabs with real ground-measurement (1934, 359–400) can now be seen to require revision, not least because he considered that those portions of the Rampart forming the northern defences of Wall-forts in this sector ought to be deducted from the given length, whereas nowadays we should allow this manipulation only in the case of primary forts. Moreover, the probability that in the sector between Castlehill and Eastermains, if not beyond, the distances recorded are in notional Wall-miles with no allowance made for the lineal measure taken up by Wall installations (even including primary forts) would seem to indicate that these sectors were built as originally planned and were not, as Macdonald thought, re-allocated hastily after a major disruption of the building scheme. The disruptive influence was identified by Macdonald as the basalt rock of Croy Hill, which he thought had so delayed the ditch-digging teams in this sector that the whole programme had slipped out of phase. While accepting that this particular task must have been exceptionally arduous, possibly demanding more time and effort than had initially been allowed, we need not assume that its effect was so serious, for it seems improbable that preliminary reconnaissance had not alerted the Roman engineers to the difficulties likely to be encountered here.

To put matters briefly, the evidence of temporary camps, Distance Slabs, and mile-fortlets may be combined to support Macdonald's contention that the Sixth Legion built the sector between Castlehill and East Millichen, and the Second Legion built the next stint to the east, both constructing three and two-thirds notional Wall-miles of the barrier. However, the distance between the easternmost end of the last-named stint and the findspot of the next Slabs amounts to four Wall miles, or four and a third Roman miles, and consequently the Slabs of the Twentieth Legion recording the completion of three and two-thirds Wall-miles may refer to the sector on the east side of Eastermains, which would have extended as far as the presumed fortlet at Girnal Hill, midway between Croy Hill and Bar Hill. Of the intervening sector to the west of Eastermains, the easternmost portion would thus have been built by the Sixth Legion, who also erected a Distance Slab at Eastermains, unfortunately with the sector-length unspecified; the identification of a labour camp at Easter Cadder could indicate that this measured about two or two and a third Wall-miles.

It is in the final sector, between Castlehill and the River Clyde, that the regular allocation of the construction-work appears, at first sight, to have broken down. The ten surviving Distance Slabs which refer to work in these parts record the measurements in feet instead of paces, as on the Slabs from sectors to the east of Castlehill. Moreover, as shown in the accompanying Table, the distances are no longer approximations to the third-of-a-mile curtain-lengths that have been recognised in the other Slabs.

TABLE 1: *Distances recorded (in Roman feet) on Slabs found between Castlehill and the Clyde*			
	Smaller Vexillation	*Larger Vexillation*	*Total*
Second Legion:	3271	4140	7411
Sixth Legion:	3240	4141	7381
Twentieth Legion:	3000	4411	7411
			22,203

There has been, however, an obvious attempt to maintain parity in the total amount of work assigned to each legion, although it seems curious that this should have failed so narrowly in the case of the Sixth Legion. A different picture is presented when the same figures are viewed in the context of the situation obtaining when the Rampart began to be built in this sector. As noted above (p. 144) the evidence at Duntocher and Cleddans makes it clear that, before the Wall-builders set to work, the fortlets and forts had already been constructed; the Rampart formed by their defences should therefore be added to the totals credited to the Wall-builders. As Fig 8.4 reveals, when this addition is made several of the sectors, or combinations of sectors, approximate very closely to standard fractions of a Wall-mile. The westernmost, constructed by the Twentieth Legion, must represent the allocation of a complete Wall-mile, in other words the interval between two mile-fortlets, yet as the map shows, the presumed position of the Mount Pleasant fortlet is some two-thirds of a mile from the bank of the Clyde, so that this sector terminated, on the east, at a position which on Hadrian's Wall would have been occupied by a turret.

The easternmost of the two sectors built by the Sixth Legion likewise approximates to a significant fraction, two-thirds of a Roman mile, while the section shared by the westernmost parties of the Second and the Sixth amounts to one and a half miles. Although the latter figure may not seem to accord with the Hadrianic 'turret' interval, it should be borne in mind that this is the sum of two-thirds of a mile and five sixths of a mile, and it may be of significance that the Second Legion sector falls short of the lower by only 62.3 ft, whereas the Sixth Legion sector (including the presumed 85 ft frontage of Carleith fortlet) exceeds the larger by almost precisely the same length. Similarly the addition of the front of Duntocher fortlet to the combined Second Legion sectors makes it evident that a total length of one and a half Wall-miles was originally to be allocated, the eastern end of the joint sector lying one third of a mile west of Cleddans fortlet. In the event, the building of the secondary fort at Duntocher probably displaced the terminus by 142 ft or so. (Incidentally it may be noted that the omission from the Wall reckoning of the frontages of both short-axis fortlets at Cleddans and Duntocher provides support for the theory that neither the Second nor the Sixth Legion was responsible for building fortlets of this type.) If the initial plan had been adhered to, however, the east end of the adjacent Sixth Legion sector would have been situated a third of a Wall-mile east of Cleddans fortlet, again at a turret position.

It may thus be seen that, taking mile-fortlets only into consideration, each legionary party was expected to be responsible for one and a half Wall-miles. When the Distance Slabs total is added to the combined frontages of Old Kilpatrick and Duntocher forts, the resulting sum of 23,169 Roman feet is only 161 ft. short of 4⅔ Wall-miles. Measurement on the 1:2500 map, with due allowance made for the loss entailed by varying relief, suggests very strongly that the total lineal measurement from the point on Castlehill (where the easternmost Distance Slab of the Twentieth Legion was found) is very close to 4⅔ Roman miles; the shortfall of 161 ft

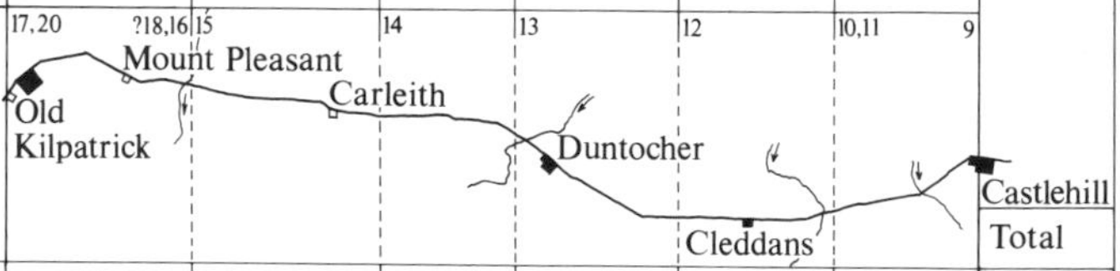

Legion	XX	VI	II	II	VI	XX	
	17,20 ?18,16 15 Old Kilpatrick Mount Pleasant	Carleith	14	13 Duntocher	12	10,11 9 Cleddans Castlehill	Total
Distance Slab length (ft.)	4411	4141	3271	4140	3270*	3000	22,233
Fort frontage (ft.)	c.484	—	—	c.142	—	—	626
Fortlet frontage (ft.)	2 x 85	85	—	85	85	½ x 85	468
Total (feet)	5065	4226	3271	4367	3355	3043	23,327
Total (Roman miles)	1 (+65ft.)	1½ (−3 ft.)		1½ (+222ft.)		⅔(−290ft.)	4⅔(−6ft.)

Fig. 8.4 Archaeological data for the Clyde-Castlehill sector.

represents an error of less than one percent and may not therefore be significant. What should be considered of some significance, however, is the apparently scrupulous attention to metrical detail that was exercised by the Roman legionaries at work on the Antonine Wall. As an indication of the virtues which, for more than six centuries, made the Roman army a force to be reckoned with, it deserves as much publicity as the records of their triumphs in battle.

In view of the changing pattern of design and construction described in the foregoing pages, it will be no surprise to readers to learn that there is no single theory about the length of time taken to build the entire Wall. Without any strain on the imagination one might sketch in any number of scenarios to fit the isolated facts relating to this problem. Although it is possible to suggest work-rates which might be achieved by labourers without the benefit of industrial machinery (cf. Hanson & Maxwell, 1983, 132–4), the need to press on with the work for military reasons, or conversely the inability to deploy sufficient manpower for the same reasons, could have materially affected the time taken on the job. The construction of Hadrian's Wall commenced in AD 122 and was still continuing on parts of the frontier-line in 137, although much of the curtain may have been in service in one form or another by 128. However, there were considerable changes of policy and structural additions on the southern barrier – the building of the Vallum, the relocation of the forts, the extension of the curtain from Newcastle to Wallsend – which may have had echoes, but no precise parallels, in the development of the Antonine Wall. We must presume that at least some of the lessons learnt on Hadrian's Wall had been taken to heart.

The earliest stage at which it is reasonable to expect that work could have started at the Forth-Clyde isthmus, is the successful termination of the campaigns of Lollius Urbicus. Presumably it was for this victory that Antoninus Pius was given his second imperial acclamation in 142 and received the congratulations of Fronto (*belli in Britannia confecti laudem*) c. 143. At any rate, from the evidence of the inscriptions on the Wall, only two of which mention Urbicus as governor (*R.I.B.* 2191–2 from Balmuildy), it would appear that by 142, the last year of Urbicus's governorship, only the primary forts had been built. The identity of his successor can only be guessed. The curious erasure of the titles presumed to be those of a governor on the Ingliston milestone (Fig. **8.5**) has recently been taken to indicate (Maxwell, 1984c) that the governor so stigmatised was Q. Cornelius Priscianus condemned as a *hostis publicus* in AD 145 while serving in Hispania Tarraconensis. There is a strong possibility that

Priscianus had been governor of Britain in 142–5 (Birley, 1981, 115–16) and accordingly it may have been his hand that steered the Antonine Wall through to completion. If that is so, it could have been the new governor who injected new ideas, in the form of additional Wall-garrisons, into the original plan, perhaps a token of the disruptive effect he seems to have had a little later in his career! Such changes must have retarded the construction programme, extending it well into its third season, if not beyond.* On the other hand, it is possible to imagine that, given a frontier-length of 42 Wall-miles, it would have been administratively convenient and attractive to have divided the barrier into three annual stints of 14 miles, each to be equally divided between the three legionary building-parties. The Distance slab measurements from the Bridgeness-Avon and the Castlehill-Old Kilpatrick sectors (the latter having doubtless been intended to stand undivided) may appear to provide some support for this, since each sector appears to have been 4⅔ miles in length, but the available evidence is hardly conclusive.

However long the construction actually took, there is evidence that it was considered by the High Command to have gone on long enough. The subdivision of the sector between Castlehill and the Clyde was surely undertaken in order to inject some urgency into the work, the

Fig. 8.5

The two conjoined fragments of the Ingliston milestone recording road-construction early in the first Antonine period. The erased portion in the middle of the inscription may once have included the name of a governor subsequently disgraced, perhaps Cornelius Priscianus (AD ?142–145).

*The absence of Cornelius Priscianus's name from the Distance Slabs (like that of Urbicus) needs some explanation. Possibly they were not carved and erected until after 145, when mention of the disgraced governor would have been impolitic.

equality of the tripartite partition serving, as Macdonald pointed out long ago, to promote feelings of rivalry between the various gangs. There are signs that this feeling of urgency was experienced some time before the programme reached Castlehill, for it has been observed that to the west of Kirkintilloch the width of the Antonine Ditch is consistently less than the quoted norm; the majority of sections reveal a standard width of 20-25 ft (6.1-7.6m), approximately half the dimensions recorded in the central sector of the Wall. Since the digging of the Ditch represented the second largest item of manpower-expenditure in the Wall-building programme, such a reduction would have had a marked effect on work-rates. At the same time, one is tempted (by a spirit of mischief, perhaps) to ask whether the same reasoning should not also be employed to the evidence for narrowing of the Ditch in the sector, say, between Bridgeness and the Avon. Since it appears to be an almost independent limb of the mural frontier, covering a coastal area that was already well-protected by nature, it too could have been a late addition, not altogether unlike the extension at the east end of Hadrian's Wall between Wallsend and Newcastle. Indeed, apart from the narrow ditch, one might tentatively claim that the same interpretation would be supported by both the curious misalignment of the Wall-terminals on either bank of the River Avon and the run of Wall-miles, which appear to *commence* at the Avon; the fortlet at Kinneil lies almost exactly two Wall-miles east of the river, while the distance to the eastern terminus of the Wall is as much as 500 yds (450 m) short of five Wall-miles. Although this represents a surprisingly close structural parallel to the eastern extension to Hadrian's Wall, the real point in drawing attention to the situation is to demonstrate that, far from being an inert mass of archaeological data, the Antonine Wall, like all field-monuments, is capable of generating problems which will occupy the interest and professional time of archaeologists yet unborn.

9

The Antonine Occupation: Homes fit for heroes

THE FORTS OF ROMAN SCOTLAND have been mentioned on innumerable occasions in the foregoing pages, but usually because of their tactical or strategic significance. It scarcely needs to be said, but, in our preoccupation with either the broader sweep or the nicer details of history, it may be forgotten that forts were more than flags on a military planner's map. For the garrisons who maintained the peace on the north-westernmost frontier of Rome these forts were home. They were no temporary bivouacs amid strange peoples and alien landscapes, but long-term postings, which perhaps only trouble further up the line, or drafts required for a distant frontier war, or possibly even retirement or death might terminate before expected. Irksome the billets might be, hardly less so the men that shared them, but the barrack-hearth to which each soldier returned after sweltering fatigues, or the long boredom of the watch, or the desperate battling with snowdrifts on a midwinter patrol, warmed him with a keener flame than was ever lit with flint and steel. The troops that marched north under Lollius Urbicus at the beginning of the Antonine occupation could have spent a dozen or more years in the same fort, acclimatising themselves to the clear moorland air of upper Clydesdale, or the salty onshore breezes of the Firth of Forth, learning to tell the time from the sun's passage across the distant peaks of Caledonia or the broad shoulders of Tinto Hill. For these men the frontier zone became their adopted *angulus terrarum*, but the ties of sentiment would have been worth nothing without the underpinning of security. This the fort could provide in two obvious respects; by the strength of its defences, and the stores of food and water with which it was generously plenished.

Since each fort derived its defensive strength from the natural position it occupied as well as the artificial fortifications by which it was enclosed, the positions chosen by the Flavian engineers in the first century, whether under the direct guidance of Agricola himself or not, were, for the most part, entirely suitable for the purposes of the Antonine occupation. Only in cases when tactical considerations had changed (as at Easter Happrew in Upper Tweeddale, or Castle Greg on the bleak moors between Lothian and Clydesdale) or where an entirely new strategy was being followed (as in the whole of Strathmore, which later lay outside the province) were Agricolan foundations not reselected for occupation. On the sites to which a Roman garrison returned, however, the military installations were completely re-built, the defences being recast, and often in such a way as to render them even more formidable than before. By the end of the Antonine occupation, when possibly further lines of defence had been added to the circuit, the depth of the fortified zone surrounding the fort might present a bewilderingly complex appearance. Such a site is Ardoch, roughly midway along the road between Forth and Tay, which as we have already learned (pp. 118–19) played an important role in guarding the outermost frontier during the Flavian period.

Ardoch in its final form, presumably as it was maintained in the second Antonine period (AD 155–63), was defended, at least on the northern and eastern sides, by a single massive rampart and as many as five ditches (Fig. 9.1). The pioneering excavation of 1895 recovered a surprising amount of structural detail from the interior and produced a plan which may still serve as the basis for discussion of the site's development. Unfortunately the sort of evidence, particularly in terms of stratigraphy, which might have indicated the relationships of the different sets of buildings and defences was not sufficiently well understood at the time to allow the excavators to form their own conclusions about structural sequence. Nevertheless, some fifty years later O.G.S. Crawford, as the leading field-worker of his day, was moved to offer a tentative interpretation of the surviving earthworks (Crawford, 1949, 30–9), basing his judgement on a careful examination of the numerous details which the practised eye can still discern amidst the apparently incomprehensible complexity of this invaluable monument. His analysis, which has been followed by most who have subsequently written about the site (e.g. Breeze, 1979, 30–2; 1983, 224–36), may be summarised as positing a consistent reduction of the area of the fort. The defences of the earliest (Flavian) fort were indicated, in

Crawford's opinion, by the two outer ditches in the north and east sides; the particularly broad bank lying inside the ditches on the latter side was taken by Crawford to represent the surviving bulk of the Flavian east rampart. The succeeding Antonine fort was of about the same dimension from north to south, but about 80 ft (24.4 m) narrower, its northern side being represented by the detached length of rampart, which was left isolated in the midst of the northern ditch-system (Fig. 9.1, c), when the

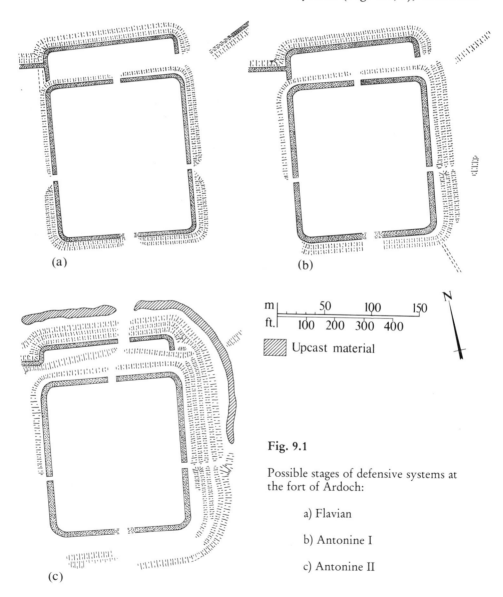

(a)

(b)

m | 50   100   150

ft. | 100 200 300 400

N

▨ Upcast material

(c)

Fig. 9.1

Possible stages of defensive systems at the fort of Ardoch:

a) Flavian

b) Antonine I

c) Antonine II

fort was again reduced in area and a new north rampart constructed some 120 ft (37m) to the south.

There are, however, several curious features which it is difficult to explain in the terms of this interpretation, and it may be constructive to examine these, if only to illustrate that the analysis of earthworks provides ample scope for the investigative fieldworker without recourse having to be made to excavation. Indeed, a critical scrutiny of the observable relationship of upstanding structural remains should form the first stage of any excavation, since it serves to generate those hypotheses whose sampling with the spade and trowel will modify, if not create, the main strategy of excavation. The possibility of the Flavian fort, in at least one phase, having been roughly coextensive with the main rampart of the surviving fort has already been argued (pp. 115–16). To recapitulate briefly, the presence of a relatively slight ditch lying in the space between the final rampart and its innermost ditch has been compared with similar occurrences on other multi-period sites, where the 'berm' ditch was identified as belonging to the earliest Flavian fortification. Moreover, it has been suggested that a meaningful and appropriate pattern of internal buildings may be fitted within the space enclosed by such defences. The alternative significance of the outlying works described by Crawford as the slighted remains of a Flavian rampart will be considered presently. For the moment, it will be sufficient to examine the nature of the isolated rampart, which is claimed to have been the northern side of the larger Antonine I fort.

Several features are immediately obvious to those examining the site on the ground, and by means of the plans and sections published in the 1897 report: firstly, the isolated northern rampart is less robust and less complex in structure than the innermost work; secondly, it does not appear to have been provided with the stone 'paving' beneath its forward lip which apparently ran round the entire perimeter of the latest rampart; and thirdly, the ditch lying immediately outside it appears originally to have been carried across the existing entrance gap without interruption. Now, if this was indeed the north side of the Antonine I fort (and possibly the Flavian too) one would have expected it to be more complex in section, particularly because the evidence of other Antonine I sites suggests that most of the major forts were the work of legionary craftsmen; it is only in the second Antonine period that 'auxiliary' workmanship — characterised, perhaps unfairly, as less neatly or less skilfully executed — is more commonly recognised. At Ardoch the application of such criteria would compel one to identify the innermost rampart, with its carefully laid stone base*, as

*Not a stone revetting-wall, as has been suggested (Breeze, 1983, 235).

belonging to the first Antonine period, leaving the outer work to be explained as the interior defence of an annexe, certainly used in the early Antonine occupation, but possibly originating in the time of Agricola (Fig. **9.1**, *a,b*). Such an enclosure would have provided an extra acre (0.4 ha) of usable space with a higher degree of security than was possible in the *procestrium*, the 25.5 acre (10.4 ha) polygonal enclosure lying to the north of the fort. There are various indications that the latter structure was also of early Flavian origin: most significantly, it appears to be transected on the east by the Roman road heading north to Strageath, which is arguably of Flavian date itself. The presence of an early temporary camp within the interior of the *procestrium*, (St Joseph, 1976, 19) not only supports this interpretation, but also suggests by reason of its state of preservation that the outer area was not long or intensively used; there would thus have been all the more need for the smaller annexe.

There is, however, an even better reason for believing that the earlier Antonine fort did not extend as far as the outlying rampart: the course of the ditches at the north-east angle of inner work (Fig. **9.1**,*c*): the three innermost lines all begin to curve round to the west at this point, but had they originally continued on to the east angle of the outwork, their course would have almost certainly driven straight ahead and there would have been no need to extend the irregular oblique ditch, from the interior of the presumed annexe. We may therefore assume that at least the two outer ditches of this trio terminated here, at the southern entrance to the annexe, probably very much as they had done in the Flavian period. The two outermost ditches of all, on this analysis, would belong to the very last structural phase, at the beginning of the second Antonine period, their course adapted to the pre-existing defensive complex; this conformity may be recognised at three points in particular − at the north-east angle, where the ditches have been drawn round the earlier annexe entrance; at the south-east angle, where the inner member of the pair skirts the southern terminal of the outermost Antonine I ditch; and at the east gate. At this last point the outermost ditch is extended outwards across the direct line of approach in what has been described as a *clavicula*. Close inspection of the ditch-extension suggests very strongly, however, that this is not the case, the feature more closely resembling a *titulum* or isolated short stretch of ditch, provided as a protection for an earlier set of defences, probably those of the first Antonine fort (Fig. **9.1**,*b*). The slight change of alignment that can be seen in the outer pair of ditches between the angle and the entrance being necessitated by the desire to incorporate the *titulum* in the new system.

It will thus be seen that it is perfectly possible to construct an alternative hypothesis about the structural relationships of the earthworks at Ardoch, using a combination of the surviving remains and the early excavation evidence. There is an attractive advantage to the newly offered version in that it provides a more credible explanation of the height of the combs of ground lying immediately inside the outermost pair of ditches, namely that it represents the accumulation of upcast from the ditches of the Antonine I (and Flavian) fort, spread successively further and further out from the fort to which it related. Therein also lies the possible explanation of the enigmatic outer bank, whose apparently sinuous course has led many to presume that it is of post-Roman, possibly mediaeval date. But it would perhaps be more sensible to suggest that it resulted from the landscaping of the site during the final reconstruction, and that it may conceivably indicate that the final touches were never added. A comparison of the nature of the ground surface on either side of this bank reveals that there has been rigorous levelling between it and the outermost ditch, but the terrain immediately outside is hummocky and of almost unaltered natural profile. Moreover, the wide gap on the north, opposite the entrance through the fort's defensive system, and the inswinging line north of the east gate to avoid encroachment upon the road, make it appear that some attempt was made to respect existing installations. Only excavation will confirm or disprove these hypotheses, but the superficial evidence suggests that even this, the best-preserved and most visited of Roman sites in Scotland has much to tell us about fort-building in the province as a whole.

The Antonine Wall fort of Rough Castle, (Fig. **9.2**), the subject of yet another of the pioneering excavations of 1895–1905, furnishes an interesting parallel and contrast to Ardoch. When first examined, the earthwork complex, which is the best preserved of any on the Wall, revealed a wealth of structural evidence, doubtless first uncovered under the watchful eye of clerk of works Mackie (see above, pp. 13–16) and carefully recorded by the equally painstaking Buchanan. The overall plan was, however, accepted without specific enquiry into the relationship of its component parts, as at Ardoch. Thus, the peculiarities of the enclosing rampart were duly noted and drawn, Buchanan observing (1905, 460) that the main fort rampart, some 20 ft (6m) in average thickness, was 'supplemented by varying margins' at the front and rear, which increased the thickness to as much as 35 ft (10.7 m); no attempt was however made to explain the intricacies of the ditch-system enclosing the series of annexes and enclosures to the east of the fort. Almost thirty years passed before the problem was considered again. This time it was Sir George Macdonald, whose limited excavations convinced him 'that the fort rampart had been uniformly increased in thickness, but in stages which coincided with the progressive diminution of the usable space within the annexe' (cf. Macdonald, 1934, 219–26). Macdonald also pointed up the complicated history of the minor enclosure located by the earlier excavators in the north-west corner of the annexe; in his opinion, it was used in at least one phase as a specially secure stores compound.

There matters rested until 1957, when the Ministry of Works, faced by the need to evaluate the structural state of the site prior to improving its appearance for display to the public, embarked upon a five-year pro-gramme of investigation (MacIvor, Thomas & Breeze, 1980). As a result of these excavations it was possible to determine that the additions to the fort

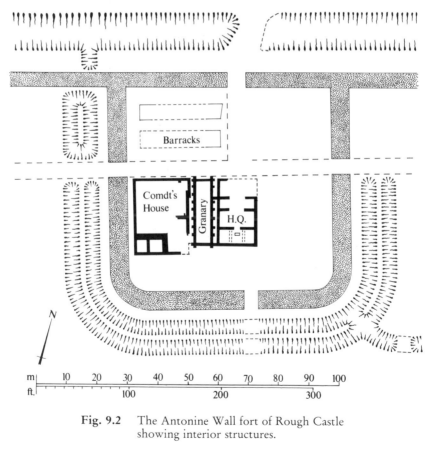

Fig. 9.2   The Antonine Wall fort of Rough Castle showing interior structures.

rampart were in reality two different features. That on the outer side was no more than a particularly elaborate re-metalling of the level platform between the rampart and the innermost ditch, while the thickening on the inner side was found to be localised to two sectors immediately north of the *via principalis*; the latter features were the remains of *ascensus*, staircases or ramps which gave access to the rampart-walk.

In addition to clarifying the obscurities of former reports, the most recent excavations recovered evidence of structures which had previously gone unnoticed. Buchanan's team, lacking the special sensitivity of a Thomas Ely, had failed to repeat the Ardoch clerk of works' achievement in identifying the traces of timber buildings. In consequence, the 1905 plan showed a blank space between the *via principalis* and the Antonine Rampart. As even the latest report comments on the difficulty in identifying the location of individual post-holes in this area, the inability of the early diggers to recover such fugitive evidence should be treated with understanding. In any event, it is in the nature of archaeological fieldwork and research constantly to be superseded by succeeding programmes of investigation, and only the irredeemably ignorant would lay it to the charge of any scholar that a future generation came to realise his limitations. There were in fact two categories of timber structures discovered during the 1957–61 excavations. Even the more permanent kind, identified as barracks, were recognised by nothing more tangible than the darker-coloured earth which had sifted into the holes once occupied by the uprights of the timber framework. Measuring approximately 98 ft (26.5m) long and from 19 ft to 21 ft 6 in (5.8-6.3 m) in width, such blocks cannot be other than sub-divided barracks – a device which, as noted at Inchtuthil, and possibly Ardoch (pp. 116–17) – might be employed to fit these long buildings into relatively confined areas. Conceivably the centuries of troops composing the garrison (the Sixth Cohort of Nervians is recorded here) were split into two parts, one being located on either side of the main north-south road, the *via praetoria*; in that case, the combined block-length would have been a maximum of about 42 m, a not inappropriate size for troops of an auxiliary infantry regiment. Consideration of the space available elsewhere in the fort suggests that, at most, another two half-blocks could have been accommodated behind the buildings of the central range; the entire complement would thus have been the equivalent of three full blocks, or exactly half the establishment of an infantry cohort. We may presume that most of the remainder will have been employed in manning the various minor Wall-installations in the vicinity of Rough Castle; between Castlecary and Falkirk it is probable that there were six mile fortlets, and at least four signalling-platforms, not to mention other works whose existence we may yet only guess at.

However, the barrack blocks were not the first structures to occupy the building-plot lying immediately to the south of the Antonine Rampart at Rough Castle. Apparently at an earlier stage a rectangular building of very slight construction, with an overall length of some 82 ft (25 m) and only 10 ft (3 m) wide stood in this position; it was surrounded by a shallow drip-trench and may have been of a tent-like structure. The purpose of such an ephemeral type of building is unknown, but its presence demonstrates the enormously complex pattern of constructional phases through which even a minor Roman site may have passed before taking on the appearance by which we know it today; it is the incidence of details like these that makes the formulation of theories about Wall-building-programmes and policies a decidedly hazardous operation. Yet these temporary hutments were not the earliest structures on the site, for Macdonald had found (1933a, 262 – 3) that there were lengths of ditch within the fort annexe, one of which extended northwards underneath the Antonine Wall itself, having been deliberately packed before the construction of the Wall began. A little way to the west of these lay the curious minor enclosure, first discovered by Buchanan and later re-examined by Macdonald; that it too belongs to an early phase of the fort's history is indicated by the fact that its presence is respected by the inner ditch on the east side of the fort, a relationship which was recognised by Macdonald. It was not until the excavation of Duntocher (Robertson, 1957) had revealed the relationship between an Antonine Wall fort and fortlet (p. 145) that another possible interpretation of the Rough Castle enclosure became apparent. As John Gillam was the first to point out, the two sites present in superficial plan a mirror-image of each other. Whether the Rough Castle structure is in fact a mile-fortlet, or whether the adjacent lengths of ditch represent the traces of an installation like those on Bar Hill and Croy Hill (Keppie, 1984; Hanson, 1979) that belong to the earliest constructional phases of the Wall, cannot yet be determined. But the fact that such questions can still be asked after almost ninety years of site-investigation and discussion amply demonstrates the continuing development and vitality of Wall-studies.

It remains to comment briefly on the tiny garrison at Rough Castle. The probability of this being a vexillation forming half of a 500-strong regiment of auxiliary infantry has already been mentioned, and the discovery of two inscriptions dedicated by the Sixth Cohort of Nervians identifies the parent unit during one of the two Antonine occupations. One of these inscriptions was a commemorative slab (*R.I.B.* 2145) recording the construction of the *principia* — a rare instance of an inscribed text actually specifiying the structure whose completion was thus celebrated; since the slab was found in a pit in the forecourt of the headquarters-building, it has been suggested that it was buried at the end of the last phase of occupation of Rough Castle, the work commemorated being the *repair* of the building at the beginning of that phase. Such an interpretation would accord well with the observation that secondary construction on most Antonine sites in Scotland, being generally of inferior quality, would more aptly be recognised as the handiwork of auxiliaries rather than legionaries. It may seem curious, therefore, that a sub-division of an auxiliary unit should have been commanded by a legionary centurion, but the altar dedicated to the goddess Victory, which was found in 1843 a little way to the south of the fort (*R.I.B.* 2144), records that the Nervians were under the command of Flavius Betto, centurion of the Twentieth Legion. The appointment of legionary centurions to the command of auxiliary units was not uncommon, although the officer in charge was customarily a prefect, a Roman citizen of equestrian rank serving in the first step of the *tres militiae*, the threefold military service requirement of all who entered upon public life. However, when a suitable candidate for the prefecture could not be found among the equestrians, the post might be filled by the secondment of a relatively senior centurion from a legion. In a situation where strategy demanded that regiments be subdivided, as on the Antonine Wall, there might obviously be a sudden demand for prefects which the normal sources could not supply.

On the other hand, it is possible that the intention from the very beginning was to assign such vexillations on the Wall to the command of legionary officers, Flavius Verecundus of the Sixth Legion at Westerwood fort and M. Cocceius Firmus of the Second Legion at Auchendavy being other possible examples. In support of this contention it may be instructive to compare the form and size of certain buildings of the central range of the fort with legionary structures. It has long been noticed that the *principia* (*a* on Fig. **9.2**), although the smallest identifiable member of this category on the Wall, nevertheless conformed in layout to the standard type, having a suite of smaller rooms at the rear and a courtyard (handsomely paved) at the front of the building. Attention has not been drawn, however, to the significance of its dimensions: 75 ft by 44 ft (23 m x 13.4 m) over the walls. As the accompanying diagram shows, this corresponds closely with the average size of a legionary centurion's quarters in the Flavian fortress at Inchtuthil (Fig. **9.3,2**); the specific example chosen for illustration is even more apt, as it was one of the two built separately in the temporary

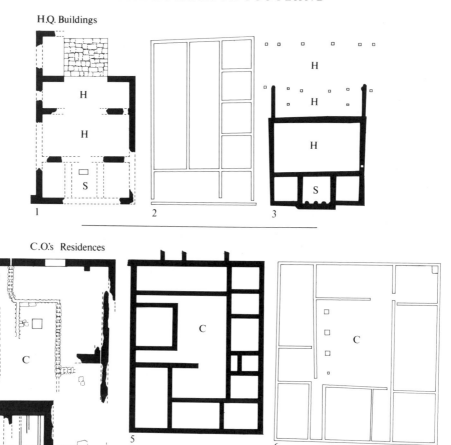

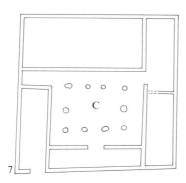

Fig. 9.3

The headquarters building and commanding officer's residence of Rough Castle and comparable buildings elsewhere:

1. Rough Castle *principia*
2. Building II, Officers' Compound, Inchtuthil
3. *Principia*, Hesselbach numerus fortlet, Upper Germany
4. Rough Castle *praetorium*
5. Centurion's quarters, first cohort, Caerleon
6. Centurion's quarters, first cohort, Inchtuthil
7. *Praetorium*, Hod Hill, Dorset. (H=Hall, C=Courtyard, S=*Sacellium*).

compound, possibly to serve as unit-offices for the guard-detachment stationed there (above, pp. 116–17). The Antonine Wall may thus furnish another analogy for the use of a standard building-plan for a purpose other than that for which it was designed, but in the case of Rough Castle, translated from timber into stone; the connexion with the Twentieth Legion in both instances may be significant.

It is surely, therefore, more than coincidental that the building identified as the commanding officer's residence, or *praetorium*, at Rough Castle (4 on Fig. **9.3**) should measure, as far as can be estimated, approximately 60 ft by 80 ft (18 m x 24 m) and have consisted of a suite of rooms ranged around a rectangular courtyard; despite the uncertainties inherent in the 1905 plan, the similarity in size and plan to the quarters of a centurion of the first cohort at Inchtuthil is most remarkable (Fig. **9.3**, 5–6). The provision of residential accommodation on this scale would have been amply appropriate for an up-and-coming legionary centurion, whether as befitting his position in the first cohort of the legion, as is most probable, or as an earnest of the further promotion for which the command at Rough Castle surely destined him.

That this practice of using legionary-derived structures was relatively widespread is suggested by two further instances, at Hesselbach in Upper Germany and Hod Hill in Dorset. In the former the garrison was a *numerus*, an auxiliary regiment of roughly half-cohort strength, examples of which multiplied on the German frontier in the late first and early second century, thus presumably much increasing the demand for commanding officers. It is perhaps not a coincidence, therefore, that the *principia* at Hesselbach (Fig. **9.3**,3) so closely mirrors in plan and proportions the Rough Castle equivalent. Similar conclusions might be drawn about the *praetorium* of Hod Hill fort, which dates to the early days of Claudian conquest. Here too the garrison appears to have been of an unusual composition, possibly attracting a legionary nominee as commander, and it would consequently have been entirely acceptable to model his personal residence (Fig, **9.3**,7) on the quarters of a centurion of the first cohort.

In conclusion it may be pointed out that there are other buildings at Rough Castle for which interesting parallels can be found. The fort's granary, (Fig. **9.2**), for example, is almost exactly the same size as that constructed in the first Antonine fort of Crawford; that, too, may have housed roughly half an auxiliary regiment.

The strategic and tactical context of the post at Crawford, discovered in 1938 but not excavated on any scale till quite recently (Maxwell, 1972), presents an interesting parallel with that of the Wall installations. Situated in the harsher lands of Upper Clydesdale, it guarded an important road-junction and river-crossing (see above, p. 86) on the south-western fringes of the territory of the Selgovae. In the first Antonine period the fort measured about 345 ft by 190 ft (105 m x 58 m) within the rampart, its capacity of 1½ acres (0.6 ha) being half as great again as that of Rough Castle. The greater size of the headquarters building, which was of orthodox plan, indicates that this was probably the 'home-base' of the regiment providing the garrison, although the comparatively small capacity of the granary indicates that not more than half the unit was ever stationed here; the rest of the troops were outposted probably in the fortlets which were disposed at intervals of some six or seven Roman miles along the roads that radiate out from this centre. The tentatively recon-structed plan of Crawford (Fig. 9.4) resembles that of Rough Castle in that the barracks, by reason of shortage of space, were built in two separate parts, each block measuring 65 ft by 28 ft (19.8 m x 8.5 m) over the walls; the overall area of each double block amounted to about 2,700 sq. ft. (250

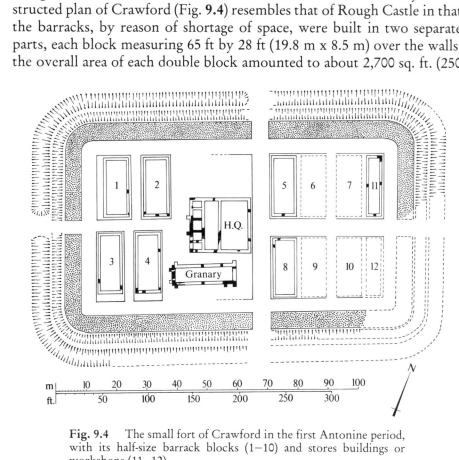

Fig. 9.4   The small fort of Crawford in the first Antonine period, with its half-size barrack blocks (1–10) and stores buildings or workshops (11–12).

sq. m), which approximates to the space theoretically available for each pair of buildings at Rough Castle. Although we may therefore presume that each pair of barracks was large enough to have accommodated a century, it would be wrong to assume that the presence of ten blocks indicates a garrison of five centuries, or some four hundred men; the restricted capacity of the granary alone would argue against this. A more reasonable interpretation would be that the regiment in garrison was half of a part-mounted cohort, which would have required eight half-size barracks and two half-size stables to house a complement of 180 infantrymen, together with 60 troopers and their mounts. It may be observed that an equitate regiment of this kind would have been particularly appropriate for deployment in the wide range of patrolling duties to be expected in this hilly terrain.

Some nine examples are known of the fortlets in which men of the Crawford garrison, and comrades from other forts, served on detached duty (Fig. 9.5). Scattered widely throughout the valleys of the Southern Uplands, they appear to vary considerably in size, and it has been suggested

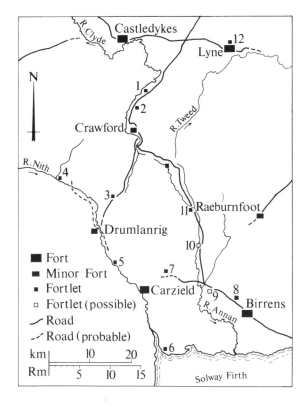

Fig. 9.5

Fortlets and 'parent' forts in SW Scotland in the Antonine period:

Fortlets

1. Lamington
2. Wandel
3. Durisdeer
4. Sanquhar
5. Barburgh Mill
6. Lantonside
7. Murder Loch
8. Burnswark
9. Torwood
10. Dalmakethar
11. Tassiesholm
12. Redshaw Burn.

(Maxwell, 1977) that this variation may reflect not only the size of the individual garrisons but also the type of unit to which they belong. For example, excavation at the fortlet of Barburgh Mill in Nithsdale (Breeze, 1974) showed that the garrison had consisted of a century of auxiliary infantry housed in a pair of barrack blocks, as at Crawford, although in this case the buildings were constructed wholly of timber. The total area provided by this double block approaches 3150 sq. ft. (290 sq. m), appreciably more than the capacity available at Crawford. Moreover, when Crawford was re-occupied in the second Antonine period (AD 158 – 163), the individual blocks appear to have been increased in length, the internal area provided by a pair then amounting to about 3,500 sq. ft. (330 sq. m). It is extremely probably that these differences reflect the observed tendency for the centuries of larger regiments to be provided with more generous accommodation (cf. Breeze & Dobson, 1969, 27-31). Thus the fortlets at Barburgh Mill and Tassiesholm with an internal area of 9070 sq. ft. and 9750 sq. ft (0.08 ha and 0.09 ha) respectively were probably manned by centuries based respectively at the recently discovered fort of Drumlanrig (Maxwell & Wilson, 1987, 16-17), where air photographs indicate the presence of larger barracks, or at Birrens, where a part-mounted milliary regiment was in garrison; Wandel and Redshaw Burn, on the other hand, the fortlets closest to Crawford, are both about 3,700 sq. ft. (0.03 ha) in area, from which one would deduce that their garrisons were about half a century, housed in barracks, of the smaller 'quingenary-regiment' type.

It has already been shown (above, pp. 118 – 21) that the troops in the fortlets probably outposted in turn part of their strength to man the watch-towers, whose surveillance and signalling-duties completed the chain of supervision over the Roman arteries of communication and the doings of the Border tribesmen. Thus, whether arranged along the mural barrier or keeping the peace in the seclusion of the upland glens, the standard pattern of major base, fort, fortlet, and tower was adapted or extended to suit the needs of the occasion. However, it would seem that the situation in the south-west eventually changed so much that it was no longer necessary or possible to maintain the smaller intermediate links of this system. When the Romans briefly withdrew from Scotland (c. AD 155), the fortlets and towers were abandoned for good. Although it is possible that they had failed to provide the required level of security, the apparent absence of permanent garrisons in the analogous mile-fortlets on the Antonine Wall during the same period probably points to a more general cause, the most likely being shortage of manpower.

As it would be inappropriate to close any consideration of Roman achievements in Scotland on such a dying note, the final pages of this book will be devoted to a brief account of the class of installations which must have made the deepest impression on the native Britons — the stone-walled forts; not that building in stone was by any means an unknown craft in native society, rather the reverse, particularly in the Atlantic Province, where the ability to construct drystone fortifications like brochs and duns was based upon a tradition that went back to the Neolithic period. The impressive novelty of the Roman skill was that it comprehended not only the cutting and shaping of stone, but also the knowledge of the principles of engineering and architecture which facilitated the rearing of structures that partook equally of practical elegance and durability. There was, too, a masterly appreciation of the logistical problems — the location of suitable building-materials, their transport from the source to the building-site, and the maintenance of an adequate work force.

To the best of our knowledge there were only five stone-walled military posts in Scotland : the Flavian legionary fortress at Inchtuthil ; the two Antonine Wall forts at Castlecary and Balmuildy; and the Antonine forts at Cramond and Newstead. The fact that the Inchtuthil base was possibly unique in Britain at the time of its construction makes the identification with the Ptolemaic place-name *Pteroton Stratopedon (Pinnata Castra* in Latin) almost unavoidable (but cf. Rivet & Smith, 1979, s.v.; *contra* Frere, 1980): the suggested meaning 'fortress with stone merlons' can only refer to the 6000-ft perimeter of Strathmore conglomerate with which the legionary base was walled (see above, pp. 100–1). The visual effect as the rising and setting sun took 'the new-cut ashlar' must have been almost literally stunning to native onlookers. Excavation by Professors Richmond and St Joseph (Pitts & St Joseph, 1985, 61-76) showed that the Wall, which was 5 ft (1.3 m) thick, had rested on a foundation of clay and cobbles and had been backed by a rampart 13 ft (4 m) thick. Its height is unknown but 12 ft (3.7 m) would not have been impossible (Fig. **9.6,***a*). When the fortress was evacuated in AD 86/7 the outer revetting wall was, as we have learned, deliberately dismantled and the defences slighted, with the result that little of the structure now remains in position.

Much more is known about the stone-built forts on the Antonine Wall. At Balmuildy (Fig. **9.6,***b*) the fort wall was based upon a cobble foundation 9 ft (2.7 m) wide, its inner face 1½ ft (0.45 m) from the rear edge of the foundation trench. A chamfered course, possibly the second, further reduced the thickness to 7 ft (2.13 m) and the Wall presumably rose vertically above this to the level of the wall-walk at a height of about 10-12 ft

(3-3.7 m); at this level there was doubtless a projecting string course surmounted by a crenellated breastwork 5-6 ft (1.5-1.8 m) in maximum height; the estimates of height are based upon the assumption that the level of the Wall walk would coincide roughly with that of the keystone of the arching above the fort entrance (see below, p. 186).

Similar structural evidence was recovered at Castlecary (Fig. **9.6**,*c*), where once again the faithful record left by Mungo Buchanan has provided later generations with a wealth of detail. In this case, a clay-packed cobble foundation 9 ft (2.7 m) wide and 9 in (0.22 m) deep was deemed sufficient. This was overlaid by a solid foundation course of exceptionally large stones

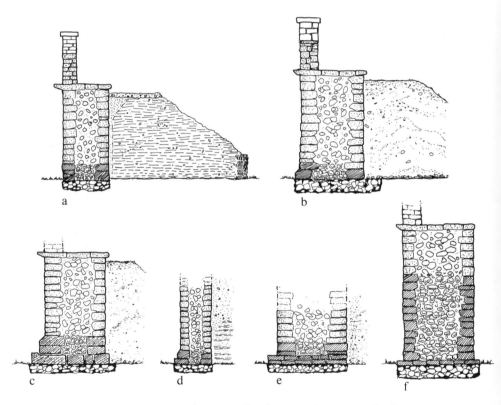

Fig. 9.6   Sections of stone walls of Roman forts in Scotland:

a) Flavian legionary fortress Inchtuthil
b) Antonine Wall fort Balmuildy
c) Antonine Wall fort Castlecary
d) 2nd-century fort Cramond
e) 2nd-century fort Newstead
f) Hadrian's Wall (narrow gauge); scale *c*.1:125.

to a maximum thickness of 8 ft (2.4 m); above this, and offset to front and rear by at least 6 ins. (0.15 m), was the lowest course of the superstructure which comprised an inner and outer face containing a rubble core held together with lime-mortar. Immediately above this again a chamfered course at the front of the wall reduced the thickness to about 6 ft 6 ins (2 m), and it is to be presumed that both faces then rose vertically to the level of the sentry-walk. Despite the sheer massiveness of the fabric employed in the wall, however, perhaps the most remarkable indication of the skills possessed by the Roman builders is the evidence of the attention they paid to detail: this manifests itself especially in the treatment of the foundation plinth, the outermost 9 ins (0.23 m) of whose upper surface is raised one inch (25mm) above the level of the rest of the stone – the purpose being to prevent outward movement of the lowest course of outer facing-stones immediately above it. The similarity in construction between the walls of Castlecary and Balmuildy is probably not accidental, for we know that the Second Legion was engaged in Antonine building-work at both, and was certainly employed on the defences of the latter (*R.I.B.* Nos. 2191-2).

The defences at Cramond were much slighter (Fig. **9.6,***d*), the wall being only 3ft 7 in (1.09 m) thick in its upper portion. Yet the treatment of its foundations recalls that observed at the last two examples, and although the inscribed slab recording work of the Second Legion builders cannot be closely dated, it is tempting to see their hand in the Antonine fort wall. (Rae & Rae, 1974, 169-73). Based on a foundation trench packed with sandstone chippings there was a scarcement course 4 ft (1.2 m) thick, above which the outer face was set back 3 in. (76mm), a chamfer reducing the thickness by a further 2 in (51 mm); from the lowest course upwards the wallcore was of rubble held together with lime-mortar.

At Newstead, where the building was presumably undertaken by a party from the Twentieth Legion, the foundations were of a different kind. Their precise nature cannot be determined from the unsatisfactory sections and confusing verbal account published in the report (Curle, 1911, plan III and p. 33), but it would appear that upon the customary cobble-packed foundation trench, and appreciably overlapping it, there had been laid two scarcement courses of red sandstone blocks, roughly shaped. On this lay the lowest course of the wall proper, which consisted of a long hammer-dressed facing stones only 4½ ins. (0.11 m) high; it was offset at least 1 ft (0.3 m) from the front of the foundation, and above it the outer face of the wall rose vertically, its fabric composed of larger, more quadratic hammer-dressed blocks, decorated externally with diamond brooching. There was no evidence of a chamfered course comparable to that at the last three sites, and the wall-core appears to have been bonded with clay mortar. With the exception of the last feature, the wall at Newstead was closely comparable in profile and dimensions with the Narrow Wall sector of the Hadrianic frontier (Fig. **9.6**,*e*,*f*).

Not that this similarity should cause any surprise, for one of the last tasks upon which the legionary working parties may have been engaged before they were summoned to participate in the Antonine campaigns was the re-building in stone of the Turf Wall sector of the Tyne-Solway barrier. It should not be forgotten, however, that with the exception of the wall at Castlecary, all the examples described above were backed by a bank of earth, clay, or turf. At Newstead the bank, representing the re-used rampart of the preceding Flavian-Trajanic fort, was as much as 38 ft (11.6 m) thick; at Balmuildy it was reckoned to be some 20 ft (6 m) thick, and at Cramond 23 ft (7 m); the purpose of such a feature was twofold – to provide greater strength and stability to the thinner walls and, just as important, give readier access to the wall-head than would have been possible by using the sentry-walk alone; the width of the latter would probably not have exceeded 6 ft (1.8 m) even on the most massive examples and must surely have been less than 3 ft (0.9 m) at Cramond. At Castlecary, where the absence of a bank precluded such ease of access, we may imagine that wooden staircases, set at intervals along the back of the Wall would have been used to supplement the normal approaches from ground level through gate-towers and angle-turrets. The free-standing internal wall which cut off the westernmost third of the fort of Newstead in the first Antonine period was only 5 ft 6 in (1.6 m) thick at its base and may not have incorporated even a sentry-walk. Since its purpose was to separate the quarters of the vexillation of the Twentieth Legion from those of the auxiliary cavalry detachment which shared the fort with them, it may be reckoned that such provision was in any case superfluous. Nevertheless, that so robust a line of demarcation should have been considered necessary speaks volumes about the gulf that lay between the auxiliary and legionary elements of the Roman army.

It has already been shown, in the brief account of temporary camps, (above, pp. 38–67) that Roman military engineers deemed the entrances the weakest point of a defensive perimeter, protecting them with elaborate patterns of *titulum* and *clavicula*. The same concern is naturally demonstrated in their treatment of the entrances of the permanent forts, the peculiarities of some of the Agricolan examples, which were built of timber, having been described in an earlier chapter (pp. 89–90). It is unfortunate that none of the entrances of the stone-walled forts has been excavated in recent times, but the fragmentary record that survives is never-theless sufficient to show that these were architectural creations of some pretension. At Newstead the remains had been robbed to their foundations, and probably because of the relative denudation, no large-scale plans were provided in the 1911 excavation report. Nevertheless, it is again possible from a conflation of the verbal record and site-plan to produce a sketch of the ground plan of at least two entrances, sufficient at least to show how imposing they must have been.

The east gate foundations are those of a single-portal entrance (Fig. **9.7,** c) measuring about 12 ft (3.7 m) between the passage-walls, the effective width doubtless being narrowed to about 10 ft (3 m) by imposts which carried the springing of the single arch. The entrance was flanked on either side by towers at least 24 ft (7.3 m) deep and about 14 ft (4.3 m) wide, whose rearward portions contained guardrooms at ground-level. Not enough is known of the other gates in the perimeter wall to make it possible to discuss their form, but the internal cross-wall which separated the legionaries from the auxiliaries appears to have incorporated a gateway of similar design to that just described, the main difference being that it was slightly smaller and flanked by towers which projected some 3 ft (0.9 m) in front of the line of the outer face.

The north gate at Balmuildy, which has furnished the greatest body of

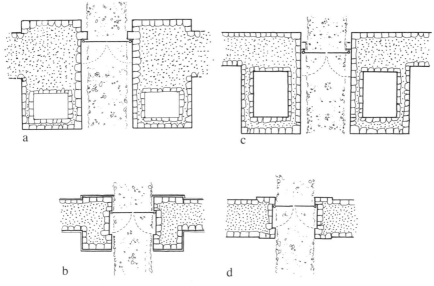

Fig. 9.7   Gateways of stonewalled forts:

a) Balmuildy   c) Newstead
b) Castlecary   d) Hadrianic milecastle; scale c.1:250.

evidence relating to stone gateways in Scotland, appears to embody design features which are common to both the cited examples at Newstead, and is closely comparable in dimensions with the larger. In this instance (Fig. 9.7,*a*) the single-portal entrance passage was flanked by rectangular towers measuring about 21 ft by 14 ft (6.4 x 4.3 m), which projected some 3 ft beyond the outer wall-face; the rear of each tower was occupied by guard-rooms of the same size as those recorded in the Newstead cross-wall gate. The general appearance is not unlike half the plan of a fort gateway on Hadrian's Wall; the gate-towers at the western entrance of Housesteads, for example, are of the same width, appear to have possessed only one pair of responds at the outer end of the passage, and their only significant difference is that they do not project beyond the outer wall-face. It is extremely probable that the legionary builders who constructed the gate at Balmuildy based their design on a drawing that had been filed in the unit drawing-office since Hadrianic times; all that required to be done was to excise one portal from the earlier plan and add about five feet at the front of each tower. Both alterations reflect the greater concern for security that is manifested throughout the Antonine Wall forts, none of which appear to have possessed the generously proportioned double-gateways, so common on the southern wall.

Similar 'off the peg' borrowings from the installations of Hadrian's Wall have been observed before in Scotland, the use of fortlets based on the Hadrianic milecastle (both on the Antonine Wall itself and in the south-west) being but one example. It should therefore cause no surprise to learn that the gateways of Castlecary may display a similar origin. Once again, the nature of gateway plan may be reconstructed from the detailed notes and drawings published by Mungo Buchanan (Fig. 9.7,*b*), although the possible significance has never been singled out for comment. The gates are all single-portal structures measuring 10 ft (3 m) in width, the passageway being formed by the inward return of the fort wall at right angles for a distance of 6 ft. (1.8 m); the total length is thus some 14 ft (4.3 m), including the 6 in. (0.15 m) projection beyond the line of the outer face. The overall plan is thus so reminiscent of the type of gateway associated with short-axis milecastles on Hadrian's Wall (Fig. 9.7*d*) and attributed to the Second Legion (Breeze & Dobson, 1976, 62; Birley, 1961, 99) that we may be reasonably confident in claiming that this was yet another 'borrowing' from the legionary draughtsman's archives. It is even possible that the two pairs of responds, supporting an archway at either end of the entrance-passage, which were present in the milecastle prototype, also existed at Castlecary. The unrebated side-walls shown on Buchanan's plan of the north and south gates illustrate the plan at the level of scarcement course, but the elevation of the west side of the north gate shows what appears to be a rebate about 3 ft 6 in from the inner end; furthermore in the small-scale plan of the east gate the north side-wall exhibits the sort of rebated plan which would be consonant with such a feature. Whatever the precise form of the passage, there can be little doubt that the builders chose to erect a gateway which resembled the Hadrianic milecastle's in being surmounted by a single tower, yet another indication that the accent was firmly upon defence.

Nevertheless, even though the scale was less ample than in Hadrian's

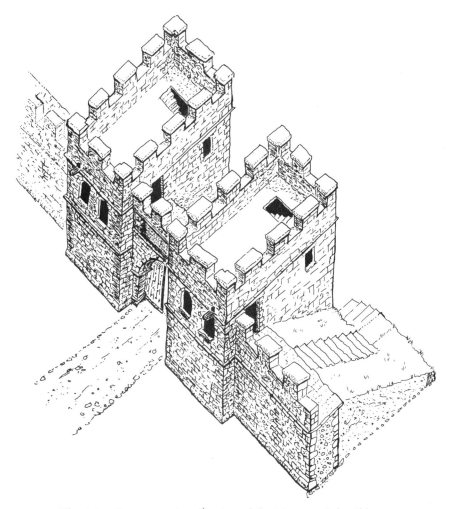

Fig. 9.8 Reconstruction drawing of the N gate at Balmuildy.

day and the designers more concerned with security, the structures that rose on the Scottish frontier were by no means devoid of architectural embellishment. Careful examination of the scattered masonry fragments around the north gate of Balmuildy enabled the excavators to reconstruct, at least in outline, the facade of what was clearly intended to be an imposing edifice (Miller, 1922, 17-20). In more recent times Dr Keppie has shown (1976a) how the monumental inscription whose fragments were found in the ruins of that gateway may be fitted into an elegant and impressive architectural design. Putting that reconstruction into an appropriate structural setting (Fig. **9.8**) we can see something of the effect which its designers must have hoped to produce. Looking proudly northward over the valley of the River Kelvin towards the tumbled foothills of the highland massif, it broadcast a message of resolute confidence in the power and achievements of the Roman army. To the native tribesmen living beyond the frontier, it must have seemed to symbolise an empire as unyielding and permanent as the massive stones of which it was wrought. Today much of the fabric of that imperial sway lies blanketed beneath the turf of a peaceful countryside. Yet it may not be unreasonable to claim that, while we in modern times still find our interest awakened by the monuments of the Roman frontier, the power and influence of Rome is not wholly dead. One of the main objects of the foregoing chapters has been to demonstrate that in their richness and variety, Roman remains in Scotland fully merit that interest and invite ever more intensive consideration and research.

BIBLIOGRAPHY

ABERCROMBY, J., T. ROSS & J. ANDERSON	1902	'Account of the excavation of the Roman station at Inchtuthil, Perthshire, undertaken by the Society of Antiquaries of Scotland in 1901', *Proc. Soc. Antiq. Scot.*, 36 (1901–2), 182–242.
ADAMSON, H.	1979	'Cleaven Dyke', in Breeze, 1979, 45
ADAMSON, H., & D.B. GALLAGHER	1987	'The Roman Fort at Bertha, the 1973 excavation', *Proc. Soc. Antiq. Scot.*, 116 (1986), 195–204.
ANDERSON, W.A.	1956	'The Roman fort at Bochastle, Callander', *Trans. Glasgow Archaeol. Soc.*, 15, 35–63
BIRLEY, A.	1974	'Roman Frontiers and Roman Frontier Policy', *Trans. Architect. Archaeol. Soc. Durham & Northumberland*, 3, 13–25
	1981	*The Fasti of Roman Britain.* London
BIRLEY, E.	1961	*Research on Hadrian's Wall.* Kendal
BRADLEY, E.	1960	'Ms Notes on aerial reconnaissance near Perth c.1940–1' National Monuments Record of Scotland
BREEZE, D.J.	1970	'Excavations at Ardoch 1970', *Proc. Soc. Antiq. Scot.*, 102 (1969–70), 122–8
	1974	'The Roman fortlet at Barburgh Mill, Dumfriesshire', *Britannia*, 5, 130–62
(ed.)	1979	*Roman Scotland, some recent excavations.* Edinburgh
	1980	'Roman Scotland during the reign of Antoninus Pius', in Hanson & Keppie, 1980, 45–60
	1981	'Agricola the builder', *Scottish Archaeol. Forum*, 12, 14–24
	1982	*The Northern Frontiers of Roman Britain.* London
	1983	'The Roman forts at Ardoch', in A. O'Connor and D.V. Clarke (eds.) *From the Stone Age to the Forty-five*, 224–36, Edinburgh
	1984	'The Roman Fort on the Antonine Wall at Bearsden', in Breeze (ed.), *Studies in Scottish Antiquity.* Edinburgh
BREEZE, D.J. & B. DOBSON	1969	'Fort types on Hadrian's Wall', *Archaeol. Aeliana*, 47 (4th series), 15–32
	1976	*Hadrian's Wall.* London
BUCHANAN, M., D. CHRISTISON, *et al.*,	1905	'Report on the Society's Excavation at Rough Castle on the Antonine Wall', *Proc. Soc. Antiq. Scot.*, 39 (1904–5), 442–99
CALLANDER, J.G.	1919	'Notes on the Roman remains at Grassy Walls and Bertha near Perth', *Proc. Soc. Antiq. Scot.*, 53 (1918–19), 145–52
CHALMERS, G.	1807	*Caledonia: or an Account, Historical and Topographic, of North Britain.* London

CHRISTISON, D., J.
BARBOUR, & J.
MACDONALD *et al.*
1895 'Account of the excavation of Birrens, a Roman station in Annandale, undertaken by the Society of Antiquaries in 1895'. *Proc. Soc. Antiq. Scot.*, 30 (1895−6), 81−199

CHRISTISON, D., J.H.
CUNNINGHAM, J.
ANDERSON, & T.
ROSS
1898 'Account of the excavation of the Roman station at Ardoch, Perthshire, undertaken by the Society of Antiquaries in 1896−7'. *Proc. Soc. Antiq. Scot.*, 32 (1897−88), 399−435

CHRISTISON, D. & M.
BUCHANAN
1903 'Excavation of Castlecary fort on the Antonine Vallum'. *Proc. Soc. Antiq. Scot.*, 37 (1902−3), 271−346

CHRISTISON, P.
1957 'Bannockburn − 23rd and 24th June 1314. A study in military history', *Proc. Soc. Antiq. Scot.*, 90 (1956−7), 170−9

CLARKE, J.
1933 *The Roman Fort at Cadder.* Glasgow

CRAWFORD, O.G.S.
1939 'Air reconnaissance of Roman Scotland', *Antiquity*, 13, 280−92

1949 *Topography of Roman Scotland North of the Antonine Wall.* Cambridge

CURLE, J.
1911 *A Roman Frontier Post and its People: the Fort of Newstead in the Parish of Melrose.* Glasgow

1940 'Sir George Macdonald, K.C.B.: 1862−1940. A memoir', *Proc. Soc. Antiq. Scot.*, 74 (1939−40), 123−32

DANIELS, C.M.
1970 'Problems of the Roman northern frontier', *Scottish Archaeol. Forum*, 2, 91−101

DAVIDSON, J.M.
1952 'From Corbiehall (Castledykes) to the Forth-Clyde Isthmus', in S.N. Miller (ed.) *The Roman Occupation of South-western Scotland*, 66−87. Glasgow

DOBSON, B.
1981 'Agricola's life and career', *Scottish Archaeol. Forum*, 12, 1−13

FINK, R.O.
1958 'Hunt's *Pridianum*: British Museum Papyrus 2851', *J. Roman Studies*, 48, 102−16

FRERE, S.S.
1979 'The Roman fort at Strageath' in Breeze, 1979, 37−41

1980 Review of Rivet and Smith, 1979, *Britannia*, 11, 419−23

1981 'The Flavian frontier in Scotland', *Scottish Archaeol. Forum*, 12, 89−97

FRIELL, G.J.P. & W.S.
HANSON
1988 'Westerton: a Roman watch-tower on the Gask frontier', *Proc. Soc. Antiq. Scot.*, 115, forthcoming

G.A.S.
1899 *The Antonine Wall Report.* Glasgow

GILLAM, J.P.
1975 'Possible changes in plan in the course of the construction of the Antonine Wall', *Scottish Archaeol. Forum*, 7, 51−6

GORDON, A.
1726 *Itinerarium Septentrionale.* London

GRILLONE, A. (ed.)
1977 Hygini *de metatione castrorum.*

HANSON, W.S.
1978 'Roman campaigns north of the Forth-Clyde isthmus: the evidence of the temporary camps', *Proc. Soc. Antiq. Scot.*, 109 (1977−78), 140−50

	1979	'Croy Hill' in Breeze, 1979, 19 – 20
	1980	'The first Roman occupation of Scotland', in W.S. Hanson and L.J.F. Keppie (eds.), *Roman Frontier Studies 1979: papers presented to the Twelfth International Congress of Roman Frontier Studies*, (British Archaeological Reports, International Series 71) 15 – 43. Oxford.
	1981	'Agricola on the Forth-Clyde isthmus', *Scottish Archaeol. Forum*, 12, 55 – 68
	1987	*Agricola and the Conquest of the North*. London.
HANSON, W.S., C.M. DANIELS, J.N. DORE & J.P. GILLAM	1979	'The Agricolan supply base at Red House, Corbridge', *Archaeol. Aeliana*, 7 (5th series), 1 – 97,
HANSON, W.S. & G.S. MAXWELL	1980	'An Agricolan *praesidium* on the Forth-Clyde isthmus (Mollins, Strathclyde)', *Britannia*, 11, 43 – 9
	1983	*Rome's North-west Frontier: the Antonine Wall*. Edinburgh
	1983a	'Minor enclosures on the Antonine Wall at Wilderness Plantation', *Britannia*, 14, 227 – 43
	1989	'A fortlet and temporary camp on the Antonine Wall at Summerston', *Proc. Soc. Antiq. Scot.*, forthcoming
JARRETT, M.G.	1985	'History, archaeology and Roman Scotland', *Proc. Soc. Antiq. Scot.*, 115, 59 – 66.
JONES, G.D.B.	1976	'The western extension of Hadrian's Wall: Bowness to Cardurnock', *Britannia*, 7, 236 – 43
	1978	'Concept and development in Roman frontiers', *John Rylands Bulletin*, 115 – 144
KEPPIE, L.J.F.	1974	'The building of the Antonine Wall; archaeological and epigraphic evidence', *Proc. Soc. Antiq. Scot.*, 105, (1973 – 4), 151 – 65
	1976	'Some rescue excavations on the line of the Antonine Wall 1973 – 6', *Proc. Soc. Antiq., Scot.*, 107 (1975 – 6), 61 – 80
	1976a	'Legio II Augusta and the north gate at Balmuildy', *Glasgow Archaeol. J.*, 4, 99 – 102
	1979	*Roman Distance Slabs from the Antonine Wall: a brief guide*. Glasgow
	1980	'The Roman forts on Castlehill, Bearsden', *Glasgow Archaeol. J.*, 7, 80 – 4
	1982	'The Antonine Wall 1960 – 1980', *Britannia*, 13, 91 – 112
	1986	'Excavations at the Roman fort on Bar Hill 1979 – 82', *Glasgow Archaeol. J.*, 12, 49 – 81
KEPPIE, L.J.F. & J.J. WALKER	1981	'Fortlets on the Antonine Wall at Seabegs Wood, Kinneil and Cleddans', *Britannia*, 13, 143 – 62
LAIDLAW, W.	1893	'On the remains of the Roman station at Cappuck, Roxburgh', *Proc. Berwickshire Natur. Club*, 14 (1892 – 3), 382 – 9
LEPPER, F.A.	1948	*Trajan's Parthian War*. Oxford

MACDONALD, G.   1916   'Two Roman camps at Raedykes and Glenmailen',
                                        Proc. Soc. Antiq. Scot., 50 (1915 – 16), 317 – 59
                             1933   'John Horsley, Scholar and Gentleman', *Archaeol.
                                        Aeliana*, (4th Series) 10, 1 – 57.
                             1933a   'Notes on the Roman forts at Rough Castle and
                                        Westerwood with a postscript', *Proc. Soc. Antiq.
                                        Scot.*, 67 (1932 – 3), 243 – 96
                             1934 \ *The Roman Wall in Scotland*. (2nd edn.). Oxford
                             1939   'Verbum non amplius addam', *J. Roman Studies*, 29,
                                        5 – 27
MACDONALD, G. & A.O.   1929   'The Roman fort at Mumrills near Falkirk', *Proc. Soc.
    CURLE   Antiq. Scot.*, 71 (1935 – 6), 396 – 575
MACDONALD, G. & A.   1906   'The Roman forts on the Bar Hill', *Proc. Soc. Antiq.
    PARK   Scot.*, 40 (1905 – 6), 403 – 56
MACDONALD, J.   1894   'Notes on the "Roman Roads", of the One-inch
                                        Ordnance Map of Scotland', *Proc. Soc. Antiq. Scot.*,
                                        28 (1893 – 4), 20 – 61, and 298 – 320
                             1895   'Notes on the "Roman Roads" of the One-inch
                                        Ordnance Map of Scotland. The Roxburghshire
                                        Roads', *Proc. Soc. Antiq. Scot.*, 29 (1894 – 5), 317 – 28
                             1897   *Tituli Hunteriani: an Account of the Roman Stones in
                                        the Hunterian Museum, University of Glasgow.*
                                        Glasgow.
MACIVOR, I., M.C.   1980   'Excavations on the Antonine Wall fort of Rough
    THOMAS & D.J. BREEZE   Castle, Stirlingshire, 1957 – 61', *Proc. Soc. Antiq.
                                        Scot.*, 110 (1978 – 80), 230 – 85
MACKENSEN, M.   1987   *Frühkaiserzeitliche Kleinkastelle bei Nersingen and
                                        Burlafingen an der Oberen Donau.* Munich
MACKIE, E.W.   1983   'The Leckie broch, Stirlingshire: an interim report',
                                        Glasgow Archaeol. J., 9 (1982), 60 – 72
MAITLAND, W.   1757   *History and Antiquities of Scotland*. London
MARGARY, I.D.   1973   *Roman Roads in Britain*. London
MAXFIELD, V.A.   1986   'Pre-Flavian forts and their garrisons', *Britannia*, 17,
                                        59 – 72.
MAXWELL, G.S.   1972   'Excavations at the Roman fort at Crawford,
                                        Lanarkshire', *Proc. Soc. Antiq. Scot.*, 104 (1971 – 2),
                                        147 – 200
                             1974   'The building of the Antonine Wall', in D.M. Pippidi
                                        (ed.) *Actes du IXe Congrès Internationale d'Etudes sur
                                        les Frontières Romaines*, 327 – 32. Bucharest.
                             1977   'A linear defence-system in south-western Scotland',
                                        in D. Haupt and H.G. Horn (eds.), *Studien zu den
                                        Militärgrenzen Roms, II: Vorträge des 10.
                                        Internationalen Limeskongresses*, 23 – 30. Cologne.
                             1981   'Agricola's campaigns: the evidence of the
                                        temporary camps', *Scottish Archaeol. Forum*, 12,
                                        25 – 54
                             1982   'Roman temporary camps at Inchtuthil: an
                                        examination of the aerial photographic evidence',
                                        Scottish Archaeol. Rev., 1, pt. 2, 105 – 13

	1983	'Roman settlement in Scotland', in J.C. Chapman and H.C. Mytum (eds.) *Settlement in North Britain 1000 BC-AD 1000* (B.A.R. British Series, 118), 233–61. Oxford
	1983a	'Recent aerial discoveries in Roman Scotland: Drumquhassle, Elginhaugh and Woodhead', *Britannia*, 14, 167–81
	1984a	'New frontiers: the Roman fort at Doune and its possible significance', *Britannia*, 15, 217–23
	1984b	'The evidence of the Roman period', in A. Fenton and G. Stell (eds.) *Loads and Roads in Scotland and Beyond*, 21–48. Edinburgh.
	1984c	'Two Roman inscribed stones from Scotland', *Proc. Soc. Antiq. Scot.*, 113 (1983–4), 379–90.
	1986	'Sidelight on the Roman military campaigns in North Britain', in *Studien zu den Militärgrenzen Roms III (Forschungen und Berichte zur Vor- und Frühgeschichte in Baden-Württemberg*, 20), 60–63.
	1987	'Settlement in Southern Pictland: a new overview', in A. Small (ed.), *The Picts: a new look at old problems*, 31–44. Dundee.
	1989	*A Battle Lost: Romans and Caledonians at Mons Graupius*. Edinburgh.
MAXWELL, G.S. & D.R. WILSON	1987	'Air Reconnaissance in Roman Britain, 1977–84', *Britannia*, 18, 1–48.
MILLER, S.N.	1922	*The Roman Fort at Balmuildy*. Glasgow
PITTS, L.F. & J.K.S. ST JOSEPH	1985	*Inchtuthil: the Roman Legionary Fortress*, Britannia Monograph Series, No. 6, London.
POSTGATE, P.E.	1930	'Notes on Tacitus', *Proc. Cambridge. Phil. Soc.* cx/v–vii, 8
RAE, A. & V. RAE	1974	'The Roman fort at Cramond, Edinburgh: excavations 1954–66', *Britannia*, 5, 163–224
R.C.A.M.S.	1963	*Stirlingshire: an Inventory of the Ancient and Historical Monuments*. Edinburgh.
	1967	*Peeblesshire: an Inventory of the Ancient and Historical Monuments*. Edinburgh
	1978	*Lanarkshire: an Inventory of the Prehistoric and Roman Monuments*. Edinburgh
REED, N.H.	1971	'The fifth year of Agricola's campaigns', *Britannia*, 2, 143–8
RICHMOND, I.A.	1940	'Excavations on the estate of Meikleour, Perthshire, 1939', *Proc. Soc. Antiq. Scot.*, 74 (1939–40), 37–47
	1943	'Recent discoveries in Roman Britain from the air and in the field', *J. Roman Stud.*, 33, 45–54
	1950	'Excavations at the Roman fort of Newstead, 1947', *Proc. Soc. Antiq. Scot.*, 84 (1949–50), 1–37
RICHMOND, I.A. & J. McINTYRE	1939	'The Agricolan fort at Fendoch', *Proc. Soc. Antiq. Scot.*, 73 (1938–9), 110–54
RIVET, A.L.F. & C. SMITH	1979	*The Place-names of Roman Britain*. London

ROBERTSON, A.S.   1957   *An Antonine Fort: Golden Hill, Duntocher.* Edinburgh

1963   'Miscellanea Romano-Caledonica', *Proc. Soc. Antiq. Scot.*, 97, (1963–4), 180–201

1964   *The Roman fort at Castledykes.* Edinburgh

1968   'Two groups of Roman *Asses* from North Britain', *Numismatic Chron.*, 8, 61–6

1974   'Roman "signal stations" on the Gask Ridge', *Trans. Perths. Soc. Natur. Sci. (Special Issue)*, 14–29

1975   'Agricola's campaigns in Scotland and their aftermath', *Scottish Archaeol. Forum*, 7, 1–12

1977   'Excavations at Cardean and Stracathro, Angus', in Haupt, D. and H.G. Horn (eds.), *Studien zu den Militärgrenzen Roms, II*, 65–74. Cologne/Bonn.

1979   'The Roman fort at Cardean', in Breeze, 1979, 42–4

1980   'The bridges on Severan coins of AD 208 and 209', in Hanson, W.S. and L.J.F. Keppie (eds.), *Roman Frontier Studies 1979: papers presented to the Twelfth International Congress of Roman Frontier Studies*, 131–140. Oxford

ROY W.   1793   *Military Antiquities of the Romans in North Britain.* London

ST JOSEPH, J.K.S.   1952   'The roads: from Carlisle to the Forth; the roads to Nithsdale, from Tweed to Clyde; the Avondale road', in S.N. Miller (ed.) *The Roman Occupation of South-Western Scotland*, 1–65. Glasgow

1965   'Air reconnaissance in Britain, 1961–64', *J. Roman Stud.*, 55, 74–89

1970   'The camps at Ardoch, Stracathro and Ythan Wells: recent excavations', *Britannia*, 1, 163–78

1973   'Air reconnaissance in Roman Britain 1969–72'. *J. Roman Stud.*, 63, 214–46

1976   'Air reconnaissance of Roman Scotland, 1939–75', *Glasgow Archaeol. J.*, 4, 1–28

1977   'Air reconnaissance in Roman Britain, 1973–76' *J. Roman Stud.*, 67, 125–61.

1978a   'The camp at Durno and Mons Graupius', *Britannia*, 9, 271–88

1978b   'A Roman camp near Girvan, Ayrshire', *Britannia*, 9, 397–401

ST. JOSEPH, J.K.S. & G.S. MAXWELL   1989   'The Roman fort at Hatton of Cargill' *Britannia*, forthcoming

SCHÖNBERGER, H.   1969   'The Roman frontier in Germany: an archaeological survey', *J. Roman Stud.*, 59, 144–97

SCHULTEN, A.   1929   *Numantia; die Ergebnisse der Ausgrabungen, 1905–12*: IV, Die Lager bei Renieblas. Munich

SIBBALD, R.   1707   *Historical Inquiries.* Edinburgh

STEER, K.A.   1952   'A Roman signal-station on the Eildon Hill North, Roxburghshire', *Proc. Soc. Antiq. Scot.*, 86 (1951–2), 202–5

	1957	'The nature and purpose of the expansions on the Antonine Wall', *Proc. Soc. Antiq. Scot.*, 90 (1956 – 7), 161 – 9
STEVENS, C.E.	1966	\ *The Building of Hadrian's Wall.* Kendal
STUART, J.	1868	'Professor Thorkelin and General Robert Melvill, on Roman antiquities in the North of Scotland, 1788 – 90', *Proc. Soc. Antiq. Scot.*, 7 (1867 – 8), 26 – 34
STUART, R.	1845	*Caledonia Romana: A Descriptive Account of the Roman Antiquities of Scotland* (1st Edn.). Edinburgh
SYME, R.	1959	\ 'The Lower Danube under Trajan', *J. Roman Stud.*, 49, 26 – 33
TODD, M.	1981	*Roman Britain 55BC – AD 400.* Brighton
WATSON, G.R.	1969	*The Roman Soldier.* London
WILKES, J.J.	1974	'The Antonine Wall fortlet at Wilderness Plantation', *Glasgow Archaeol. J.*, 3, 51 – 65
WILSON, D.	1851	'Roman camp at Harburn', *Proc. Soc. Antiq. Scot.*, 1 (1851 – 4), 58 – 9
	1863	*The Prehistoric Annals of Scotland.* London and Cambridge
WILSON, D. & D. LAING	1873	'An account of Alexander Gordon, A.M., Author of the *Itinerarium Septentrionale*, 1726', *Proc. Soc. Antiq. Scot.*, 10 (1872 – 4), 363 – 82.

INDEX